Goodbye, Europe? Hello, Chaos?

Goodbye, Europe?
Hello, Chaos?

Merkel's Migrant Bomb

J. Michael Springmann

DAENA PUBLICATIONS LLC
4005 Wisconsin Avenue NW
#9771
Washington, DC 20016

ISBN-13: 9780990926221
ISBN-10: 0990926222
Library of Congress Control Number: 2017938499
Daena Publications LLC, Washington, DC

Also written by J. Michael Springmann

Visas for Al Qaeda: CIA Handouts That Rocked the World

To the peoples of Europe whose governments abandoned them.
To the unfortunate millions driven from their homes by American foreign policy.
These were individuals and families weaponized as migrants, pushed into foreign lands and cultures they did not understand.
They were expected to fit in. Yet some were intended to fail.

One refugee is a novelty, ten refugees are boring, and a hundred refugees are a menace.

—Kelly M. Greenhill, *Weapons of Mass Migration*

Contents

Foreword

"IF YOU REALLY want to help refugees, stop feeding them. Let a few of them die of starvation, war injuries, and disease on the sidewalks of Western Europe. Then go organize the ensuing public outrage to pressure the governments to stop the wars responsible for producing such refugee streams. If you keep taking them in and feeding them, you are complicit in cooperating with the aggressor because you aid and abet in the process of them becoming permanently dislodged from their countries. You are helping the aggressor win."

These unexpectedly contentious 1992 words of a seasoned emergency physician unsettled me. He had spent years in a military intelligence role, building a medical first responder NGO with tent clinics in conflict zones from Afghanistan, under Soviet invasion, to later Africa and the Balkans. Had I just heard this well-known philanthropist call for direct sacrifice of a percentage of refugees, whom I was supporting in the Balkans war, for the greater political good? He delivered these words during a planning meeting in Chicago as we were organizing his humanitarian clinics in the first war zones of what was still Yugoslavia. At that time, I was a new and very enthusiastic director of a small humanitarian NGO delivering aid to the conflict regions of the Balkans. As part of this role, I fed and housed refugees, and his words had shocked me. Such early encounters with the deep state under US foreign policy's humanitarian mask raised my growing awareness of the world of NGOs in war zones, many of which serve as mere CIA front operations—essentially, tools in the deconstruction of country after country. Refugees in such settings have been routinely used as a coercive weapon.

Over the next twenty-five years, I watched other nations fall victim to the ongoing nation-building methodology developed into the current blueprint. Yugoslavia was successfully fractured by a concentrated effort of Western intelligence and NGOs riding shotgun while the seven new Yugoslavias were absorbed by the CIA, NATO, the European Union, and their collective industrial and political interests, all of whom worked seamlessly with networks of NGOs on creating the demise of Yugoslavia.

The methods Western intelligence field-tested and widely used to destroy Yugoslavia proved so successful that in the new millennium, the teachings of Gene Sharp, professor and author of a rulebook on how to create a revolution, were combined with the well-funded Soros-organized color revolutions using rent-a-rebels. Organized Western-funded protest groups operated in vast networks, including human rights groups all the way to violent protesters, followed by death squads, all under the umbrella of Western intelligence, which controls this entire spectrum of agents provocateurs.

Entire networks of Western NGOs cooperated under CIA overhead support to construct the fatal recipe of Problem-Reaction-Solution that methodically deconstructed Yugoslavia from within. After the deconstruction of the Balkans was so successful, even its deconstruction techniques and results became famous under the political term of "balkanization."

Following the demise of Yugoslavia, the United Nations created a "commitment" named Responsibility to Protect ("R2P") in 2005, which allowed for Western invasion and expansion via military "peacekeeping" missions to allegedly help populations under war or ethnic attack. Western intelligence had gained much practice in creating heated protests, escalating to civil wars, with death squads required in order to invoke R2P. This strengthened intelligence-run NGOs as coup enablers and migrant herders alongside accompanying military interventions in target countries undergoing such unfortunate CIA power remodeling.

After creating Otpor (a Serbian resistance organization) as a working prototype of a Sharp/Soros color revolution, the CIA program consisting of manufactured violent protests leading to transition to civil war, the same recipes were next applied in Libya and Syria with the same brutality and the same grim success. By perhaps premonitive anticipation of coming wars that would be ignited once again under humanitarian and human rights protest cover, former President Obama, new in office in 2009 and lacking any record of peacekeeping, inexplicably received a Nobel Peace Prize. This would serve to inoculate his series of nation-building wars as peacekeeping missions and protect them from scrutiny by rebranding arsonist as savior and creating a false aura of humanitarianism and peacekeeping purposes as backdrop to the increasingly bloodthirsty expansion of the CIA's nation-building schemes, now under the Nobel Peace President Obama. In tandem, the CIA's friend German Chancellor Angela Merkel influenced the European Union to facilitate the CIA plan to drown Europe under a tsunami of migrants. The entire agenda visibly serves various economic and political agendas, resulting in dramatic long-term changes to the social, cultural, demographic, and legislative restructuring of Europe's future. In classic CIA fashion, this is being carried out without the consent of the involved populations.

As someone who spent a number of years working directly in war zones with refugees and migrants, I was immediately suspicious as to the agenda's official narrative being laden with familiar foreign policy plots being responsible for it. Everything I had learned professionally by working with the same UN and philanthropic agencies made it clear that there was a synthetic whiff emanating from this allegedly spontaneous migrant crisis. The fact that millions of people were being collected and professionally herded toward Western Europe raised my suspicions. Having worked with refugee populations for years, I knew that refugees are commonly and preferably organized in camps near their countries of origin in anticipation of return to their homes. Encouraging millions of people to embark on such a march as many NGOs do results in increased mortality and stress on countries of origin, transit countries, and target countries alike. It bypasses all sensible solutions and serves primarily covert political motives and is counterproductive to responsible professional refugee management. The migrant crisis can only be resolved by extinguishing the wars that are largely its cause, not by forcing millions of socially dependent people toward Europe, where they ignite a predictable backlash and growing clashes with the native populations as their numbers grow larger.

Polarization and intense media spin were soon in full force, with protests and clashes organized between various far-left and far-right groups in Europe, with the migrant crisis serving as political football. A well-prepared media spin with messages from Big Sister Merkel's propaganda arm reaching into the media began molding German minds about what to think of the migrant crisis. Many aggressive leftist protest groups involved are well-known tools of Western intelligence, such as Antifa and the Black Bloc being formed of the remnants of the New Left of the 1960s and 1970s, as well as a host of intelligence-controlled far-right groups, all seemingly having received marching orders to engage in heated protests with each other throughout Europe. Meanwhile, most migrants, who are victims of the manufactured wars in their countries, attempt to integrate into Western culture, which is easier for some than others.

While many Western countries have helped migrants extensively by taking large numbers of refugees, their resources, patience, and domestic stress tolerances are not infinite. A growing political right is rising as a direct backlash while xenophobia flourishes. Islamist attacks across Europe are on rise and bear a familiar pattern of previously known Western-manufactured terrorism. A number of anti-Western attacks on Western women, culture, or religion occur on a regular basis now and produce growing tensions. While radical groups such as Daesh have been creating "special ops migrants" and hiding them among the streams of ordinary migrants, a number of group attacks of migrants against each other or against German citizens were found to have been well coordinated via Facebook and Twitter straight to the iPhones of such "migrants" with directives to cause violence and simultaneous mass rapes in several European cities and step up pressure along political fault lines across Europe. "Attack their culture, rape their women, and break them" is one of the oldest military intelligence strategies. But who is directing such events in Europe?

In 1925, Richard von Coudenhove-Kalergi, a Japanese Austrian who became famous as one of the men who helped found the bedrock of what was to become the European Union, wrote: "The man of the future will be of mixed race. Today's races and classes will gradually disappear owing to the vanishing of space, time, and prejudice. The Eurasian-Negroid race of the future, similar in its appearance to the Ancient Egyptians, will replace the diversity of peoples with a diversity of individuals." In 2010, Merkel received the prestigious Coudenhove-Kalergi Award for her great vision in European integration. Merkel's Europe is beginning to look a whole lot like Kalergi's vision from nearly a century ago. Had the process been natural, it would likely have resulted in much more diversity and harmony. But the process was introduced rapidly, and large populations traumatized and uprooted by wars are being introduced into an increasingly less willing Europe. It is not happening naturally, and migrants and native Europeans alike barely have a chance to adjust to the rapid cultural changes in both worlds as this cultural merger is being steered with increasing velocity toward major clashes.

While dramatically changing the demographics of Germany, this strategy of tension accompanying the migrant streams also allows the state to introduce more surveillance of the total population and restrictions on freedom and serves as robust excuse to usher in totalitarianism in "necessary" increments. Perhaps the greatest danger to Europe is not even this latest creation of terrorism itself, which has been afforded broad cover among the sea of migrants, but the increasing control measures declared necessary by those in power pretending to fight terrorism.

While the ideologically impoverished political Left exploits and romanticizes the migrant crisis to advance its own complex set of covert political agendas, it does its masters' bidding as it obediently spars with its designated kabuki partner, the rising Alt Right. Both are under the heavy influence of Western intelligence control, sparring with each other on command. From Brexit to the Trump/Bannon phenomenon and the rise of Alt Right parties and leaders springing up in Europe like mushrooms after a hard rain, traditional establishment fascism is making a fresh new salon comeback dressed up in Alt Right revolutionary drag.

We should consider that perhaps the best way to manage a migrant crisis is to not create one in the first place. Identifying the men behind the curtain and addressing our growing number of wars and engaging in a constructive dialog across the political spectrum is perhaps more effective than joining any political movements on the left or right, as both are being manipulated. We are inadvertently complicit if we turn migrants into a political football while not recognizing the agenda they become a tool for when engaging on either side of the controlled political battle lines.

In this new book, J. Michael Springmann examines the roots and waystations of the migrant crisis of Europe. He analyzes Kelly M. Greenhill's academic writings, which serve as strategic CIA think tank templates and methodology cookbook for creating a migrant crisis and effectively coercing entire nations into policy knee-jerk synchronicity with it, and he exposes the agencies who are controlling these events.

Silvia Germek
February 23, 2017

Author's Note

I wish to acknowledge, with great thanks, the extremely useful research assistance I received in writing this book. I would like to single out Silvia Germek, a knowledgeable expert on Central Europe and the Balkans, as well as Glynn Custred, professor emeritus of anthropology at California State University. Miss Germek's English, German, and Serbo-Croatian language proficiency proved invaluable in producing this work. Professor Custred's interest in frontiers, borders, and borderlands, along with his writings for the Association of Borderland Studies, was most helpful.

Additionally, I would like to recognize Silvia Germek for her most generous aid in reading and rereading the drafts of *Good-Bye, Europe? Hello, Chaos?* Her sagacious analysis, comments, and suggestions immeasurably strengthened this effort. Indeed, it was her suggestion about the migrants concept that sparked this tome.

I also want to express my gratitude for the encouragement and support of Andrew Kreig and Wayne Madsen, two very successful, well-informed, and extremely experienced investigative journalists.

What's this Book About?

THIS BOOK COVERS Europe's migrant crisis: the flood of aliens, mostly refugees, real and otherwise, fleeing American wars in South Asia, Southwest Asia, and North Africa.

The work devotes a significant amount of ink to Germany. That country, after all, "invited" the refugees to come, tried to parcel them out to other members of the European Union, and savaged anyone and any organization that opposed that concept.

Introduction

What?

WHAT'S HAPPENING IN Europe? What is this wave of people? Alien invaders? Clash of cultures? Migrants? Refugees? Asylees? Terrorists? Is it really a "refugee crisis"? And who are the hundreds of thousands of fit young men with iPhones, all aiming for Germany like homing pigeons? Where are their wives and children? Is some invisible force coordinating them?

This mass migration does look remarkably well organized, indeed, suspiciously so. Who or what could be directing this movement of peoples? And why? Could it be an engineered effort to prop up a falling German tax base in the short run? Or, perhaps, is it a well-planned campaign by someone to divide and weaken Europe in the long run? Could it be both? And how does it connect to the United States?

There are signs of American and European military and intelligence services' involvement. Real or remarkably well-made counterfeit passports have turned up in the hands of migrants. The US government has paid for boats to carry the alien invaders to Europe. Thousands upon thousands of illegals have disappeared without a trace once inside Europe. American companies have set up Wi-Fi networks along the migrant route to Germany. George Soros groups created iPhone apps that guide the migrants on their journey across Europe. They also helped with interpreters and other aid. UN officials, think tank directors, and Dutch politicians have said that the European Union must become more multicultural.

It is definitely not a spontaneous refugee crisis. By all signs, it may be an attempt to keep tax money flowing in Germany, a country with a falling birthrate and once-extensive social welfare benefits. An aging, declining workforce can no longer fund such generous public assistance. It also appears to be an organized program to set not only European against European across demographic, political, and socioeconomic lines but also Europeans and "migrants" against each other in a wildly diverse but visibly organized pattern of divide and conquer.

As we will examine in this book, the goal appears to be to weaken Europe, weaken the migrants' home countries, and provide for increased American influence over international affairs. Covertly imposed conflicts along religious, ethnic, cultural, and national lines will aid in this. Thanks to simultaneous "terrorist" attacks with oddly perfect timing, traditionally antiwar Europe has now joined the United States' Forever War mind-set. Is this through "coincidence" or intelligent design?

Who?

German chancellor (prime minister) Angela Dorothea Merkel is a key player in the migrant crisis. Geli, or Angie, Merkel might be a very public figure, but she is also a very private one. In fact, she is so private that her background is almost nonexistent. Only the bare facts are mentioned:

- She was born in Hamburg, in what was then West Germany, in 1954.
- She is the daughter of a Lutheran minister.
- She moved with her parents to Templin, East Germany, the Communist German Democratic Republic (GDR), just a few months after her birth.

- Her father, Horst Kasner, was instrumental in creating a separate Lutheran Church in the GDR, allowing its government to keep a closer watch on its members; he was seen as pro-regime.
- Her family received perks from this: two cars (when other citizens were lucky to get even a Trabant, the car that gave Communism a bad name) plus travel to West Germany and Italy.

During her thirty-five years of living in the Communist state, she

- joined the *Freie Deutsche Jugend* (Free German Youth, FDJ), the official Communist youth association;
- studied at prestigious schools and went on to take a PhD in physics at a time when the clergy's children were routinely refused such advantages;
- had Lothar de Maizière, the last GDR non-Communist head of government, as her mentor;
- turned into his government's spokesman in 1990;
- became protégé of Helmut Kohl, West German Chancellor and head of the Christian Democratic Union (CDU), a large, right-of-center party;
- received several ministries in his government; and
- eventually became deputy party leader in 1991.[1]

Despite being seen as a motherly figure, Merkel, according to Jonathan Powell, appears to be a ruthless, canny political operator. Powell, who had served as British prime minister Tony Blair's chief of staff, pointed to her wrecking Helmut Kohl's career as head of the CDU. Somehow Kohl's involvement in black money, illegal financial transactions, and hidden donations came to light, causing him to resign as head of the CDU in 1999. Lothar de Maizière, once in line to succeed Kohl, appeared to stumble badly in 1990. Somehow his background as an unofficial

1 Encyclopedia.com (*Encyclopedia of World Biography*).

member of the GDR's State Security Service (*Staatssicherheitsdienst*, also known as the Stasi) appeared. Domestic spies were officially out of favor, and Geli suddenly had no opposition in her climb to the top.

Somehow the protégé and mentee succeeded where others had failed. Somehow deadly secrets became known from someone on the inside. Any guesses who?

Yet other old Stasi did quite well with Angie. Anetta Kahane (code name Victoria), with State Security from 1974 to 1982, took indirect charge of Germany's war on hate speech. Merkel's justice minister, Heiko Maas, recruited her and the organization she founded, Network against Nazis (*Netz Gegen Nazis*), to define and control controversial language. Kahane also began the Amadeu Antonio Foundation, which works against xenophobia, anti-Semitism (when directed at establishment Jews like herself), and right-wing extremism.[2]

Adara Press came out and accused Chancellor Merkel of being a Stasi informant. The site charged her with being an "unofficial associate" with the Security Service. Merkel always maintained that she was only involved in cultural affairs with the FDJ and rejected the one Stasi recruitment attempt she received. However, Wilhelm von Pax asserted that she was an agitator and propagandist in the youth movement, quite unlike the apolitical physics PhD she claimed to be. How else, he says, can you explain her rapid rise in the GDR?[3]

This concept continued. A former colleague from the Academy of Sciences, Gunter Walther, asserted that she propagated Marxism-Leninism. Moreover, she had been secretary for agitation and propaganda (*agitprop*) while in the FDJ. These and other comments went to the authors of *The First Life of Angela M.* Another came from Günther Krause. He had been a one-time German transport minister and, earlier,

2 Bodissey, Baron. "The Stasi Never Died, It Just Went to Work for Angela Merkel," gatesofvienna.net, July 16, 2016. Also see Watson, Paul Joseph. "Ex-Stasi Agent Hired to Censor 'Xenophobic' Facebook Posts—German Government Cracks Down on Dissent against Migrant Influx," infowars.com, September 16, 2015.

3 Von Pax, Wilhelm. "Was Angela Merkel a Stasi Informer? Some Say, 'Ja,'" Adara Press, October 19, 2015.

a GDR politician. He had worked with Merkel in East Germany's waning days. Noting that she does not admit her closeness to the old GDR system, he commented that she was very useful as the pastor's daughter. Merkel was supposed to have said, "If we reform the GDR, it won't be in terms of the Federal Republic."[4]

Perhaps some of the old ways of thinking and doing in the GDR have not disappeared. They still survive in Angela Merkel's mind. If so, they may well have influenced her involvement in the migrant tsunami.

4 Spiegel Online. "How Close Was Merkel to the Communist System?," May 14, 2013.

1

Weapons of Mass Migration

The Beginning

CHANGE FIRST BEGAN with the destruction of Afghanistan in 1979. The wrecking of Yugoslavia, Iraq, Libya, Syria, Yemen, Pakistan, and Afghanistan continue to the present day. You might be able to include postcoup Ukraine in this mix as well. The United States and its repressive, often repulsive, "allies" have thus far destroyed a good bit of South and Southwest Asia, the Balkans, and North Africa. This was not done for what used to be "truth, justice, and the American way" but, rather, for the unbelievably titled Global War on Terror (GWOT, sounding very much like a cat coughing up a hairball). Under the aegis of that awful acronym, the United States created (vomited out?) the mujahideen, later rebranded as Al Qaeda and, still later, as its successor, ISIL or ISIS or IS or D'aish. Choose one, whichever sounds most like cat puke. An extensive background on how this came to be is set forth in *Visas for Al Qaeda: CIA Handouts That Rocked the World.*[5] (The work also discusses how the author became embroiled in the CIA's visas for terrorists program. It

5 J. Michael Springmann, *Visas for Al Qaeda: CIA Handouts That Rocked the World* (Washington, DC: Daena Publications LLC: 2014).

recounts how, through misadventure, he became all too familiar with black intelligence operations, lending him an expertise that few have.)

America achieved this drastic transformation of Europe not through atomic bombs, marching armies, or fleets of warships but through a concept in asymmetric warfare: using directed mass migration as a weapon. That's a sword that cuts in two directions at once: against the targeted recipient group as well as against the migrant outflow country.[6]

Weapons of Mass Migration?

Kelly M. Greenhill, an academic with close ties to the national security establishment, summarized methods of how migrants have been successfully used to achieve certain goals. There appears to be evidence that Greenhill's work is being used as a cookbook for creating Europe's current migrant crisis. According to Stanford University's Center for International Security and Cooperation (CISAC), she is an associate professor of political science and international relations at Tufts University and a research fellow at Harvard University's Kennedy School of Government. She holds a PhD and an SM from MIT, a CSS from Harvard University, and a BA from UC Berkeley. Greenhill previously held pre- and postdoctoral fellowships at Harvard University's Olin Institute for Strategic Studies and Belfer Center for Science and International Affairs and at CISAC. Outside of academia, Greenhill has served as a consultant to the Ford Foundation and to the United Nations High Commissioner for Refugees (UNHCR), as a defense program analyst for the US Department of Defense, and as an economic policy intern in the office of Senator John F. Kerry.

In her book *Weapons of Mass Migration,* Greenhill obfuscates the quoted concept by calling it *coercive engineered migration* (or migration-driven coercion).[7] This is subtle chisel work. Greenhill hammers out this

6 Kelly M. Greenhill, *Weapons of Mass Migration: Forced Displacement, Coercion, and Foreign Policy* (Ithaca, NY: Cornell University Press: 2010).

7 Ibid., 2

coercive process, naming it and graving it into the stone of receptive minds in the intelligence services.

Basically, her concept of this migration is a "two-level, generally, asymmetric coercion by punishment strategy, in which challengers on the international level seek to influence the behavior of their targets by exploiting the existence of competing domestic interests within the target state(s) and by manipulating the costs or risks imposed on their civilian population(s)." Military coercion is not necessarily cheap. Soldiers, bullets, and bombs have their costs, political and otherwise. However, Greenhill talks about another kind of bomb: a population bomb. "Costs are inflicted through the threat and use of human demographic bombs to achieve political goals that would be utterly impossible through military means."[8]

How does this work? Look at her chapters.

Weapons of Mass Migration opens with a descriptive introduction, defining and clarifying her coercive concepts. The first chapter is "Understanding the Coercive Power of Mass Migrations." In it, she defines, measures, and identifies some sixty-four coercive engineered migrations by year, target, and group. Chapter 2 looks at "The 1994 Cuban *Balseros* [Rafters] Crisis," with thousands sailing toward Florida. The Yugoslav disaster is recounted in chapter 3: "'Now the Refugees *Are* the War': NATO and the Kosovo Conflict." The next installment of this engineered-migrant cookbook, "An Invasion to Stop the Invasion: The United States and the Haitian Boatpeople Crises," is chapter 4. In it, Greenhill recounts how you can conduct coercion from afar, the dangers of grandstanding, and the "emerging norms of justified intervention."[9] The fifth chapter concerns "North Korean Migrants, Nongovernmental Organizations, and Nuclear Weapons" (i.e., how you can destabilize a country through an outflow of its people). The sixth and last chapter is devoted to "Conclusions and Policy Implications." This deals with the efficacy of coercive engineered migrations and how to handle them.

8 Ibid., 3.

9 Ibid., 182–183.

Here's the gist of coercive engineered migrations: one country or group imposes international costs or risks on another. The aim is a coercive strategic outcome. Instead of bombs and bullets, the weapon of choice is people. The kinetic force of large groups of people on the move is, indeed, a multihandled club. By sending, or threatening to send, a wave of refugees or asylees or migrants to the recipient state or group, the transferring entity imposes costs on its target. One such cost is simply an overwhelmed physical capacity to digest the influx. A second is political blackmail, aimed at the target's society or its professed liberal values.[10] This translates to, "If you're so tolerant, why do you oppose people fleeing oppression? They just want to work, pay taxes, and live the good life." These objections Greenhill terms *hypocrisy costs.* She notes "that liberal democracies should be particularly vulnerable to the imposition of hypocrisy costs and to coercive engineered migration, more generally."

Why is this effective?

Target states often threaten to deport illegal aliens en masse. Alternatively, they frequently try to turn them back at the frontier. However, somewhere along the way, they've undoubtedly made statements or commitments to protect people fleeing persecution or violence. To quote Greenhill again, hypocrisy costs "serve as effective force multipliers for weak challengers, allowing them to punch above their weight and to influence the behavior of actors normally outside their ambit."[11]

You can read about this type of latter cost—propaganda, really—any day in any American newspaper article about illegal aliens moving to the United States. They're just "undocumented immigrants"! But it's still a psychological operation, or PSYOP, to use the jargon. Think about it. Phrase it differently: "Only racists would oppose our helping these new citizens in training." That's called a double-bind strategy, another bit

10 Ibid., 3.

11 Ibid., 4.

of psychological jargon. In plain English, this is "the feeling that whatever decision you make, you are wrong." It brings about confusion and anxiety.[12]

Here are two examples of this from the *Washington Post.*

In an article from November 18, 2016, the *Post* presents as news a story about an Idaho town dependent on its illegal aliens. The paper asserted that employers in Twin Falls, Idaho, "would be lost without the low-wage workforce from Iraq, Afghanistan, and sub-Saharan Africa." Continuing, the *Post* asserted that "people in meat-packing towns and agricultural areas are wondering whether their communities will hold on to a supply of Hispanic workers and other foreign laborers crucial to those industries." The piece briefly mentioned the tensions that have grown up, in part as problems with digesting outsiders not attuned to the local culture. Additionally, it commented on (and minimized) the crime that came along with the migrants.[13]

In its report, the *Post,* as always, omitted key facts. On January 1, 2016, the US population stood at 322,761,807 (US Census Bureau). According to an undated Gallup poll, the real US unemployment rate was 10 percent as of October 1, 2016.

There you have it. In a country of more than 300 million people and with 10 percent of its workforce without a job, more illegal aliens are desperately needed. Why? There is absolutely no one available to labor in its plants and on its farms.

Later, the *Washington Post* provided another story designed to garner sympathy for another illegal alien. US District Judge James C. Cacheris ruled November 22, 2016, that a teenager should be returned to his mother in the United States. The boy had been jailed for three years after an immigration judge determined he did not have to be deported. It's not until the story jumps to an inside page that the paper provides important background. Without saying how the detainee came to the

12 Berry LMHC, CAP, William. "The Relationship Double Bind: From Frustration to Enlightenment," *Psychology Today*, August 3, 2011.

13 Harlan, Chico. "A Point of Pride or Fear," *Washington Post,* November 18, 2016.

United States, the narrative notes that he "fell in with members of a drug cartel...He was arrested for theft and assault, among other crimes, and was addicted to drugs."[14] Yet noncitizens can be deported for possession of more than an ounce (thirty grams) of marijuana. If they have been convicted of having, using, abusing, or being addicted to any other controlled substance, they are deportable.[15]

He's obviously needed to work in a plant or in the fields, processing and growing opium poppies and marijuana.

US citizens are quite conditioned to this. For years, they've been hearing about waves of people from the Caribbean or south of the Rio Grande (known as Rio Bravo to Mexicans) or elsewhere. Playing up American "exceptionalism," the wave's proponents point to public figures with questionable immigrant backgrounds or to the advantages of hardworking people fleeing tyranny. (It must be said, these people provide a distinct advantage for business: they work for the minimum wage with few, if any, benefits.) Unfortunately, those drumming up the advantages of admitting "undocumented immigrants," in violation of the Immigration and Nationality Act,[16] patently ignore the consequences of American foreign policy south of the border.

Since the end of World War II, the United States has

- overthrown the government of Guatemala (1954);
- sought to overthrow the government of Cuba (1959 to the present);
- organized death squads in Guatemala (the 1960s through the 1980s);
- overthrown the government of the Dominican Republic (1963);

---

14 Weiner, Rachel and Marimow, Anne E. "Teen to Be Freed after Years in Legal Limbo," *Washington Post*, November 23, 2016. NB The judge's brother, Plato, often appeared before his court, the US District Court for the Eastern District of Virginia, representing clients on national security issues.

15 Immigration and Nationality Act/US Code: Sec. 237 1/ [8 U.S.C. 1227].

16 Title 8, US Code.

- overthrown the government of Brazil (1964);
- overthrown the government of Bolivia (1971);
- overthrown the government of Chile (1973);
- attacked the people of Nicaragua with a proxy army, the Contras (1979 through 1986);
- helped fight democratic dissidents in El Salvador (1980 through 1992);
- invaded Grenada (1983);
- invaded and overthrown the government of Panama (1989);
- sought to overthrow the government of Venezuela (2002 to the present);
- overthrown the government of Haiti (2004); and
- supported overthrow of the Honduran President Zelaya (2009).

Is there any wonder that "undocumented immigrants" are migrating north?

How Does Using People as Weapons Work?

Leaping over Greenhill's chapters on Cuba, Yugoslavia (essentially US and NATO propaganda), and Haiti, let's take a look at her remarks on North Korea.

Essentially a how-to-do-it guidebook on engineering mass migrations, the section shows how aggressive *agents provocateurs*, between 2002 and 2005, sought to replicate, in the Hermit Kingdom, the tidal wave of East Germans that roared through Hungary and into West Germany in 1989. These agents, a coalition of activists and nongovernmental organizations, including at least seven international human rights NGOs, saw how this had resulted in regime change in Europe. It not only ended the existence of the German Democratic Republic (East Germany) but also brought on the collapse of the Iron Curtain, Winston Churchill's term for the barrier between Western Europe and the USSR's sphere of influence. "As one UNHCR [United Nations High Commission for Refugees] official put it, 'These guys are serious. Regime change by refugee flow; this could be the next big thing.'"[17]

According to Greenhill, "'The theory [is] that if UN refugee camps are established on the China-North Korea border, they will incite a flood of North Korean refugees who want to escape political oppression in North Korea, leading to the same type of regime collapse in North Korea that occurred in East Germany,' just without the Berlin Wall."[18] One of the key players in this operation was Norbert Vollertsen, "a German who witnessed the fall of the Wall." He declared, "I understand the destabilizing impact an exodus of refugees can have on totalitarian regimes."[19] And it wasn't just Vollertsen who was caught up in this. Several religious figures were also deeply involved, such as Rev. Tim Peters and Rev. Douglas Shin. Peters was an evangelical pastor and head of a Seoul-based charity, and Shin led the Los Angeles–based Korean Peninsula Peace Project. Shin noted, "Some people will perish, but the majority will get out...There will be a continuous flow until the end [of the North Korean government]."[20]

Force as a Political Instrument

Central to Greenhill's concept is the use of force (or the threat of force) as a political instrument. Stephen Kaplan, a one-time official of the US National Intelligence Council (NIC), contributed to this view of power. (The NIC supports the Director of National Intelligence in his role as head of the American intelligence services.) In a body of work the Brookings Institution produced for the US government's Defense Advanced Research Projects Agency (DARPA), Kaplan wrote

17 *Weapons of Mass Migration*, 232–233, citing UNHCR official, personal communication, December 2002.

18 Ibid., 233, citing Brad Glosserman and Scott Snyder, "Borders and Boundaries: The North Korean Refugee Crisis," *PacNet Newsletter* 21 (2002).

19 Ibid., 234, citing Norbert Vollertsen, "Prison Nation: Why North Koreans Cheered Bush's 'Axis of Evil' Designation," *Wall Street Journal*, February 5, 2003.

20 Ibid., 234–235.

about the "use of discrete military moves to influence particular foreign situations."[21]

With American armed forces deeply involved in Afghanistan, Iraq, Libya, Syria, and what was once Yugoslavia, there was ample opportunity to manipulate their governments along with "the hearts and minds" of their people. In all of these countries, particularly in Yugoslavia, the United States played ethnic, religious, and linguistic groups against each other.

In Afghanistan, according to the CIA's *World Factbook* (September 28, 2016, update), there are many tribal groups: Pashtun, Tajik, Hazara, Uzbek, and "other" (which includes smaller numbers of Baloch, Turkmen, Nuristani, Pamiri, Arab, Gujjar, Brahui, Qizilbash, Aimaq, Pashai, and Kyrgyz). Language additionally divides these groups: 50 percent speak Afghan Persian, or Dari (the official language), 35 percent speak Pashto (another official language), 11 percent speak Turkic languages (primarily Uzbek and Turkmen), and 4 percent speak thirty minor languages (primarily Balochi and Pashai). There is much bilingualism, but Dari functions as the lingua franca. Afghanistan is primarily 99.7 percent Muslim, with a breakdown of Sunni at 84.7–89.7 percent and Shia at 10–15 percent. So, along religious fault lines, Afghanistan was and is a divided country.

How did this work? Once the war between the US-backed mujahideen and the Soviet Union began,

> Afghanistan was split and divided into different ideological groups, resulting in bloodshed, killing, destruction, suffering, and hatred among Afghans…
>
> The number of religious schools (madrassas) educating Afghans rose from 2,500 in 1980 at the start of Afghan resistance

21 Stephen S. Kaplan, *Force without War: The United States' Use of the Armed Forces as a Political Instrument.* Washington, DC: Brookings Institution, 1977, 2. Brookings is a nonprofit public policy organization based in Washington, DC. It appears to have close ties to the Democratic Party and to the US foreign policy establishment.

> to over 39,000. The United States encouraged the Saudis to recruit Wahhabist ideologues to come join the resistance and teach in refugee institutes...
>
> The Hezb-e-Islami faction, a relatively small group among the resistance to the Soviets and their Afghan allies, received at least 80% of U.S. aid. According to Professor Barnett Rubin's [congressional] testimony...the militia—led by the notorious Gulbuddin Hekmatyar—conducted a "reign of terror against insufficiently Islamic intellectuals" in the refugee camps of Pakistan. Despite all this, Rubin...noted how "both the ISI [Pakistan's Inter–Services Intelligence] and CIA considered him a useful tool for shaping the future of Central Asia."
>
> ...During the 1980s, the United States was so focused on defeating the Soviets and the Afghan communists that an alliance was made with Islamist extremists...In this decade [2000–2010], the United States has been so focused on defeating the Taliban and al-Qaeda it's made alliances with an assortment of drug lords, opium magnates, militia leaders, and other violent and corrupting elements which have contributed to the country's devastation still further.[22]

In the Federal Republic of Yugoslavia, another former country of varying religions, ethnicities, and induced hatreds, US policy was to capitalize on internal tensions, helping pit Croats and Slovenians against Serbs, Roman Catholics against Orthodox, Slavs against non-Slavs (modern Albanians), and all against Muslims. While imported fighters from Afghanistan and elsewhere were wreaking havoc in the Republic, the Americans were insisting something had to be done to "protect" the various groups being exploited. As tensions rose, the different states of Yugoslavia declared (or were encouraged to declare) their independence through direct Western influence. Germany, a US client state, hastened

---

22 Zunes, Stephen and Arsala, Kushal, edited by Greco, Emily Schwartz. *The U.S. and Afghan Tragedy–Remembering Recent History*. Foreign Policy in Focus, February 18, 2009.

and directly helped facilitate the breakup of the country through its 1991 recognition of the most economically developed states of the Yugoslav Federation, Slovenia and Croatia. This was an initiative that Germany's then foreign minister, Hans-Dietrich Genscher, led directly. The Americans, for their part, wanted to control the other parts of the confederation in order to command routes to Caspian Sea oil resources, among other goals.[23]

Similar things have taken place elsewhere, such as in Iraq.

In "American Terror Strategy in Iraq," Dr. Elias Akleh flatly stated that the American aim in Iraq was *divide et impera* (Imperial Rome's principle of divide and rule). With a goal of "spreading a sectarian hatred between the three major Iraqi sects, Kurds, Shiite, and Sunnis," American agents, ably assisted by Israeli intelligence, have been executing Sunni and Shiite leaders while blowing up their mosques and setting off explosives in their communities. This diverted the groups from fighting the American invaders to battling each other.

Additionally, Dr. Akleh wrote that US forces targeted civilians and tried to link the attacks to the resistance, attempting to cut them off from the Iraqi population that sheltered them. The assailants weren't the Anglo-Saxon Christians from the American Midwest but were "Al Qaeda," "al-Zarqawi," or "foreign terrorists." Following the lead of a similar Nazi SS strategy in wartime Czechoslovakia, and as they had done with Operation Phoenix in Vietnam, the Americans destroyed entire villages for protecting opponents of the invasion.

US officials such as James Steele and Steve Casteel, as Dr. Akleh perspicaciously wrote, created sectarian, vigilante militias, placing them under the control of Iraqi politicians such as Iyad Allawi, "for their protection." Akleh further asserted that directing Kurdish Peshmerga and Shiite militias against the Sunni "increase[d] the likelihood of sectarian hatred and civil war." To its everlasting discredit, the US Marine Corps

---

23 *Visas for Al Qaeda*, 99, citing Michael Parenti, "The Rational Destruction of Yugoslavia," www.michaelparenti.org. Michel Chossudovsky, "Dismantling Former Yugoslavia, Recolonizing Bosnia-Herzegovina," *globalresearch.ca*, February 19, 2002.

created its own Iraqi militias. Dr. Akleh stated that, in January 2005, the 7th Marines established a group called the Iraqi Freedom Guard, paying each member $400 a month (at the 2005 exchange rate, that was nearly 600,000 Iraqi dinars). This was an exceptionally high salary at a time of rapidly plummeting incomes.[24] The 23rd Marines also set up a militia, mostly from Basra, called Freedom Fighters. Both groups, Dr. Akleh said, were used in attacks in Anbar Province in Western Iraq. Continuing, Elias Akleh said that the American forces had worked out an agreement with Moqtada al-Sadr's Mahdi army, always described in the US press as "anti-American," to pursue and seize members of the resistance.

As Robert Dreyfuss explained in "Phoenix Rising," Congress had given $3 billion to the CIA to create militia-run paramilitary units. The object was to kill "nationalists, other opponents of the US occupation, and thousands of civilian Baathists, up to 120,000 of the estimated 2.5 million former Baath Party members in Iraq." Furthermore, Dreyfuss asserted that the lion's share of this money would help "create a lethal, and revenge-minded Iraqi security force."[25]

Libya was a good target for *divide et impera.*

> The inhabitants of Libya are a mixed people of various stocks from Africa, the Mediterranean Basin, Europe, and Southwest Asia. [They are] Berbers, Egyptians, Greeks, people of Italian descent, people from the Levant, Iranians, Arabs, Turks, Vandals, Hadjanrais, Tuaregs (the Kel Tamajaq or Kel Tamashq), and several other groups…
>
> [This led to] internal fighting [stoked by Western intelligence]…replicating the same divisive scenarios that occurred in the former Yugoslavia and in Iraq…

---

24 The median income in Iraq in 2003 was about 366,000 dinars (ca. $255). It slid in the first half of 2004 to approximately 207,000 dinars (roughly $144). CNN: "Report Paints Grim Picture of Iraqi Life," May 12, 2005.

25 *Visas for Al Qaeda*, 126–128, citing Elias's undated article appearing originally at www.inmediares.dk. and Dreyfuss, Robert, *The Prospect*, December 10, 2003.

> Anyone who understands Libyan society also understands the heavy political weight and representation the tribes have.
>
> This war [sought] to create divisions within Libyan society. Admiral Stravridis, the U.S. commander in charge of NATO, [said to Congress] in March 2011 that he believed that Qaddafi's support base would shrink as the tribal cleavages in Libya came "into play" as the war proceeded. [That is] NATO operations in Libya will cause further internal divisions through igniting tribal tensions that will cement regional differences...The U.S. and NATO also know full well that if Colonel Qaddafi is gone... the Libyan tribes would bicker amongst themselves for power and be politically divided...
>
> The U.S., Britain, France, Italy, and NATO...are also very well aware that any tribal conflicts in Libya will spread from North Africa into West Africa and Central Africa [in a pattern of engineered strife].[26]

Like Libya, Syria is a land of easily exploited divisions, which fits the American concept of encouraging internal disagreement.

Syria was and is a country of varying sects, ethnicities, and loyalties. It fits the American idea of divide and rule, according to the same devastating recipe.

Syria is about the size of the US state of Washington (185,180 square kilometers/71,498 square miles). Like Washington, it is made up of a humid coastal zone, deserts, semiarid plains, and mountains. Syria averages twenty-five centimeters (not quite ten inches) of rainfall per year.[27]

Take a look at just the religious groupings. The Alawites (part of Shia Islam) are generally poor and live in rural areas, primarily in the

---

26 Nazemroaya, Mahdi Darius. *The War on Libya: An Imperialist Project to Create Three Libyas.* Global Research, July 29, 2011.

27 Federal Research Division, Library of Congress for the US Army, *Syria, A Country Study,* Area Handbook Series (Washington, DC: US Government/Secretary of the Army, 1988), 53–55, 57.

west and center of the country. Christians, Druze (a mix of Shiism, Christianity, and paganism), and Circassians (a Caucasian people) inhabit the southwest. And in the north dwell Assyrians (a Semitic people ethnically distinct from Arabs and Jews), Shi'a, and Sunni. Also in the center are Shi'a and Sunni. There are also Jews and Kurds, along with Ismailis (another branch of Islam). Christians break out into Greek Orthodox, Syrian Orthodox, and Greek Catholics.[28] In short, Syria is like a pizza with everything on it.

The consciousness of Syrian nationalism is not well defined. A person's loyalty is to his or her family, ethnic group, or religious community. People tend to cooperate with those known and trusted, such as traditional family members and their own ethnic and religious factions.[29]

By the end of the 1970s, the Syrian economy had expanded beyond its traditional agricultural base to include services, industry, and commercial sectors.[30] All in all, Syria fit the strategic pattern for American disruption: religious groups with little in common, emphasis on the family and ethnicity, a weak economy, and a government trying to hold it all together. This proved too juicy a target for seasoned nation wreckers in the West.

To Sum Up

Beginning with Afghanistan and ending with Syria, the US government assiduously worked to exploit countries riven by religious, ethnic, linguistic, and cultural differences. Creating alliances with drug lords, warlords, and fanatics of every stripe, America, the "City upon a Hill," in Massachusetts Bay Colony Governor Winthrop's words, fashioned or exploited existing tensions to divide and rule. In Afghanistan, it was warlords and the mujahideen, sustained by Saudi Arabia and Pakistan. In Yugoslavia, it was al-Qaeda inserted into the Bosnian Muslim *Ljiljani*

28 Ibid., 62–64.
29 Ibid., 63.
30 Ibid., 109.

paramilitary force and the empowerment of the Kosovo Liberation Army. Both were supported and supplied by NATO. In Iraq, it was al-Qaeda, backed by Saudi Arabia. In Libya, it was Afghan War–trained al-Qaeda operatives assisted by NATO countries' intelligence services. In Syria, it is the latest group of rebranded terrorists buttressed by the Gulf States, Israel, Jordan, Saudi Arabia, and Turkey. Their weapons of choice were bombs and bullets.

But there was method to this madness. (The author had been in Jeddah when the whole lunacy began. As time went by, he recognized the birth of al-Qaeda and its subsequent variations as they moved from country to country.)

The United States and NATO had developed a practice of picking the best terrorists from each country and loosing them upon their targets. Once that operation was over, they aimed them at the next country for the next attack. Along with the usual weapons, the West's homicidal maniacs added the region's oldest methods of brutal slaughter to structured special operations training, which their Western mentors provided.

As a result of the foregoing, the dead are countless, and the refugees and those internally displaced number in the millions. This is American policy in Latin America and the Caribbean on a global scale.

2

The Next Step: Using Weapons of Mass Migration

The Seething Masses

MORE THAN HALF (54 percent) of all refugees worldwide come from just three countries: the Syrian Arab Republic (4.9 million), Afghanistan (2.7 million), and Somalia (1.1 million). Iraq and Libya, following their destruction, have contributed 4,746,100 and 471,653 people respectively. Officially, they are populations "of concern" (i.e., refugees, asylees, or citizens in like situations). Regarding the parts of old Yugoslavia, Bosnia and Herzegovina produced 157,662 more individuals. Croatia still has 17,631 in such a state, while other republics count extra, such as Montenegro with 15,875, Serbia and Kosovo with 259,023, and Slovenia with 399. Fifteen years after war's end, the total for what was once a whole country still comes to 450,590 people, classed as either refugees, asylees, or those in similar conditions. (NB Macedonia and Vojvodina are not listed.)[31]

Lesser numbers of inhabitants came from other countries subject to US policy decisions. Albania, Pakistan, Eritrea, Nigeria, Iran, and the

31 UNHCR.org, 2015.

Ukraine together poured a total of several hundred thousand citizens into the mix going to Europe.[32]

Where did they go? Germany got more than 476,000 asylum applications in 2015 alone. However, German officials claimed they had counted more than a million such incoming migrants in 2015. Hungary, in second place, picked up 177,130 applications by the end of that year, the highest number on the continent relative to its population. Austria became host to slightly fewer, about 100,000 asylees. France, Italy, and Sweden found themselves with 100,000 or slightly fewer people each.

Adding in the rest of the continent, asylum claims in Europe totaled 1,321,560. The bulk of these (1,011,700) arrived by water, and almost 34,900 arrived by land. The previous year, 2014, saw only 280,000 land and sea arrivals. (And those are just the people who bellied up to the applications counter. Not counted are the ones who simply walked across the border and disappeared.) Unsurprisingly, the European Union's external border force, Frontex, asserts that the numbers crossing into Europe in 2015 amounted to more than 1.8 million souls.[33] If you look at the figures from the European criminal intelligence agency (Europol), there are 10,000 more that have gone missing. These are unaccompanied child refugees who disappeared after arriving in Europe. Europol asserts that 27 percent of the million-plus arrivals in Europe constituted youngsters—that's 270,000 minors.[34]

And is all this a pickup, uncoordinated affair, or do the migrants get help?

> Experts say the main assistance migrants ask for when they arrive at junctions in their journeys is information.

32 BBC. "Migrant Crisis: Migration to Europe Explained in Seven Charts," March 4, 2016.

33 Ibid.

34 Townsend, Mark. "10,000 Refugee Children Are Missing, Says Europol," *The Guardian*, January 30, 2016.

> "They keep asking where can they go, where can they go for protection," said Melita Sunjic, spokeswoman for the UN's refugee agency UNHCR.
>
> Many are increasingly turning to smartphones and social networks such as Whatsapp and Facebook to share advice on routes.
>
> Getting a local Sim card or connecting to wireless internet allows the migrants to use GPS maps, search engines and booking sites.[35]

Spooks or Mooks?

Throughout *Visas for Al Qaeda: CIA Handouts That Rocked the World*, we drew attention to the various intelligence agencies' role in creating and directing the bewildering number of terrorist organizations. Besides, and in connection with, their actions abroad, the spooks had great influence in America. They made palatable concepts such as increased domestic surveillance and gradual loss of civil liberties, all of which resulted in a "strategy of tension."

Al-Qaeda "tensions" proved successful in achieving carte blanche for domestic policy. So much so that external wars and infringement on civil rights to protect us from terrorist attacks made it easier to mask creating, funding, and directing a myriad of allegedly extremist Islamic groups. This became one of the fine dark arts of the CIA, MI6, and Mossad, with a little help from Saudi money.

Is it then not just a tiny step further to tie those groups into the seething masses?

Early in 2016, *RT* asked this writer's opinion on whether an estimated five thousand jihadists had moved into Europe as part of the migrant flood. The author disputed the proposed number but thought that many might well have infiltrated the continent. As time went by,

35 Coleman, Jasmine. "Migrant Crisis: What Is the Next Route through Europe?," *BBC News*, September 22, 2015.

more and more reports surfaced about extremists "going with the flow." And yet the German borders became more open.

Germany seems to have gotten its share of terrorists, but that unfortunate country's government does not link the migrant wave to its unsavory membership. However, occasionally this discrepancy gets highlighted. On November 8, 2016, *New Europe* reported that police in North Rhine-Westphalia arrested five members of a "terrorist recruiting network." Operating on behalf of the Islamic State, the organization enlisted and supported "volunteers" seeking to fight in Syria. One of those arrested was Abu Walaa, also known as Ahmad Abde, a preacher and a major figure in Germany's jihadist movement. Unfortunately for Germany's internal security service, the Federal Office for the Protection of the Constitution (*Bundesamt für Verfassungsschutz*, or BfV), neither it nor the police fingered the preacher. "The arrest appears to have been facilitated by a former IS fighter, Anil O., 22, who identified Walaa as Germany's IS leader."[36]

Fox News identified Walaa as a thirty-two-year-old Iraqi. The network also claimed that two other suspects (Hasan C., a fifty-year-old Turk, and an unnamed thirty-six-year-old German Serb) were responsible for teaching Arabic and radical Islam to those recruited.[37]

On November 30, 2016, the Associated Press (AP) reported another black eye for the BfV. In April 2016, the internal security service had hired a former bank employee, a recent convert to Islam. The fifty-one-year-old mole sought to use his position to "help the brothers" attack his employer. The BfV caught on to this only after another of its officers, pretending to be an Islamic extremist, found the infiltrator in an Internet chat room.[38]

The article claimed the BfV had followed its normal procedures during the interview and hiring process. If so, the service (1) is remarkably

---

36 "Germany Arrests IS Leader, Abu Walaa," *New Europe Online*, November 8, 2016.

37 "Five ISIS Suspects Arrested in Germany," *Fox News*, November 8, 2016.

38 Rising, David. "Islamic Extremist Mole in German Intel Agency a Recent Hire," *AP*, November 30, 2016.

incompetent, or (2) tried to use the spy as an unwitting double agent, or (3) simply planned an intelligence coup to keep the fear alive. There is a fourth possibility: it was a propaganda effort designed to show the government is acting against the Muslim migrant flood.

But, as time went by, more discomforting details emerged. The mole, "of Spanish descent," turned out to be a homosexual who acted in gay pornographic films, hardly employment for a devout Muslim. Hans-Christian Ströbele, on the German parliament's intelligence oversight committee, was sharply critical. Noting that this happened to the counterespionage agency, he said, "It's not only a rather bizarre, but also a quite scary story." Ströbele, a member of the Green Party, added that the agency "needs to tell us immediately what exactly happened and how it could happen that somebody like this was hired."

The BfV's response? One was, oh, the spy might have been mentally ill, with multiple personalities. Another was, it's almost impossible to prevent a breach like this.[39] What's clear is that the German internal intelligence service can't or won't or is not permitted to do its job. Are they really that incompetent? Or is there political pressure from Chancellor Merkel?

The United Kingdom's *Telegraph* soon noted that ISIL was smuggling terrorist sleeper cells throughout Europe. The paper asserted that British intelligence officials feared that group was equipping its fighters with counterfeit Syrian or Iraqi passports "so sophisticated it is almost impossible to distinguish between genuine refugees and terror suspects." Additionally, the paper said that those suspects, under intelligence agencies' surveillance in Raqqa, Syria, "suddenly vanish."[40]

Really? Truly? Muslim fanatics sophisticated enough to produce a large supply of nearly genuine travel documents in war-torn countries? Alleged crazies able to vanish into thin air while under the watchful eyes

---

39 Mekhennet, Souad and Faiola, Anthony. "German Spy Was Gay Porn Actor—and Secret Islamist," *Washington Post*, December 1, 2016.

40 Whitehead, Tom and Coughlin, Con. "Isil Exploiting Migrant Routes to Smuggle Jihadists Back to Britain Using Fake Documents," *The Telegraph*, January 26, 2016.

of a multitude of supposedly experienced, trained, professional espionage services? Either the *Telegraph*'s story is tongue in cheek, or Her Britannic Majesty's Secret Intelligence Service can't do its stated job. Or is it that MI6 is working hand in glove with the terrorists? Or, perhaps, Queenie's spooks and the bad boys have a fabulous working relationship with each other. You choose.

And there are still more choices.

Global Research carried a report from Gearóid Ó Colmáin connecting the United States and French governments to the "refugee" wave.

> Austrian intelligence officials have reportedly revealed that US government agencies are paying for the transport of migrants to Europe. On August 5th, 2015 [the] Austrian magazine *Infodirekt* reported:
>
> "It has come to our knowledge that US organisations are paying for the boats taking thousands of refugees to Europe. US organisations have created a co-financing scheme which provides for a considerable portion of the transportation costs. Not every refugee from North Africa has 11,000 Euro cash [*sic*]. Nobody is asking where is the money coming from?"
>
> French government officials have also been caught selling life boats to refugees in Turkey. France's *France 2 Television* station filmed honorary pro-consul Françoise Olcay in Turkey *in flagrante delicto.*

While Mme Olcay justified her actions by asserting that hundreds of Turkish officials were involved with the lifeboat scheme, no one denied that the French government had printed Syrian passports prior to 2011. Did that same government provide travel permits to the flood of migrants somehow using false Syrian documents?[41]

41 Ó Colmáin, Gearóid. "Imperialism's Migration Agenda: Who Is Funding the Refugees Transport into Europe?" *Global Research*, February 2, 2016 (from *Dissident Voice*, January 24, 2016).

Some of these passes, genuine ones, have come from the Syrian embassy in Berlin. In Germany, Syrian refugees have better success in applying for asylum. *Focus* quoted the *Berliner Zeitung* as saying that staff at the legation would issue travel documents to anyone proving to be Syrian. For an extra €150 (ca. US$160), embassy employees would make up a genuine passport for anyone who wanted such a document. There was no need to check for citizenship. Given that many genuine Syrian passports have been lost, stolen, or taken by traffickers, there are many real travel documents floating around. And many Syrians had an actual need for a replacement. Moreover, the German state's attorney doesn't yet know how many authentic passes have been sold to non-Syrians.[42]

We Thinks They Doth Protest Too Much

Iraq, since the American invasions of 1991 and 2003, has been repeatedly rocked by protests: against war, against religion, against politics. This author recounted the sordid tale of refugees and internally displaced, who number in the millions, in "Between Iraq and a Hard Place."[43]

> Well, there are roughly 2 million of these [internally displaced] who fled such situations [devastated infrastructure], who have been forced out of their homes (or what's left of their homes), to seek shelter and sustenance, where and when and however they might find them. And those are the ones still in Iraq.
>
> There are also an estimated 2 million more who navigated the radioactive, poisonous, depleted uranium dust from expended U.S. munitions and found refuge in neighboring countries, lands such as Syria, denounced by the United States

42 "Syrische Botschaft soll falsche Pässe gegen Extragebühr ausgestellt haben" (Syrian Embassy Supposed to Have Issued False Passports for an Extra Fee), *Focus.de*, January 27, 2017.

43 Springmann, J. Michael. "Between Iraq and a Hard Place," *The Public Record*, March 21, 2009.

> and Israel as supporting terrorism, and Lebanon, a country devastated and destabilized by American and Israeli pressures and policies. Unlike Israel and America, Syria, bleeding Lebanon, and nearby Jordan are poor countries, short of water, food, and resources, barely able to feed and shelter their own people.
>
> Iraq once numbered about 25 million inhabitants. The approximately 4 million "internally displaced" and "refugees" together comprise about 15% of the population. The ones abroad are mostly members of what was once the Arab world's most educated and populous middle class, the very people needed in any country for stability and growth, the very people that a devastated Iraq cannot afford to lose.

Libya had its own refugee crisis following protests, supposedly beginning in 2009 and exploding in February 2011. The latter gave the pretext for the US-French-British-Italian attacks on the country, using bombs, bullets, and spooks. It ended six months later in October with the murder of the country's director, Moammar Gaddafi. Besides the number of people displaced or forced into exile by the 2011 fighting (ca. 435,000),[44] Libya has lost still more citizens through external meddling and internal strife.

> Libya has struggled to rebuild state institutions amid rising violence since the ouster and subsequent death of Colonel Muammar al-Qaddafi in October 2011. The strength of rebel militias has increased—approximately 1,700 armed groups, including fighters loyal to the Islamic State—especially since the attack on the U.S. consulate in Benghazi on September 11, 2012...
>
> As a result of the continued fighting, more than 434,869 people have been internally displaced as of June 2015—double the

44 ScienceDirect. Citing "Libyan Armed Conflict 2011: Mortality, Injury and Population Displacement," *African Journal of Emergency Medicine,* September 2015 (Volume 5, Issue 3, Pages 101–107).

> number of displaced persons from the previous year. Given its proximity to Europe, Libya has also been used as a passageway for Libyan refugees and refugees from other North African and sub-Saharan African countries. In 2015, half a million people had sailed by boat from Libya as of September.[45]

Syria's protests supposedly "began in the southern city of Deraa in March when locals gathered to demand the release of 14 school children who were arrested and reportedly tortured after writing on a wall the well-known slogan of the popular uprisings in Tunisia and Egypt: 'The people want the downfall of the regime.'"[46]

Mark you, the "dissent" did not begin in the political capital, Damascus, the oldest continuously inhabited city in the world. Given its population of over 1.5 million people (according to the 2004 census)[47] and Damascus University, with 110,000 students,[48] you'd think the unrest would have begun there. Or it could have started in Aleppo (Halab), the largest metropolis in the country, with more than 4 million souls (from the 2004 census)[49] and 65,000 students at its university.[50]

No, it began in Deraa, a town of less than 100,000 people (from the 2004 census).[51] It sits on the Jordanian frontier, twenty miles (roughly thirty-two kilometers) from Israel. The two universities in the municipality don't report their student enrollment.[52]

A remarkable coincidence, is it not? It looks more like Middle Eastern puppetry. The Hashemite Kingdom and Israel are so close to the United States and so far from democracy. Jordan, of course, is a US client state receiving billions of dollars in military and economic aid throughout

45 Council on Foreign Relations. "Conflict Tracker," October 18, 2016.

46 BBC News. April 9, 2012.

47 citypopulation.de.

48 http://eacea.ec.europa.eu/tempus/participating_countries/higher/syria.pdf.

49 citypopulation.de.

50 http://eacea.ec.europa.eu/tempus/participating_countries/higher/syria.pdf.

51 citypopulation.de.

52 http://www.4icu.org/reviews/11906.htm.

the years ($15.83 billion since 1951).[53] Israel is a terrorist entity having far too much control over US foreign policy. It has a plan, the Yinon Plan, for balkanizing the Middle East.[54] And Syria is part of it.

Yet the state-run BBC claimed,

> The peaceful show of dissent was, however, too much for the government and when people marched through the city after Friday prayers on 18 March, security forces opened fire, killing four people. The following day, they shot at mourners at the victims' funerals, killing another person.
>
> Within days, the unrest in Deraa had spiraled out of the control of the local authorities. In late March, the army's fourth armoured division—commanded by the president's brother, Maher—was sent in to crush the emboldened protesters. Dozens of people were killed, as tanks shelled residential areas and troops stormed homes, rounding up those believed to have attended demonstrations.[55]

But *Global Research* tells another story:

> Five Years ago Daraa, mid-March 2011.
>
> "I have seen from the beginning armed protesters in those demonstrations...They were the first to fire on the police. Very often the violence of the security forces comes in response to the brutal violence of the armed insurgents."—*Jesuit priest Father Frans Van der Lugt, January 2012, Homs Syria*
>
> "The claim that armed opposition to the government has begun only recently is a complete lie. The killings of soldiers,

53 Sharp, Jeremy M. 2016 *Jordan: Background and US Relations.* CRS Report No. RL33546. Washington, DC: Congressional Research Service. https://www.fas.org/sgp/crs/mideast/RL33546.pdf.

54 Shashak, Israel. "Greater Israel: The Zionist Plan for the Middle East," *Global Research*, April 23, 2016.

55 BBC News. April 9, 2012.

police and civilians, often in the most brutal circumstances, have been going on virtually since the beginning."—*Professor Jeremy Salt, October 2011, Ankara Turkey*[56]

To summarize the foregoing, Greenhill asserted that people seeking to coerce the decision-making of their targets use different mechanisms. They can erode the government's power base (cut the regime's links with its supporters). If they can, they try to develop unrest. Dissatisfaction with the government will weaken it. Also, they can debilitate the country as a whole. Or they can prevent military victories and political successes.[57]

Doesn't Syria match this concept perfectly? And wouldn't driving its citizens into Germany fit as well? As for Greenhill's comments on "capacity swamping" and "political agitation," they tally with what's happened in Europe. Swamping manipulates the ability of "targets to accept/accommodate/assimilate a given group of migrants or refugees...Political agitation [manipulates] the *willingness* of targets to do so."[58] Moreover, "migration crises tend to split societies into (at least) two mutually antagonistic and often highly mobilized groups: the pro-refugee/migrant and anti-refugee/migrant camp."[59] Doesn't this describe Germany?

Refugees, Asylees, Migrants—Why Are They in Europe?

From the North Cape to the Peloponnesus, Europe prides itself on being filled with democracies. As Kelly Greenhill astutely observes, albeit in her trademark convoluted language, "With respect to hypocrisy costs, the higher the (anticipated) costs targets face, the *more likely* [emphasis in original] it is that they will back down."[60] And Europe backed down.

56 Anderson, Professor Tim. "Daraa 2011: Syria's Islamist Insurrection in Disguise," *Global Research*, March 16, 2016.

57 Greenhill, 38.

58 Ibid., 38.

59 Ibid., 40.

60 Ibid., 10.

Didn't the other Arab countries take in the Iraqis, the Libyans, and the Syrians? Initially, some did. Lebanon, Jordan, and Syria helped resettle a number of Iraqis after the Bush crime syndicate's "awesomely shocking" attack on the Land between the Two Rivers in 2003. Lebanon and Jordan strained their economies with Syrians after the United States began to destabilize that country early in 2011. But America's loyal "allies"—the Gulf States, Saudi Arabia, Morocco, Egypt, and Turkey—didn't help much with relocation. They ignored ties of culture, language, religion, and climate[61]—or, in Turkey's case, took them in and sent them on.

Israel, an ever-helpful architect of chaos, did nothing to resolve it. Its view was, "Israeli Prime Minister Benjamin Netanyahu on Sunday [September 6, 2015] rejected a call to host refugees from Syria and elsewhere, saying that while Israel is 'not indifferent to the human tragedy of the refugees,' it is not in a position to take them in."[62]

And, as for the Arabian Peninsula states, here's the report from Germany's international broadcaster, *Deutsche Welle*: "Yet, while...boatloads of the destitute are making their way to Europe, the Gulf states have taken only a few hundred refugees, according to data from the UN's refugee agency (UNHCR). Led by the Saudis and Qatar, the Gulf states push the line that the refugee crisis is the outcome of Western inaction and the Syrian regime's brutality, even as they throw billions of dollars in supplies and weaponry into the Syrian jihadist cauldron to oust Assad at all costs."[63]

In the end, they are there because of Turkey and the Federal Republic of Germany.

---

61 A sprinkling ended up in Morocco: "Syrian Refugees Seek Sanctuary in Morocco: Hundreds of Refugees Have Entered Morocco across the Algerian Border, with Many Aiming to Reach European Shores." *Al Jazeera* (No author, no date).

62 Sobelman, Batsheva. "One Country That Won't Be Taking Syrian Refugees: Israel," *Los Angeles Times*, September 6, 2015.

63 "Arab Monarchies Turn Down Syrian Refugees over Security Threat," *Deutsche Welle*, January 25, 2016 (No author).

Greenhill says: "Coercive engineered migration is often embedded within mass migrations strategically engineered for dispossessive, exportive, or militarized reasons."[64] There is another advantage to this subterfuge: the more the migrants are seen as "victims and the more they can provoke moral outrage on behalf of their group, the higher the probability that international assistance will be forthcoming."[65]

How does this play out?

Turkey, a member of NATO with close ties to the United States and Israel, has an 899-kilometer/559-mile border with Syria. Its boundary with Iran runs 534 kilometers/332 miles. The Turkey-Iraq frontier stretches 367 kilometers/228 miles. Kurds, with no love for Turkey, Iraq, or Iran, heavily populate the periphery of those countries' borders with Anatolia. Kurds in northern Iraq work closely with America and Israel.

Consequently, if you are a migrant from East of Suez and you want to go to Europe, you go to Turkey first, with help (or at least no hindrance) from the local Kurds. Walking or riding is easier than traveling to a port and taking your chances with the Mediterranean Sea—or with one of the countries located on that body of water.

The government of Recep Tayyip Erdoğan could have blocked the wave of migrants into Turkey. Yet he allowed the tsunami to crest. Beyond that, he is now encouraging a greater migrant flow, blackmailing Europe with his own policy agenda, demanding Turkey's entrance into the Schengen-area visa-free travel zone as well as aid. In 2000, there were 1,281,000 international migrants in Anatolia. In 2015, the number had nearly doubled, reaching 2,964,900 (including 1.6 million refugees), with the median age being thirty-four years and thirty-five years, respectively.[66] (In September 2015, *Politico* reported that there were 2.2 million Syrian refugees lodged in Turkey.)[67] According to an *InfoWars*

64 Greenhill, 14.

65 Ibid., 23.

66 United Nations. *International Migration Report*. 13, 34.

67 Karnitschnig, Matthew. "European Leaders Seek Refugee Deal with Turkey," *Politico*, September 20, 2015.

piece, Turkey "planned and financed the mass migration." Citing a Polish media claim, the website asserted that Erdoğan supplied the migrants with the resources needed to realize their dream of living in Europe. Thomas Otłowski, writing for *Wiadomości*, a popular television news program, opined that Turkey did this because of Syrian-caused social and economic problems. Continuing, the Polish station noted that the Turks had "turned a blind eye to 'the activities of organized gangs of smugglers' who assist the effort to move thousands of migrants by sea to the Greek islands of Lesbos, Kos and Samos where they then travel to Europe." (This provided an added fillip to long-standing Greek-Turkish tensions.)[68] "Earlier, speaking of migration flow control, "Frontex's *Operation Poseidon* teams...[photographed] a Turkish Coast Guard cutter escorting a boatload of illegal migrants toward Greek waters."[69]

It is also possible to argue that the Turks used their country as a holding tank for refugees until such a time as it was possible to do the most damage to Europe. A trickle of illegals has no effect, really. However, a bolus of millions gets attention—and produces effects. The wave of migrants destabilized Europe and brought efforts to pay the Turks for closing the tap—or even to take some refugees back. The migratory wave even produced public discussions about admitting Turkey to the European Union, following years of denying it entry.

Turkey—or, rather, the new Ottoman sultan wannabe, Recep Tayyip Erdoğan—is still threatening Europe with a new migrant wave. According to the *Washington Post*, Sultan Erdoğan is extremely unhappy that the European Union sought to suspend membership talks. Fuming that Turkey's chances of membership were jeopardized after Erdoğan's crackdown following a questionable coup, the sultan is evidently seeking payback. In a television address on November 25, 2016, he said, "If you go any further, those border gates will be opened." The *Post* reported

68 Nimmo, Kurt. "Turkey Responsible for Flood of Illegal Immigrants in Europe," *InfoWars*, September 22, 2015.

69 Germek, Silvia. Unpublished 2015 MS citing "Turkish Coast Guard Caught Escorting Smugglers," *Sofia Echo*, September 21, 2009.

that Erdoğan specifically meant Turkey's frontier crossing with EU member Bulgaria. (The paper did not mention migrants using Turkish Aegean Sea islands, as in the past.) The *Post* estimated that there are still 2.7 million Syrians and 300,000 Iraqis, plus others, still in Turkey.

According to a ranking European government official contributing comments especially for this book, Erdoğan will likely do this:

> Turkey as the first stop to Europe tried to negotiate with the EU about requirements for retention of refugees. But the promised three billion Euros per year plus the liberalization of the visa regime for Turkish citizens has not yet been realized. Now it's just a matter of days when Ankara will release a new wave of refugees to Europe, i.e. Germany. After an unsuccessful coup in Turkey significantly soured the Ankara-Washington relationship, this opened a new chapter between Ankara and Moscow.[70]

Additionally, the Washington paper noted that more illegals from Africa are sailing across the Mediterranean to Europe. The *Post* touched on increasing unrest in migrant camps along the closed borders from the Aegean to northern Europe. Asylum seekers have already battled police on the Greek island of Lesbos, the paper said. Continuing, the journal reported that authorities had arrested four hundred refugees, mostly Afghans, in Bulgaria following imposition of quarantine.[71]

This fits into Kelly Greenhill's migration puzzle. In her chapter on North Korean refugees, she notes that one of the ways illegals get publicity is to take to the sea. Expecting to be rescued by passing ships, they end up in a place where they can claim asylum.[72]

---

70 Official statement by Pavle Kalinic, European government official, for this publication, December 23, 2016. Translation. He is equivalent to Croatia's DHS chief, and he is also their top terrorism specialist.

71 Birnbaum, Michael and Murphy, Brian. "Erdogan Issues Warning over E.U. Political Snubs," *Washington Post*, November 26, 2016.

72 Greenhill, 239.

Others added to this concept of sinister underhandedness. Citing an undated *World Net Daily* article, *InfoWars* recounted Dr. Mark Christian's statement that "the media is making this out to be a spontaneous refugee crisis when this is actually a very well organized event." In the article, Christian, an Egyptian-born former Muslim, asserted that the underlying purpose was regime change in Syria. He was quoted as saying that the flood of refugees into Europe is designed to put pressure on the West and provide a pretext for an invasion of Syria, the removal of Bashar al-Assad, and the installation of a Sunni government.[73]

73 Nimmo, Kurt. "Refugee Crisis: Planned Invasion of Europe," *InfoWars*, September 19, 2015.

3

Migrant Waves

A Balancing Act

The migrants also are remarkably unbalanced. It's not families that are marching to salvation; it's young, single men. "According to official counts, a disproportionate number of these migrants are young, unmarried, unaccompanied males. In fact, the sex ratios among migrants are so one-sided—...[worse than those in China, in some cases]—that they could radically change the gender balance in European countries in certain age cohorts." Sweden, which has been very open about its asylum seekers, is representative of the current European trends:

> According to Swedish government statistics, as of the end of November, 71 percent of all applicants for asylum to Sweden in 2015 were male. More than 21 percent of all migrants to Sweden were classified as unaccompanied minors, representing more than half of all minor migrants to the country. For *accompanied* minors, the sex ratio was about 1.16 boys for every one girl. But for *unaccompanied* minors, the ratio was 11.3 boys for every one girl. In other words, the Swedish case confirms IOM's [the International Organization of Migration] statistic that more than 90 percent of unaccompanied minors are male. Indeed, on

> average, approximately 90 unaccompanied boys entered Sweden every single day in 2015, compared with eight unaccompanied girls.[74]

There's also another problem: violence. *Politico* continued its analysis with disturbing details:

> Societies with extremely skewed sex ratios are more unstable even without jihadi ideologues in their midst. Numerous empirical studies have shown that sex ratios correlate significantly with violence and property crime—the higher the sex ratio, the worse the crime rate. Our research also found a link between sex ratios and the emergence of both violent criminal gangs and anti-government movements. It makes sense: When young adult males fail to make the transition to starting a household—particularly those young males who are already at risk for sociopathic behavior due to marginalization, a common concern among immigrants—their grievances are aggravated.
>
> There are also clearly negative effects for women in male-dominated populations. Crimes such as rape and sexual harassment become more common in highly masculinized societies, and women's ability to move about freely and without fear within society is curtailed.[75]
>
> Fully 72% of the "refugees" from the Syrian Civil War are males. Only 15% are children, and even fewer are women—13%.
>
> So why is this important? Because many are beginning to wonder if this is really a refugee problem, or if it's an orchestrated invasion of Europe by young males of fighting age.

74 Hudson, Valerie. "Europe's Man Problem—Migrants to Europe Skew Heavily Male—and That's Dangerous." *Politico*, January 5, 2016.

75 Ibid.

> They don't even pretend to deny that the reason they're trying to get to Europe is for the welfare and benefits the socialist countries will bestow on them.[76]

This was not unusual. Back when activists were trying to destabilize North Korea by flooding China with migrants, the Chinese made similar objections. They argued that the Koreans streaming across their borders were economic refugees seeking a financial advantage. To quote Kelly Greenhill, "The Chinese Foreign Ministry steadfastly maintained, 'these people entered China's territory illegally because of economic reasons and they are not refugees and they cannot be considered as refugees.'"[77]

And That Brings Us to Germany

While the predecessor governments of the current Federal Republic never ruled a country of immigrants, there were still inflows from outside. In the past, these were mostly workers from neighboring countries or ethnic Germans once settled in Hungary, Czechoslovakia, the Balkans, or the USSR. There was the guest worker (*Gastarbeiter*) wave of the 1950s, 1960s, and early 1970s. They came from neighboring countries such as Greece, Yugoslavia, Turkey, and Italy, filling jobs in Germany's postwar economic boom.

According to the German Federal Office for Migration and Refugees, 2014 "witnessed the highest level of immigration and the highest net migration since 1992 [from the destruction of Yugoslavia]." Immigration jumped 19 percent over the previous year, while asylum applicants leaped 60 percent to 203,000. For the first eleven months of 2015, asylum seekers bounded ahead to 425,000 persons, soaring 134

---

76 SOOPERMEXICAN (El Sooper is an anonymous blogger who has broken many national stories.). "Here's the ONE Fact That Dismantles the 'Syrian Refugee' MYTH," *The Political Insider*, undated article, Fall 2015.

77 Greenhill, 249.

percent over asylum seekers in 2014. However, according to numbers recorded under Germany's EASY system (First Allotment of Asylum Seekers) during the same period, there were 965,000 people seeking assistance. The report asserted that Poland was the legal immigrants' chief country of origin, as it had been since 1996.[78]

In late summer 2015, Germany opened its borders to all comers. On Tuesday, August 25, the Federal Office for Migration and Refugees tweeted, "We are no longer enforcing the Dublin procedures for Syrian citizens." (An asylum seeker must apply for that status in the first EU country entered.) Following that tweet, Arabic references to Angela Merkel, the German chancellor, jumped from less than five hundred a day to more than two thousand. More importantly, twenty thousand asylum seekers swarmed across the German frontier, many from Hungary, where they had been squatting in front of Budapest's railroad station. (Hungary had refused to let them through.)

The throngs formed columns of thousands, organized by Syrians and an Iraqi. The Hungarian government then chartered buses, transporting them to Austria, where German trains carried them west. "The protests were expressing personal freedom," said Abu Mohammed, forty, from Dhi Qar, Iraq. "They were about human rights, our right to be here."[79]

Asylum applications in Germany had been steadily building for the previous two years: from less than twenty thousand a month in January 2014 to over twenty thousand a month by the end of 2014. Beginning in 2015, the waves rose higher, from nearly thirty thousand in January to forty thousand monthly by September. By the end of the year, it was nearly sixty thousand every thirty days.[80]

---

78 German Federal Office for Migration and Refugees. *The 2014 Migration Report.* (Berlin: Bundesdruckerei GmbH 2016).

79 Thomas, Andrea; Bradley, Matt; Geiger, Friedrich. "Obscure German Tweet Helped Spur Migrant March from Hungary." *Wall Street Journal,* September 10, 2015.

80 German Federal Office for Migration and Refugees, 2016.

There's Small Choice in Rotten Apples

Initially, the migration of peoples caused what appeared to be minor culture clashes: defecation in the streets, brawls with drunken Oktoberfest goers, and conservative Muslim outrage against (what were to them) revealingly clad German teenagers. As time went by, this resulted in great resentment of the migrants and later culminated in the rapes, robberies, and beatings on the night of December 31, 2015.

On New Year's Eve 2015, things changed drastically. Once, just a few years ago, the event, called *Silvester* in German, was an evening of parties, fireworks, and plenty of champagne. It had been a fine and safe occasion. (While assigned to the US Consulate General in Stuttgart, the author went every year with friends to the Bismarckturm, a tower overlooking the city. He always had a clutch of skyrockets in one hand and a bottle of champagne in the other. The view was spectacular and the participants gleeful, and it was a wonder that the Swabian metropole didn't burn to the ground.)

But that year, things, just like Germany, changed—for the worse.

According to the *Washington Post*, "About 1,000 men described by officials as being largely of 'Arab or North African origin' [meaning migrants] had congregated in the square outside Cologne's main train station that night [New Year's Eve], with groups reportedly breaking off and assaulting women." Furthermore, the paper commented that females reported a sense of "lawlessness." One woman told BBC News that "they grabbed our arms...pushed our clothes away and tried to get between our legs or I don't know where."

As noted by an observant German contact, women had also been celebrating outside Cologne's impressive cathedral. They tried to flee their attackers but, owing to the press of people, couldn't. Besides being sexually molested, they had their cell phones and money stolen.

Our source added that Cologne's lord mayor, Henriette Reker, who ran as an independent aligned with the leftist Green Party, had caused a massive outpouring of scorn and contempt when she would not criticize the migrants. Instead, she advised women to keep an "arm's length" from strange men. People wanted to know just what is an "arm's length" and how you can keep an arm's length away from anyone in a huge crowd. Reker, once a member of Merkel's CDU party, had been elected from a hospital bed after a throat slashing alleged by a man ostensibly opposed to migrants. She is now the subject of mocking Facebook posts. One such came from a German Jew who shared a *Junge Alternative für Deutschland* (youth group of the *Alternative für Deutschland* AfD) poster. (AfD is a right-wing party critical of the German chancellor's efforts to bring in one million migrants.) The picture shows a woman sighting along the barrel of a large revolver held at arm's length, with the caption "We've checked it out, an arm's length is security. Reker is right."[81]

Cologne was not an anomaly.

German journalist Manuel Ochsenreiter posted a Facebook video of migrant assaults in Berlin, with the caption "This is not April/May 1945—this is New Year's Eve." The disquieting film clip showed Merkel's "invitees," her "children," firing strictly controlled handguns in the air and loosing rockets and other explosive fireworks horizontally into the crowd that packed the pavement. Fire trucks, which the author had never seen in operation during five years in Germany, were roaring through the streets, sirens howling.

In Hamburg, the *Frankfurter Allgemeine Zeitung* (FAZ) reported on January 5 that the situation there resembled Cologne. Young women between the ages of eighteen and twenty-four were verbally and sexually molested and then robbed of money and cell phones. The attackers, migrants in various-sized groups, surrounded the women who sought to flee the scene. The paper quoted Rainer Wendt, federal chairman of the German police union, as saying that the attacks weren't organized. The migrants simply used the crowd, the darkness, and the shock effect for their actions.

Another interlocutor told us that there were *Silvester* outbreaks in Stuttgart, on a smaller scale than Cologne yet also with sexual gropings, robberies, and theft of cell phones. The Stuttgart attacks took place in

81 Springmann, J. Michael. "Germany: Not for Those with Weak Constitutions," *Hausfrauleaks.com*, January 11, 2015.

the town square, the picturesque Schloßplatz, according to the FAZ. It added that two eighteen-year-old females were set upon by a group of fifteen men. The *Stuttgarter Zeitung* announced a second attack by a similar group wherein a twenty-year-old male migrant groped two girls: one fifteen, the other eighteen.

In Weil am Rhein, a town in the far southwest of Baden-Württemberg, four Syrians, including two asylum seekers between the ages of fourteen and twenty-one raped two German girls, fourteen and fifteen years old. SWR (Southwest Radio), in reporting the New Year's Eve crime, noted that the police downplayed any connection with the Cologne events and quoted the state police and the state's attorney's office as saying that a group of underage girls had willingly gone to the home of the underage boys and had engaged in "an exchange of tendernesses," implying they had voluntarily participated in sex.

In Singen, in the south of Baden-Württemberg, the local paper wrote that, on the late afternoon of January 4, 2016, two "dark-skinned men" attacked and attempted to strip naked a thirty-year-old woman sitting on a park bench behind City Hall. She fought them off, and they ran.

In Munich, principal city of relaxed Bavaria in Germany's southeast, *Rosenheim24*, an online news service, reported that ten to fifteen men swarmed two women who were taking a cigarette break outside a disco at 2:00 a.m. One was groped, and the other held tightly. Both eventually broke free and fled into the disco.

The foregoing accounts may well be only the ones reported. There is a sense, according to some contacts, that the German federal government was pressing news outlets around the country to downplay the events of *Silvester* 2015.

What's the real background to this? Kelly Greenhill wrote "targets will be most vulnerable...when there is broad and intense disagreement about the way a target should respond to an...ongoing migration crisis."[82]

82 Greenhill, 50–51.

Others suggested that the police simply didn't exert themselves. News outlets commented that the Cologne police were slow to act but quick to hide their reasons for doing so. One individual we know asked why the police didn't use water cannons on the thousand or so migrants attacking women. Yes, it was cold, but, she asked, was there a quicker way to disperse those criminals? She emphasized that the Cologne police routinely used water cannons to break up street protests and wondered how it was that the police "forgot" about their crowd-control weapon that night. Indeed, a quick check of the Internet showed that other cities in Germany, such as Hamburg and Leipzig, routinely employed them. In Stuttgart, in the fall of 2010, according to another longtime contact, the police, under the direction of Merkel's center-right Christian Democratic Union, were plenty fast in using water cannons. They sprayed women, children, and pensioners in protests against redeveloping the city's main railroad station. While the police were clearly slow and perhaps unwilling to act in Cologne against migrants, it was another story when the German Right mounted a massive demonstration against Merkel's proasylum policy. The British newspaper the *Independent* reported on January 9, 2016:

> Water cannons and pepper spray have been used to push back more than a thousand anti-immigration protesters in Cologne as anger mounted in a demonstration following attacks on New Year's Eve.[83]

One knowledgeable source from what was once Yugoslavia asks how it was possible to coordinate thousands of simultaneous migrant attacks on women all over Germany and throughout Europe.

Was it synchronized and stage-managed just as the ISIL attacks in the Middle East are, with US and European intelligence service cooperation? The earlier propaganda campaign in Germany in favor of the

---

83 Dearden, Lizzie. "Cologne Attacks: Police Use Water Cannon and Pepper Spray on Anti-Immigration Pegida Protesters," *Independent*, January 9, 2016.

migrant wave is now morphing into a movement targeting opposition to that wave. The good man (*Gutmensch/Gutbürger*) now opposes the old, stubborn, angry person (*Wutbürger*, with *Wut* meaning anger). Others might define the *Wutbürger* as someone fed up with political actions at the expense of the citizenry, such as the Stuttgarters who opposed the station redevelopment or those appalled at Merkel's migration of peoples.[84]

Coercion is the norm, not the exception. The Europeans are forced apart, and the migrants are targeted as Arabs and Muslims, "people not like us."

The attacks in Paris on November 13, 2015, followed the January 7, 2015, gunfire at the allegedly satirical magazine *Charlie Hebdo*, an anti-Muslim, anti-Semitic rag. But the shootout helped build a worldwide climate of hatred and fear of Muslims.

What appears to be the basis for a rising tide of fear and hatred is the mounting wave of migrants from Arab and Muslim countries. According to a German contact, they've even reached Süßen, a small town of some ten thousand people forty-five kilometers (ca. twenty-seven miles) east of Stuttgart. The municipality is housing them in a sports hall, she said.

And this war of cultures has other untoward effects.

In Garmisch–Partenkirchen, the Bavarian winter resort town, one father objected to his daughter being "'forced' by teachers to memorise the Islamic chants" during a school ethics lesson. This happened not long "after parents complained to German newspaper *Hessian Niedersächsische Allgemeine*...that their children's nursery was refusing to acknowledge 'Christmas rituals' to accommodate the 'diverse cultures' of other pupils."[85]

Perhaps this is making a mountain out of a molehill. However, there is a difference between acquainting the native Germans with other cultures and imposing those cultures on them. The Kassel daycare

84 Greenhill, 50–51.

85 Efstathiou, Zoe. "Fury as German Primary School 'Forces' Children to Chant 'Allahu Akbar' in Muslim Prayer," *Express*, October 30, 2016.

center without Christmas rituals had a surprising defense. It maintained there was no need for them because most children attending were not Christian. "Migrants now outnumber native children at many schools in Germany as the country has been inundated with migrants in recent years."[86] This proves the migrant wave is now crashing into the basics of local society. It also puts a new twist on multiculturalism. Germany is promoting a "separate but equal" view of society, one where each group is free to observe but not share its own traditions.

This is entirely at odds with the author's knowledge of the Arab world. His Arabic teacher, a Muslim, has told him that Christians and Muslims in the region celebrate each other's holidays. A Muslim TV producer in the Middle East echoed this, noting that she must replace her broken Christmas tree.

But who and what are coming?

> Europe...will face substantial demographically driven migration pressures from across the Mediterranean for decades to come. Although these projected inflows would triple the first-generation immigrant stocks of larger European countries between 2010 and 2040, they would still absorb only a small fraction of the 800-million-person increase in the working-age population of Sub-Saharan Africa that is projected to occur over this period.[87]

That's just the population overpressure. Stout border controls can manage this. But when the migration is organized, when the migrants are economic, not political, when the Europeans don't grasp this, what then?

As stated by *Deutsche Welle*, Czech President Miloš Zeman has compared the refugees arriving in Europe to a Trojan horse. He called the influx an "organized invasion." The news service continued, quoting

---

86 Ibid.

87 Hanson, Gordon and McIntosh, Craig. "Is the Mediterranean the New Rio Grande? US and EU Immigration Pressures in the Long Run." *Journal of Economic Perspectives*, 30(4) (2016): 57–82.

from Zeman's December 24 Christmas message, that he "warned against welcoming asylum seekers and described the European culture of hospitality as naïve." The Czech president added he was profoundly convinced that his country is not facing spontaneous movement of refugees. Zeman, elected as head of state in early 2013, further noted, "A large majority of the illegal migrants are young men in good health, and single. I wonder why these men are not taking up arms to go fight for the freedom of their countries against the Islamic State."

Zeman was not alone in castigating this migration of peoples, *die Völkerwanderung*.

Viktor Orbán, Hungarian prime minister, described the refugees entering Europe as "looking like an army." Quoted in the *Guardian* while speaking at a gathering of conservative parties from across the continent, Orbán said, "What we have been facing is not a refugee crisis. This is a migratory movement composed of economic migrants, refugees and also foreign fighters. This is an uncontrolled and unregulated process." He added, "The right to human dignity and security are basic rights. But neither the German nor the Hungarian way of life is a basic right of all people on the Earth."

According to Euractiv.com, a summit of the Visegrad Four countries—the Czech Republic, Slovakia, Hungary, and Poland—was held in Prague on September 4, 2015. It rejected mandatory quotas for taking refugees but said the group wanted to contribute to tackling the crisis and protect the Schengen border-free zone. (The 1985 Schengen, Luxembourg, agreement guaranteed free movement of people within most of the European Union.) Polish prime minister Ewa Kopacz claimed refugee quotas would attract further migrants to the European Union. Czech prime minister Bohuslav Sobotka, who chaired the meeting, asserted discussions about refugee quotas did not go to the point. The core of the problem is the European Union's incapability to regulate migration and the situation in countries like Syria and Libya, he argued. "We agreed that the debate on quotas has only one purpose. It diverts attention from the real core of the problem. Europe [has] lost [the] capability to regulate migration," Sobotka said.

And it's not just the smaller states of Europe who speak out against this *Völkerwanderung*.

According to CNN, Russian President Vladimir Putin "point[s] the finger at Europe and the United States for what has now become one of the biggest mass migrations of people in modern times." Putin further noted, "In talking to reporters Friday [September 4, 2015], it's the West's wrong-headed foreign policy in the Middle East and Northern Africa that's at the root of the crisis."

CNN added, "Putin, speaking to the Russian news agency TASS, said he warned the West about the possible consequences of its Mideast and Africa policy several years ago. 'What is this policy about? This is imposing its standards without taking into consideration historic, religious, national and cultural specifics of these regions,' Putin told...TASS at the Eastern Economic Forum in Vladivostok. 'This is first of all, the policy of our American partners. I am looking with surprise at certain American mass media now criticizing Europe for an excessively tough, as they believe, treatment of migrants,' Putin added." Europe is "blindly following U.S. instructions" and suffering greatly, he said.[88]

Well, just how did this supposedly spontaneous migration come to Europe? We could suggest that this is similar to the mujahideen migrating to Afghanistan to change the attitude of the Soviet Union. Besides recruiting terrorists and "migrants" in Saudi Arabia, using American consular offices in Dhahran, Jeddah (where the author had witnessed this), and Riyadh, there were fifty-two hiring offices in the United States, including one in Washington, DC. Overseen by the al-Farukh mosque in Brooklyn (with the aid of Omar Abdel Rahman, "the Blind Sheikh," a CIA recruit), the various bureaus transferred money as well as recruits abroad. Who's to say these organizations were never shut down? Who's to say these organizations were never expanded? Who's to say these organizations don't still operate in the Middle East and South Asia?

---

88 Springmann, J. Michael. "Fear Furcht Vrees Peur," *Hausfrauleaks.com*, January 1, 2016.

4

Destabilization with a Purpose

And Why Is This Happening?

"The surge of migrants into Germany since early spring 2015 has left a trail of clues pointing to its origins in a clandestine human-smuggling operation, planned, funded and coordinated by foreign intelligence agencies of the United States and its petro-dollar club. The evidence so far indicates the human waves crossing European borders were prompted and managed at the highest level by the U.S. National Intelligence Council (NIC), the British Secret Intelligence Service (MI-6), and the Turkish espionage service *Milli Istihbarat Teskilatı* (MIT), with covert support from jihadist-sponsoring Gulf states."[89]

The destabilization effort is definitely working.

According to Germany's Federal Criminal Police, migrants committed 142,500 crimes in just the first half of 2016. A 40 percent increase over the previous year, this amounts to 780 crimes committed by migrants daily. These include every citizen's nightmares: rapes, physical and sexual assaults, stabbings, home invasions, robberies, burglaries, and drug trafficking. The Gatestone Institute (an allegedly nonpartisan, not-for-profit international policy council) claimed that police in many parts of

89 Germek, Silvia. "'Weapons of Mass Migration' Were Targeted at German Leaders." Unpublished 2015 MS.

the Federal Republic are stretched to the limit. It noted one particularly gruesome case, the rape of a ten-year-old girl in Leipzig, the largest city in Saxony, as having drawn more attention to violent migrant crime.

In all of 2015, migrants engaged in 208,344 misdeeds, as noted in a confidential police report provided to *Bild* (a German tabloid). These numbers, an average of 23 crimes per hour, are an eighty percent jump over the number of crimes in 2014. According to an October 24 YouGov poll, 68 percent of Germans thought that "security in the country has deteriorated during the past several years."

As noted earlier, thousands of asylum seekers or refugees have disappeared. Gatestone characterized them as economic migrants who entered Germany under false pretenses, later turning to a life of crime. One cause of this spike, noted Freddi Lohse of the Hamburg Police Union, is the lenient German justice system. He claimed that the migrants saw the nonauthoritarian procedures as a green light to continue their offenses. Continuing, Lohse said that "they are used to tougher consequences in their home countries. They have no respect for us." Furthermore, one police officer, a woman, commented that law enforcement is under attack and that the courts are "a joke."[90]

Not only law enforcement is under attack. Germany's constitution is as well.

Chancellor Angela Merkel seems to have made executive changes to Germany's Basic Law (guaranteeing freedom of speech). According to the *Washington Post* of January 7, 2016, "Prosecutors are launching investigations into inflammatory comments as judges dole out fines, even probation time, to the worst offenders." Then, the *Post* noted, "German authorities, meanwhile, have reached a deal with Facebook, Google, and Twitter to get tougher on offensive content, with the outlets agreeing to apply domestic laws, rather than their own corporate policies, to review of posts." The paper omitted just how and who would be "reviewing"

90 McFadyen, Siobhan. "We Are Losing Control of the Streets. Merkel's Germany Descends into Lawlessness," *Express*, November 1, 2016.

the posts. The companies themselves? Or the German federal and state security services? Or both?

And the terrible crimes under investigation and the punishments doled out? The Washington, DC, paper added that the German state had fined a man €300 (about US$322) and sentenced him to five months' probation for daring to post on his Facebook page that refugees should "burn alive" or "drown" in the sea. A Berlin woman also got five months' probation for posting remarks on her Facebook page about asylum seekers raping a German woman. She called the rapists "Filth" and pressed for stronger measures against the migrants, writing that if this was not done, "more asylum seekers' homes will burn." The newsmagazine *Der Spiegel* reported the most extreme case: a Bavarian court sentenced a man to twenty-seven months' imprisonment for posting a suggestion that Chancellor Merkel and her helpers be stood up against a wall and shot for betraying the German people (i.e., supporting unrestricted immigration).[91]

Even the German Government Is Overwhelmed

According to the *Washington Post*, Stephan Dünnwald, speaking for the Bavarian Refugee Council, "said that there is a danger of the German authorities sweepingly rejecting certain groups of asylum seekers because they are overburdened or because of political decisions made in Berlin." He added that there are many new, inexperienced officials pressed for time. Dünnwald further noted that interpreter quality has also fallen.

The *Post* also asserted that some migrants are more equal than others, with Syrians and Iraqis gaining asylum far more often than Nigerians or Pakistanis. In fact, the paper said that if you were from the war-torn Arab world, asylum was a virtual certainty, whereas if you'd traveled from elsewhere, even halfway across the world, you'd likely done so in

91 "Germany: Not for Those with Weak Constitutions."

vain. In the mix as maintained by politicians favoring more controls on asylum are applicants using flimsy evidence to buttress purely economic claims. Others, they asserted, could simply avoid problems by going to their local police or moving to another part of their country.

The *Post* also declared that the German government is rejecting almost 37 percent of all asylum claims, including 96 percent of Pakistani ones. Likely as the result of ten thousand Nigerians applying there for asylum, the *Post* said Germany is now negotiating deportation agreements with Afghanistan and Nigeria.[92]

This happened before—in Korea. "Neither the South Korean government nor society is ready to accommodate the refugees [those encouraged to leave the North to destabilize its government]...We have about 1,300 defectors and refugees living in South Korea, but we are failing to give good treatment to them. If we can't handle 1,300, how can we handle so many more?"[93]

And *La Belle* France?

Save for those camping out in Calais[94] while trying for Britain, France has not had to cope with waves of aliens like Germany has. Indeed, according to the European Resettlement Network, "France has not been perceived as a country of asylum for Syrians. In 2013, only 1300 Syrian nationals sought asylum in France and, even if there has been a dra-

92 Kirchner, Stephanie and Faiola, Anthony. "Not All Migrants Equal in Germany," *Washington Post*, October 31, 2016.

93 Greenhill, 253, citing Chao, Julie. "Neighbors Balk at North Korean Refugees," *Atlanta Journal-Constitution*, December 29, 2002.

94 BBC. "How Is the Migrant Crisis Dividing EU Countries?," March 4, 2016. Four thousand migrants in a wretched campsite are avoiding registration. Most are from Syria, Iraq, Afghanistan, Eritrea, or the Sudan. Melander, Ingrid. "More Migrants Pitch Tents on Paris Streets as Calais Camp Shuts," *Reuters*, October 28 2016: "The number of migrants sleeping rough on the streets of Paris has risen by at least a third since the start of the week when the 'Jungle' shanty town in Calais was evacuated, officials said on Friday...This means there are some 2,000–2,500 sleeping in the area, up from around 1,500 a few days before, [Colombe Brossel, a Paris deputy mayor] said.

matic increase since the beginning of the conflict, Syria still ranks 17th on the list of countries of origin of asylum seekers in France." In 2014, French President François Hollande promised that he would admit 500 more migrants from the Syrian Arab Republic.[95]

This is truly astonishing, given France's political and cultural influence on Syria and Lebanon. Growing out of the infamous World War I Sykes-Picot Agreement, *la Republique Française*'s cultural imperialism has been extremely effective. This writer knows a Lebanese woman who counts in French rather than her native Arabic and who sent her daughters to French medium schools. They then attended college at Montréal in Québec.

Yet somehow, for some reason, in some manner, France's government suddenly changed its mind. According to Quartz.com, "French president Francois Hollande has made a heartfelt [November 18, 2015] promise to accept 30,000 refugees from war-torn Syria into France in the next two years. That's even more than the 24,000 he promised to take in, in September [2015]." In his statement, Hollande asserted that France had a humanitarian duty to aid those fleeing the (alleged) Syrian civil war.[96] According to the *Washington Post*, "He [Hollande] announced this at a gathering of mayors from French cities, where he received a standing ovation...'Our country has the duty to respect this commitment... He indicated that resettled refugees would undergo rigorous security checks, according to ABC News. He said there would be a 50 million euro [nearly US$54 million] investment fund used to support housing for refugees."[97] Reaction to this was swift, with anti-immigrant and other groups expressing strong opposition. Quartz.com termed it a dangerous culture war, a *Kulturkampf*, that "had been brewing for decades."[98]

---

95 Tardis, Matthieu. "Admission of Syrian Refugees into France," European Resettlement Network, n.d.

96 Wang, Amy X. "France Has Doubled Down on Its Promise to Syrian Refugees after the Paris Attacks," Quartz.com, November 19, 2015.

97 Tharoor, Ishaan. "France Says It Will Take 30,000 Syrian Refugees, while U.S. Republicans Would Turn Them Away," *Washington Post*, November 18, 2015.

98 "France Has Doubled Down on Its Promise to Syrian Refugees after the Paris Attacks."

Yet no one made the connection that the second tranche of migrants was welcomed after the alleged terrorist attacks in Paris on November 13, 2015. The perpetrators were, presumably, Arab Muslims living in Europe.

Nevertheless, in the aftermath of the November 13 Paris attacks, a *Syrian!* passport emerged. The *Washington Post* wrote of "rumors of Syrian refugee involvement in the Paris terror attacks." It asserted that the travel document was falsified. The paper claimed, "Authorities in multiple countries are pretty certain that the passport, found near the body of an unidentified attacker who died during his suicide assault of France's national soccer stadium, is fake. It carried the name of 'Ahmad Almohammad,' a 25-year-old Syrian. French officials have indicated that Almohammad was a loyalist soldier in the regime of Syrian President Bashar al-Assad and died a few months ago."[99]

Oh, my. Initial reports claimed that someone from Bashar al-Assad's army had helped mount a terrorist attack on the City of Light. Do you think that someone knew of the proverb that a word, once written, cannot be cut out with an axe? Was the purpose of that "rumor" to inflame hatred toward the Syrian government—and to generate support for war?

The *Post* continued:

> On Tuesday, Serbian police arrested another man at a refugee camp carrying a passport with the exact same details. It's not clear at all if he has any connection to the case, other than having used the same shadowy process of obtaining a forged Syrian passport. There is a great deal of precedent for migrants pretending to be Syrians to gain safer passage and sanctuary in Europe.
>
> Thomas de Maiziere, Germany's interior minister, suggested on Tuesday that the fake passport found at the bombing site could have been part of an Islamic State attempt to create a "false trail."[100]

99 Tharoor, Ishaan. "Were Syrian Refugees Involved in the Paris Attacks? What We Know and Don't Know," *Washington Post*, November 17, 2015.
100 Ibid.

During the author's time in the US Department of State, officers were fond of the management slogan "Never let the whores run the whorehouse." Isn't that what happened in France? The wrong people were running the country, creating bizarre effects: (1) Exclude the Syrians, with whom you've had nearly a century of close, if not amicable, relations. (2) Suddenly admit them by the thousands. (3) Claim they are terrorists. (4) Use this as an excuse to attack the Islamic State in Syria. Consider the comments the French populace made about the November attacks: "On the 13th, the France24 Facebook page was full of posts such as 'send them home,' 'they are bringing their quarrels with them,' etc."[101]

And attack the French did.

François Hollande sent the nuclear-powered aircraft carrier *Charles de Gaulle* and its planes to bomb Syria along with the *Armée de l'Air.*[102] "The French air force carried out bombing missions on ISIS targets in Raqqa, Syria, for a second day in a row. France is retaliating against Islamist extremist terror attacks that killed at least 129 people in Paris."[103] Following an attack in Nice, French and American warplanes bombed near the city of Manbij, killing more than one hundred civilians. This prompted a Syrian foreign ministry complaint to the United Nations.[104]

And so it goes.

---

101 Springmann, J. Michael. "In the Wake of the Terrorist Attacks. Paris: The City of Light or the City of Darkness?," *Global Research*, December 7, 2015.

102 Ibid.

103 Brumfield, Ben; Lister, Tim; Walsh, Nick Paton. "French Jets Bomb ISIS Stronghold of Raqaa, Syria; Few May Have Been Killed," *CNN*, November 20, 2016.

104 "Beyond a Massacre: France Deliberately Bombed Syrian Civilians after Nice Attack," *RT*, July 20, 2016.

5

Country-By-Country Crises

How Did Europe Deal with the Tsunami?

GREECE (*YUNNAN*, TO romanize the Arabic word for the country) has been the main focus for migrants. Swarming out of Turkey, thousands of settlers made for the Hellene islands. In January and February of 2016, more than 120,000 alleged asylum seekers poured into the Peloponnese and nearby isles. The tally in those months was nearly as many as in the first six months of 2015. (The total for that year was 856,723.)

The European Union accused Greece of intentionally passing these people into the rest of the continent, in violation of the Dublin agreement. In turn, Athens asserted it could not stockpile all the migrants for the rest of Europe. The country demanded that the European Union share this heavy burden. (Left unsaid were Germany and the European Union's demands that Greece shrink its economy to reimburse bankers for loans made in more prosperous times.)

There are plans afoot for the European Union that would give Greece €700 million (ca. US$769 million) in emergency aid to defray crisis expenses.[105] However, in a classic example of Kelly Greenhill's coercion costs, this hasn't produced the desired effect:

105 "How Is the Migrant Crisis Dividing EU Countries?"

> Clashes erupted at Greece's northern border for the second time in three days on Wednesday [April 13, 2016], with the Macedonian police firing tear gas on scores of migrants as they protested border closings that have left more than 12,000 stranded in a makeshift refugee camp.
>
> The protests in Idomeni, a town in Greece on the border with Macedonia, came as Greek authorities arrested 14 activists there, saying that they had incited the migrants to storm the razor-wire fence dividing the two countries.
>
> The police accused the activists, from Britain, Germany and other European countries, of encouraging the migrants to protest by telling them that doing so would arouse sympathy among European governments and in that way help reopen borders and let them proceed on what was once the main migrant path to Germany, where most say they want to go.[106] [This is just like in Greenhill's Korea chapter.]

The waves of migrants are nothing if not ingenious—unless, of course, they have help. Do they get this aid from those who flooded in before them? Do they obtain it from NGOs assisting them? Or do they acquire it from the governments facilitating their movement? (We'll cover this point in some detail in the next chapter.)

Here's a Greek problem that's become an EU issue.

Migrants are now suing all and sundry to prevent Greece from sending several illegals back to Turkey.

"Members of two Syrian families detained in Greece after fleeing the besieged city of Aleppo [Halab] have taken an unprecedented action in the Irish courts against the European Council, EU and Ireland over alleged breaches of their human rights."[107] The Syrians asserted that the European Council (the heads of the twenty-eight member states) over-

---

106 Alderman, Liz. "Greece Holds Activists as Migrants and Police Clash Anew at Macedonia Border," *New York Times*, April 13, 2016.

107 Carolan, Mary. "Syrian Families Held in Greece Sue Ireland, EU over Rights Breaches," *Irish Times*, November 7, 2016.

stepped its authority. When the Council agreed with Turkey to return "all new irregular migrants" arriving after March 20, 2016, they violated various EU treaties and the European Convention on Human Rights. According to the plaintiffs, that deal and Ireland's support of it violate Ireland's legal obligations. The Syrians insist on their transfer to Germany to join other family members already there. However, the Syrians were not in Ireland; they are in Greece—and have been since March 20, 2016. They assert that the Greek government is holding their passports.[108]

The Balkans—Passageway to the Promised (?) Lands

The main route for migrants seeking Austria, Germany, and points north and west starts with the Turkish islands. The flow moves through Greece and then into Macedonia, Serbia, Croatia, and Slovenia. The aliens then seek admittance to Austria.

There are two alternative paths as well. One moves from Turkey through Bulgaria and joins the main line in Serbia. The second one diverges from the chief channel in Greece and then skirts the Adriatic coast. It slips along the seaboards of Albania, Montenegro, Bosnia-Herzegovina, Croatia, and Slovenia before ending up at the Austrian frontier.

> The majority of refugees arriving in Europe today are doing so via the so-called Balkan route. More and more EU states want to channel this flow—if not stop it entirely. Since the summer of 2015, an informal "Coalition of the Willing" has been discussing a plan to go to the refugees directly in Turkey and divvy them up among member states. The discussions are being held by Germany, Belgium, Finland, Greece, Luxembourg, the Netherlands, Austria, Sweden, Portugal, Slovenia and France.
>
> In the opposite corner sits the eastern European Visegrad Group—Hungary, the Czech Republic, Poland and Slovakia—who

108 Ibid.

are calling for border closures. They want to seal the border between Greece and the Balkan states and assist those affected countries by sending additional personnel...

Nearly nine percent of those refugees who traveled through Serbia last summer arrived not via Macedonia but Bulgaria. That's according to the [unnamed] Serbian newspaper, which was asked to compile a report by a Belgrade NGO that serves as an assistance central for asylum seekers. At its highest, that means that tens of thousands of refugees have already entered Western Europe via Bulgaria.

One glance at a map and the route appears inviting. Bulgaria shares a 240 kilometer (149 miles) long border with Turkey, a border that is only fenced off at certain places. The path from Istanbul and the Turkish border town of Edirne is overland, sparing the migrants the life-threatening boat trip across the Aegean along with the average bill of $1,200 [ca. €1,116] that is to be paid to the traffickers organizing the passage...

Romania, on the other hand, has seen remarkably few refugees cross its borders. Yet the ways they do come are much more creative. In January, 60 people from Pakistan, Iraq, Morocco, Afghanistan and Somalia outfitted with night vision gear were arrested as they arrived from Serbia. Since last June, hundreds of people who wanted to cross over via the Danube river bridges—or, more rarely, via a boat over the Danube—have been taken into custody.

The Black Sea was the site of two attempts made in 2014 to travel directly from Turkey to Romania. More recently, there have been a number of refugees who are being documented as coming in via Ukraine or Moldova. Most of these are Afghans using Central Asia as a transit route. The next stage on their journey would have been Hungary...

"New routes now via Albania have already opened. From there, the path leads through Montenegro and Croatia, something that we want to prevent," Ranko Ostojic, Croatia's outgoing interior minister, said in January. With that statement, he was the first official to have mentioned the Adriatic route. Until that point, there was only speculation.

"In winter, we expect to see a new direction leading over the Mediterranean region and Montenegro," Croatian migration expert Anđelko Milardovic appeared to prophesize in September in the newspaper "Jutarnji list."

The reason for the shift is the remarkably warmer temperatures along the coastline, compared to those in the heart of the Balkans. The only problem is that such a route crosses a number of additional borders; not including Greece, there is Albania, Montenegro, Croatia, Bosnia and Slovenia, before reaching Austria.[109]

Macedonia

While Macedonia wants to join the European Union, the migration of peoples is putting obstacles in its path. Before and after Germany's August 2015 tweet opening its borders, Macedonia had been holding to the Dublin Regulation.[110] It even put up a razor-wire fence at the border crossing with Greece (Gevgelija-Idomeni). With a goal of reaching northern Europe, over ten thousand migrants had set up camp there. Two thousand people a day queued up for food.

Several of Macedonia's neighboring states sent border guards to help control the Greek frontier. Yet the news media asserted that its border control policy was discriminatory, "letting in small numbers of Syrians and Iraqis, but not Afghans."[111]

Forbidden to buy public transport tickets, migrants either walk or bike through the country on their way to Serbia. Enterprising Macedonians

109 Rujevic, Nemanja. "More Than One Refugee Route through the Balkans," *Deutsche Welle*, February 18, 2016.

110 Asylum claims to be processed in first country entered.

111 "How Is the Migrant Crisis Dividing EU Countries?"

sell them bicycles for between US$169 and US$225 each (€158 to €211). The bikes, abandoned at the Serbian frontier, are then returned to the Greek border. There they are resold to the next lot of migrants.[112]

In 2014, most of the 42,000 migrants illegally entering Hungary came through Serbia by way of Macedonia. By June 2015, the number had leaped to more than 60,000.[113] But this is only part of the picture. According to a February 2016 statement by the Macedonian ambassador to the United States, Vasko Naumovski, "Some 800,000 people have passed through Macedonia [in the past year]. Of those 800,000 only 80 have applied for actual asylum within Macedonia. Most migrants choose to apply for asylum in Austria, Germany, or Sweden." Naumovski continued, saying that the "migrants' travel is highly organized. Many are using smartphones to locate routes and checkpoints. A large percentage of migrants possess the financial resources necessary to…aid their passage through Macedonia." The UNHCR estimates the breakdown of the torrent to be 35 percent men, 21 percent women, and an astonishing 44 percent children.[114]

Bulgaria

A troublesome alternative to the main line into Germany, France, or Scandinavia is Bulgaria. A country of slightly more than seven million people with a fifth below the poverty line, Bulgaria is saddled with "inflation, unemployment, corruption, and crime."[115] It is also saddled with migrants.

Those aliens who slip across the border from Turkey depend on smugglers to get them to the Western welfare states. The route is through Serbia. Although the price is usually €600 to €900 per person (about

---

112 Pleasance, Chris. "Now They're Coming in by Bike! Syrian and Iraqi Migrants Cycle through Macedonia as They Head toward Britain," *Daily Mail*, June 17, 2015.

113 Amnesty International. *Europe's Borderlands*, 2015.

114 Gallagher, Liam. "SPECIAL UMD REPORT: Macedonia's Involvement in the Migrant Crisis," Washington, DC: *United Macedonian Diaspora*, March 18, 2016.

115 CIA World Factbook, 2016.

US$650 to US$980), some traffickers have made as much as €2400 (ca. US$2,600) in a single day. One smuggler, an asylum applicant in Italy, specialized in moving Afghans out of Bulgaria. Enlisted as a Dari speaker in Milan, he could communicate with the people he was trafficking. While Bulgaria places restrictions on migrant rights, the country is probably the cheapest route into benefit-rich Germany or France.

One smuggler, recruiting outside a mosque in Sofia, noted they transport a lot of twelve- and thirteen-year-olds who pay full price. He added, "Usually we move people in groups of twenty or thirty. It depends on how much they can pay: the more they pay, the smaller will be the group. I have fixed costs to cover, you know." Also, he said that there are many people-moving teams who work separately, and each has its contacts in Turkey. When a call goes to a known number, the group readies its transportation.[116]

And it's not just the individual smugglers who are engaged in people shuffling. The Bulgarian police are involved.

> For months now, rumors have been circulating about questionable business dealings to do with refugees in Bulgaria. Just one week ago, former Bulgarian border police chief Valeri Grigorov told DW [*Deutsche Welle*] in an interview that corruption was a big problem among the country's police. "One could say that there is a 'business partnership' between human traffickers, the border patrol and the Bulgarian police. The partnership is tolerated by those in charge," Grigorov said.[117]

Worse, the border police head signed a €100,000 (not quite US$110,000) contract with a company, Edelvais 0707, to transport refugees. That

116 Montanari, Ambra and Piazzese, Giovanni. "Smuggling Migrants through Bulgaria," *Deutsche Welle*, August 23, 2016.

117 Andreev, Alexander. "Border Police Officials in Bulgaria Fired for Cooperating with Human Traffickers," *Deutsche Welle*, August 16, 2016.

same firm had been involved in human trafficking and was under investigation for it.[118]

Complicating Bulgarian affairs are Serbia, Croatia, and Hungary. Suffused with migrants themselves, they are sealing their borders with the Bulgars. And if the outflow is blocked, the inflow builds up.

> Human trafficking through Bulgaria is very well organized, as Valeri Grigorov, the former director of Bulgaria's border police told DW. "Immigrants and refugees are taken from the Turkish border to the Serbian border within 72 hours. In the first leg of the journey smugglers send them to Sofia by car, where people pay 20 euros ($23) per person to spend the night, usually in the houses of Gypsies." Grigorov says that there have been violent clashes between Gypsy clans over this increasingly lucrative business.[119]

Montenegro

According to a Montenegrin police report, the country is a way station for migrants from Pakistan, Algeria, Morocco, Afghanistan, Syria, and Tunisia. Kurds are also well represented in the mix. They pass through on their way to Serbia and, ultimately, Western Europe. The report, focused on organized crime, noted that local traffickers are managing the illegal aliens' movements. They are said to be native citizens working with former fellow countrymen, there with either asylee or temporary residence status. Turkish and Montenegrin citizens charge €3,500 to €4,000 per head (slightly more than US$3,700 to nearly US$4,300). The traffickers use taxis to move their charges. The police see a threat to Italy from the stream of illegals, normally moving on foot from Istanbul to Austria or Italy. However, the gendarmes fear the Turks will use small boats to smuggle the migrants from Montenegro directly to the Italian coast.

---

118 Ibid.

119 Andreev, Alexander. "Bulgaria Fears a Tide of Refugees," *Deutsche Welle,* August 16, 2016.

Most migrants stream into the country on foot, over mountain roads and trails. And their numbers are increasing. Montenegro's Directorate of Asylum figures show that illegal migrants through the country jumped 2,600 percent, from just 115 people in 2011 to 3,000 in 2013.[120]

As always, prognostications on Montenegro's migrants, as elsewhere, seemingly require a crystal ball (or a Gypsy fortune-teller). For example, on October 10, 2016, Austrian Foreign Minister Sebastian Kurz said that Montenegro *could* become part of the migrant transit route *should* his country close its borders (emphasis added).[121]

Serbia

"On a dusty road in Kelebija, a Serbian village just south of the Hungarian border, groups of Syrians gather round a table outside a minimarket to *charge their mobile phones* [emphasis added] and weigh decisions: wait in line at the border for an asylum hearing or disappear with a smuggler." The traffickers there charge £100 a head (ca. US$125 or just more than €115) to convoy a migrant through the woods to a hole in the border fence.[122]

The George Soros–sponsored Central European University is helping. Here and elsewhere, "students who could speak Arabic, Farsi, Pashto, and other languages provided much-needed translation services on a volunteer basis. Wi-Fi and mobile phone-charging stations were set up, providing refugees with a crucial lifeline to family and friends."[123] Besides George Soros, there are other organizations helping keep migrants wired. "Noticing the importance of access to information, [the] Belgrade Centre for Human Rights, an aid group in Serbia

120 Tomovic, Dusica. "More Illegal Migrants Are Crossing Montenegro," *BalkanInsight*, September 3, 2014.

121 Hina. "Kurz Says Montenegro Could Become Part of Migrant Transit Route Should Austria Close Its Border," EBL News, October 10, 2016.

122 Connelly, Andrew. "Hungary and Serbia Turning a Blind Eye to Thousands of Migrants Using 'Closed' Balkans Route," *Telegraph*, June 12, 2016.

123 Central European University Annual Report, 2015.

has set up Wi-Fi networks for refugees, while the UN Refugee Agency has distributed thousands of SIM cards at Jordan's refugee camps."[124]

And big business has jumped into migrant support:

> Cisco's Tactical Operations (TacOps) team supported by the volunteer Disaster Response Team (DRT) from the U.K. and Ireland, Google, and NetHope have installed Meraki-based Wi-Fi networks and device charging stations at more than 17 sites along the migration route in Southern and Central Europe. Through an employee matching program, Cisco has donated a total of $745,000 to organizations aiding in the refugee crisis—including $630,000 worth of equipment to support these deployments and $200,000 in grant funding to NGO partners NetHope and Mercy Corps.[125]

According to Frank Schott, the managing director of global programs for NetHope, the organization "has_assisted refugees by setting up 24 Wi-Fi hot spots and charging stations in six countries along the European migration route as well as developing a website with maps and transit information to which refugees are directed when accessing the Wi-Fi at certain camps."[126]

Why?

Serbia, once part of Yugoslavia, lies on the Balkan route that hundreds of thousands of people traversed on their way to Western Europe. (In 2015, one estimate put the figure at one million.)[127]

---

124 Hague, Audrey. "The Syrian Refugee and Her Smartphone," *Wiredcraft*, October 11, 2015.

125 US Chamber of Commerce Foundation, September 21, 2016.

126 Wendle, John. "For Asylum Seekers, a Cellphone Is a Bridge to the Future and the Past," *Al Jazeera America*, January 18, 2016.

127 Pantovic, Milivoje and Marusic, Jakov Sinisa. "Serbia, Macedonia, Boost Controls to Stop Migrants," *BalkanInsight*, July 18, 2016.

Serbia, destroyed by American and NATO forces in the 1990s, is obviously under attack again. Migrant waves are assaulting the country, migrants that US policy has pushed out of the Arab world and elsewhere. According to Serbian authorities, the government there has registered 102,000 refugees and migrants since January 2016—more than 500 a day. Prime Minister Aleksandar Vučić claimed that nearly 2,700 refugees and migrants—including Afghans, Pakistanis, and Syrians—are still in Serbia.[128]

Serbia's interior minister, Nebojša Stefanović, "said that some 80 per cent of migrants crossing Serbia from Bulgaria and Macedonia are from Pakistan and Afghanistan, and the EU has made clear they cannot seek asylum in the EU."[129]

Speaking on Saturday, July 16, 2016, Vučić asserted Serbia cannot become a "parking lot" for refugees and migrants heading to Western Europe. One cause of this was the growing number of refugees and migrants stuck in Serbia after Hungary introduced new border controls. Although the route was effectively closed in March 2016 when the European Union and Turkey reached a deal to halt the flow of refugees to Europe, many people still continue to make the treacherous journey, usually with the help of human smugglers.[130]

The migrants in Serbia seem to have an attitude apparently calculated to garner the best press.

> Hundreds of refugees from Asia and the Middle East marched through the Serbian capital, Belgrade, on their way to the Hungarian border, launching a hunger strike to demand free passage to Western Europe.

---

128 "Hungary and Serbia Turning a Blind Eye to Thousands of Migrants Using 'Closed' Balkans Route."

129 "Serbia, Macedonia, Boost Controls to Stop Migrants."

130 No author. "Serbia to Tighten Borders amid Refugee Build-Up," *Al Jazeera*, July 16, 2016.

A group of migrant men, mainly from Afghanistan, Pakistan and Iran, consisting of 200-300 people, according different estimates, marched through Belgrade's city center and crossed the bridge to the Novi Beograd district, escorted by a police car.

There were no women or children in the group which started the march to the Hungarian border, about 200 km [about 120 mi.] to the north, according to a Ruptly producer at the scene...

Earlier on Friday, the group staged a hunger strike in Belgrade, demanding Hungary open its borders and allow them to travel into the EU. The hunger strikers left food brought by the Serbian aid groups untouched, according to NewsGram.

The migrants that joined the strike also staged a sit-in protest in Belgrade holding placards that read *"Open the border," "We are responsible global citizens"*...

Similar sitting hunger strikes were launched by refugees and migrants in Serbia in 2015, after Hungary erected a razor-wire fence on its border with Serbia and strictly limited the inflow of refugees and migrants.

At that time, the protesters refused to take food or water, also demanding Hungary open its borders, with men, women and children taking part in the protests.[131]

Croatia

By November 2015, about four hundred thousand migrants had passed through the former Yugoslav republic, but just ten applied for asylum. "Migrants and refugees enter the country from Serbia, pass by a transit camp, and they are then escorted to the Slovenian border and onward."[132]

Sure.

131 No author. "Refugees in Serbia Stage Hunger Strike, Demand Hungary Opens Border," *RT*, July 22, 2016.

132 Bradbury, Paul. "Croatian Tourism and the Migrant Crisis: What You Need to Know," *total croatia news*, November 16, 2015.

One of the alleged Paris attackers of November 13, 2015, traveled through Croatia as well. That country's registration process in the town of Opatovac approved him on October 8, a point Croatian Interior Minister Ranko Ostojić confirmed. "It was a Syrian who came from Greece, where he was also registered, passed through Macedonia, Serbia and Croatia, and then moved on to Hungary and Austria. The person had not been highlighted as a potentially suspicious individual in any police records."[133]

That is beyond passing strange. Six countries, suffused by migrants, missed the background on a *Syrian*? But then hundreds of thousands of migrants somehow got waved through the lines. Who instructed the Balkan states to send them on? Was it the EU Commission? What was the purpose? What were the instructions?

They were on their way to Germany anyway. Why apply the aforementioned Dublin Agreement, making them apply for asylum in the first EU country entered? Germany had canceled it but might later enforce it, in which case all those moved through the corridors could well come back and settle in. With no passports or national identity cards (most having been thrown away at this point), it's another case of don't ask, don't tell. And without papers, there's nothing to tell.

Hungary

More than fourteen thousand migrants pushed into Hungary in the first six months of 2016.[134] As noted earlier, Viktor Orbán, Hungarian prime minister, strongly opposed the migrant flood, seeking to block it from his country and divert it elsewhere. In 2015, Hungary had become a sluice gate for aliens streaming toward Germany. In response, Magyar riot police used water cannons and tear gas on an agitated colonist column at the Serbian frontier in September 2015. Orbán's government, despite great criticism, built a razor-wire fence along its Serbian and

133 Pavlic, Vedran. "Paris Terrorist Passed through Croatia on October 8, Confirms Croatian Police," *total croatia news*, November 16, 2015.

134 "Serbia to Tighten Borders amid Refugee Build-Up."

Croatian borders. Slovakia, to its north, and the Republic of Hungary refuse to accept any European Union–imposed quota plan.[135]

In fact, in a joint press conference with his Austrian counterpart, Orbán said "refugees are less than welcome in Hungary, calling them 'a poison' and 'terror risk.'" He added,

> "Hungary does not need a single migrant for the economy to work, or the population to sustain itself, or for the country to have a future," he said, stressing, that, on the contrary, "every single migrant poses a public security and terror risk..."
>
> As far as Hungary is concerned, "migration is not a solution but a problem...not medicine but a poison, we don't need it and won't swallow it," he argued.[136]

Orbán hits the nail on the head. He does not tout the advantages of migrants making the European economy work or filling the coffers of Germany's failing social security system. He does not claim they are needed to reverse a falling birth rate. Orbán is going straight to the real reasons behind the migrant crisis.

The Hungarian prime minister expanded on his remarks in the United Kingdom's *Telegraph*: "The problem is not a European problem, the problem is a German problem." Orbán went into more detail:

> "Everything which is now taking place before our eyes threatens to have explosive consequences for the whole of Europe," Orbán commented in the *Frankfurter Allgemeine Zeitung*. "Europe's response is madness. We must acknowledge that the European Union's misguided immigration policy is responsible for this situation.
>
> "Those arriving have been raised in another religion, and represent a radically different culture. Most of them are not

135 "How Is the Migrant Crisis Dividing EU Countries?"

136 *RT*. "'Not Medicine, but Poison': Hungarian PM Says His Country Does Not Need 'a Single Migrant,'" July 27, 2016.

Christians, but Muslims," he said..."There is no alternative, and we have no option but to defend our borders."

"Irresponsibility is the mark of every European politician who holds out the promise of a better life to immigrants and encourages them to leave everything behind and risk their lives in setting out for Europe. If Europe does not return to the path of common sense, it will find itself laid low in a battle for its fate."

Orban said the EU should tell people "not to come" and said that the EU redistribution quotas were an "invitation."

"We Hungarians are full of fear, people in Europe are full of fear because they see that the European leaders, among them the prime ministers, are not able to control the situation," [said] Orban during the press conference.[137]

Austria

Casting about for definitive figures for migrants moving through Austria, we contacted that embassy here in Washington, DC. However, according to a November 9, 2016, e-mail from the Information Office at the legation:

> There are no such numbers about migrants moving through Austria to Germany and elsewhere in Europe. In 2015 when all the refugees came to Europe, Austria and Germany abolished the law temporarily. Refugees didn't need to register at the Austrian border and could go to every country in Europe. The observation wasn't possible at this time, because too many refugees came to Europe, arrived at a country and moved to another European country without registration.

However, the embassy did provide extensive data on asylum applicants. In 2014, there were 28,027, a jump of more than 60 percent over 2013. In

137 Holehouse, Matthew and Badcock, James. "Hungary: Migration Crisis Is Germany's Problem—Not Ours," *Telegraph*, September 3, 2015.

2015, 88,912 asylum hopefuls turned up, leaping 213 percent over 2014. But through October 2016, presumably as the result of border controls in Austria and elsewhere, the number fell substantially to 37,256 people (but still 33 percent higher than the number from 2014).[138]

In 2015, nearly one million migrants streamed into the Republic of Austria on the way to Germany. The Austrian government did not send them away. In just one day, ten thousand of them poured into the country from Slovenia and Hungary. Naturally enough, Austria reimposed border checks, as did Germany and Slovakia to Austria's northeast. This, then, disrupted road and rail travel between Austria and its neighbors.[139] Blaming German Chancellor Merkel for his country's woes, Austrian Defense Minister and Socialist Party MP Hans Peter Doskozil called her "irresponsible" for saying, "We can do it!" In blunt terms, the defense minister held her accountable for her actions. In effect, he characterized Merkel's remarks as a hog call to all the migrants in the world. Buttressing his statements, he pointed to photos of migrants being cheered and showered with gifts. Doskozil continued, saying, "Austria is not the waiting room for Germany." The defense minister went on to say that Europe must enforce its common borders against migrants and not leave lands like Greece and Italy in the lurch.[140]

Between January and October 2015, there were 68,589 asylum applicants in Austria (i.e., those that didn't pass through on the way to somewhere else). Syrians (20,441), Afghans (16,549), and Iraqis (11,190) formed the largest contingents.[141]

These numbers don't tell the whole story and don't explain Minister Doskozil's fury. However, the following figures do:

---

138 Austrian Federal Ministry of the Interior. Asylum Applications.

139 "How Is the Migrant Crisis Dividing EU Countries?" Chan, Sewell and Karasz, Palko. "Thousands of Migrants Flood into Austria," *New York Times*, September 19, 2015.

140 Tomlinson, Chris. "Austrian Defence Minister: Merkel Is Irresponsible," *Breitbart.com/London*, August 27, 2016.

141 Knapp, Amy. *Country Report: Austria.* Asylum Information Database, December 2015.

> A new report on migrant crime reveals that for every 100 people who attempt to claim asylum in Austria an average of 55 criminal offences are committed, with some communities significantly more represented in statistics than others.
>
> The Austrian agency of federal statistics report shows that during the period of 2004 to 2014 almost every other migrant had committed some kind of criminal offence after coming to the country and seeking asylum.
>
> The majority of the crimes were perpetrated by Algerians, who have been held as responsible for many of the high profile migrant crimes like the mass sexual assaults on New Year's Eve [2015] in Germany.
>
> Algerians commit a staggering 155 crimes per 100 asylum seekers, with Georgians close behind at 151 per 100, and Nigerians at 129 per 100, reports *Kronen Zeitung*. Syrians are presently reasonably low on the list at only around 8 offences per 100 applicants, but the federal statistics agency says that because the study only covers up to 2014 it doesn't account for the mass influx of Syrians experienced during 2015.
>
> The report also notes 80 per cent of the criminals were young men.[142]

Here are some examples of this activity. On April 14, 2016, the Austrian paper *Kronen Zeitung* reported that an Afghan asylum applicant had sexually abused two children in a refugee home in Villach, in Carinthia. Both victims, a ten-year-old boy and a thirteen-year-old girl, were from Iran.[143] The same paper wrote that a thirty-five-year-old Algerian had tried to rape a woman in Linz at a bus stop, beating her senseless after she broke

---

142 Lane, Oliver and Tomlinson, Chris. "In Austria, over Half of All 'Asylum Seekers' Commit Crimes," *Breitbart.com/London*, March 10, 2016.

143 No author. In translation, "Two Children in Asylum District Abused," *Kronen Zeitung*, April 14, 2016.

his nose in self-defense.[144] In Salzburg, two North African men sexually molested a woman next to the railroad station. According to the newspaper *Kurier*, they severely beat a man who tried to protect her.[145]

And yet another instance of refugee crime follows.

According to the *Telegraph*, "An Iraqi migrant has admitted raping a 10-year-old boy at a swimming pool in Austria because he had not had sex in four months and it was a 'sexual emergency.'" The incident was initially hushed up, allegedly to protect the victim. Viennese police spokesman Thomas Keiblinger denied this, asserting that the Iraqi being a migrant played no role in the matter. However, the official report surfaced only after details of the December 2, 2015, incident appeared on Facebook and in the *Kronen Zeitung*. Unfortunately for the promoters of making Austria safe for illegals, "in Austria there were 126 convictions for rape in 2014, 58.7 per cent of which were committed by Austrian nationals, while 34.9 per cent were committed by non-EU citizens, according to the country's federal agency for statistics."[146]

Austria, gateway to Germany and the rest of Europe, was and is at the funnel's spout. Let's take a look at the rest of the funnel, the route(s) the migrants took to get there. They moved from Greece through the Balkans. The United States and its repressive and often repulsive allies followed their success in Yugoslavia, creating waves of human carpet bombings.

Kelly Greenhill gives us the background on beginning coercive migrations in Yugoslavia.

> As the numbers of refugees languishing in the muddy stinking fields to which they are confined grows with sickening speed, NATO countries have closed their doors. We don't mind images of them on the television screens but the people themselves are

144 No author. In translation, "Linz Woman Broke His Nose—Sex Criminal Arrested," *Kronen Zeitung*, April 30, 2016.

145 No author. In translation, "Two Men Sexually Molest Woman in Salzburg," *Kurier*, April 21, 2016.

146 Hall, Melanie. "Iraqi Migrant Admits Raping Boy in Austrian Pool after Having 'Too Much Sexual Energy,'" *Telegraph*, February 6, 2016.

> not welcome. That would make the story entirely too personal... Let them stay in the Balkans, we say.[147]

NATO's first military operation in its history was a failure. It did not accomplish its goals: to demonstrate its seriousness, to protect Kosovars, and to damage the Serbian military. However, it did succeed in creating "the largest strategic engineered population movement in Europe since World War II, in which more than 800,000 Kosovars fled or were driven from their homes in less than two months."[148]

Slovenia

Slovenia, an Alpine state of two million, tackled a torrent of migrants, using an entirely new approach. The government sought to control them through a beggar-my-neighbor policy. Instead of razor-wire fences, Slovenia created an internal transit corridor, channeling the flow from Croatia to Austria.

> Between October 2015 and January 2016, 419,205 migrants crossed through Slovenia using this corridor; only about 100 of them actually applied for asylum in Slovenia. The corridor—which is less a physical structure than a system whereby migrants arrive in Slovenia and the state helps usher them farther north—has no basis in law.

Let's look at a smaller number, the illegals who poured into the country in a single day:

> A record 12,676 migrants have crossed into Slovenia in the last 24 hours, Slovenian authorities announced Thursday. Migrants started flowing into the small European state Saturday, after

147 Greenhill, 131, citing Hilton, Isabel, "We Imagine War as a Hollywood Film," *Guardian*, April 5, 1999.

148 Ibid., 131–132.

> Hungary sealed off its border with neighboring Croatia, effectively blocking one of the main routes used by refugees to reach Western Europe.[149]

In the passageway, the migrants are registered, provided unspecified support, and transported to the Austrian frontier. Yet some alleged transients get to stay. The government gives them a "permission to remain." This goes, usually, to people who can't apply for asylum but who also can't return home. The document enables them to remain in Slovenia without providing any legal status.

While this concept delights the Slovenian government, it does not enthrall the population. Elites and the man in the street both object to the wave of migrants. And, naturally enough, they are denounced as racist, Islamophobic, and anti-immigrant. Most offensively, they do not "reflect on the positive effects of migration." Refusing to make their territories available to foreigners is seen as outrageous and contravening international human rights treaties.[150] (This idea comes from a George Soros Open Society operation.)

One such "positive" effect was made manifest in Austria: "April 15 [2016]. A 42-year-old migrant from Slovenia was arrested for attempting to sexually assault two 18-year-old women in Leibnitz."[151]

But illegal migration through Slovenia is nothing new. And migration's security threat is also old hat. Consider the situation not long after the destruction of Yugoslavia ended. And think about Turkish involvement:

> The problem of illegal migrations is getting increasingly out of control in Slovenia and is seriously undermining the national security of the country. The "Balkan Route," which runs through Slovenia,

149 Auburg, Lucie. "Slovenia Asks EU for Help after a Record 12,000 Migrants Pour into the Country in 24 Hours," *Vice News*, October 22, 2015.

150 Šalamon, Kogovšek Neža. "Slovenia Built a 'Corridor' to Move Refugees Straight through the Country," *Open Society Foundations*, February 20, 2016.

151 Kern, Soeren. "Migrant Rape Epidemic Reaches Austria," *Gatestone Institute*, May 5, 2016.

is the avenue via which migrants are looking for a better life in Western countries; as a result, the Slovenian border is illegally crossed by hundreds of migrants daily. Last year alone more than 35,000 illegal migrants were captured, which is a 91% increase on 1999. Of these, 20,000 came to Slovenia from Croatia. The greatest numbers of illegal migrants originally come from Iran, Romania and Turkey. The magnitude of illegal mass crossings of the national border, as part of migration flows, has escalated to the extent that it is posing a general threat to the safety of people and property, health and the environment, while reflecting itself in the level of crime. Given the directions specified in the Resolution on the Starting Points of the National Security of the Republic of Slovenia, these conditions have reached the point at which they threaten the internal security of the Republic of Slovenia.

Furthermore, illegal migrations have a number of other negative effects: an increase in primary crime, i.e. criminal offences committed directly by illegal migrants (burglaries, car thefts, robberies, abductions, assaults on the police) as well as in secondary crime (organised crime related to the smuggling of people, white slavery, prostitution, illegal trade in human body parts).[152]

But why are the Slovenians unhappy now?

Ivan Molan pulls out a map to explain what has been happening over the past 10 days [in late October 2015] in Brezice, the quaint town of 25,000 in eastern Slovenia where he has been mayor for more than a decade.

He points to what is called the "green" border, where at least 84,000 refugees have arrived from nearby Croatia through patches of wheat, corn, and mud en route to northern Europe. Along that boundary there is a tiny municipality of only 200

152 Republic of Slovenia, Government Communications Office. "ILLEGAL MIGRATION—A THREAT TO SLOVENIA'S NATIONAL SECURITY," January 2001.

> residents called Rigonce, the 52 year-old says, where ordinary life has all but come to a halt.
>
> "Croatians bring them in trains and buses and just tell them, 'Go for the marshes, go for the fields: on the other side is Slovenia, which is close to Austria,'" Mr. Molan says. "What people say in the village is that they have a feeling that they have become like the dump of the European Union," he adds.[153]

But there are some migrants in Slovenia that are not discussed.

According to the Macedonian English-language news agency Independent, "Terrorist cells will not only be located in Syria, but in European Union an[d the] Balkans as well " It cited the intelligence sources of an Austrian paper (*Die Presse*) as claiming that Slovenia is on a list of such potential hosts of terrorist cells. The Independent alleged that a jihadist center is located near Ljubljana.

> The article also stated that after the borders in Slovenia have been reopened, a number of the Islamic State members entered the country, and that convoys of automobiles left for the forest areas near Ljubljana.
>
> Salafists from Germany, Luxembourg, and Austria were registered, radicalized and trained to shoot firearms, Jutarnji daily reported, citing *Die Presse.*
>
> According to the daily, the program of Islamic State for militant training is highly professional, including a 70 pages long guerilla fighting manual.[154]

Kosovo

Kosovo is a legacy state left over from NATO's destruction of Yugoslavia. "Kosovo declared independence [from Serbia] in February 2008. 22

153 Politi, James. "Slovenia Struggles to Cope with Migrant Crisis," *Financial Times*, October 27, 2015.

154 No author. "Jihadists Start Training Camps in Europe and Balkans," *Independent*, January 26, 2016.

EU member states have recognized it so far. Kosovo has around two million inhabitants, predominantly Albanians." Independence has not been kind to the country. As a Yugoslav republic, it had the support of the entire federation. Now the statelet is reaping the "benefits" of the Kosovo Liberation Army's policies. "It is still the poorest country in the region, with around 30% of the population living in poverty, 10% of them in extreme poverty, living off less than one dollar per day." The unofficial unemployment rate is 40 percent, and among young people aged fifteen to twenty-four, it is nearly 60 percent.[155]

Now the native Kosovars are joining the migration tsunami, along with other peoples driven out of their lands by American foreign policy. Media estimates assert that one hundred thousand Albanians have left the country between August 2014 and February 2015. Their aim was Hungary via Serbia and then other parts of Europe. "The number of illegal migrants from Kosovo seeking asylum in the EU had gone up 40% since December [2014], which surpasses the hitherto largest groups of immigrants from Syria and Afghanistan arriving illegally, or crossing the Union's outer borders." This has greatly distressed the European Commission (the European Union's executive body). That august organization then requested that Priština "prevent sudden mass, illegal departures of Kosovars to the European Union."[156]

Yet Germany, which had tweeted "y'all come" on August 25, 2015, suddenly and quietly reversed itself—against Kosovo. It sent policemen to the Hungarian-Serbian border to help with controlling the influx. Further targeting Kosovars, the Teutons rejected about 99 percent of their asylum applications in 2014. In January 2015, that number fell to 99.3 percent. Germany's Interior Ministry even suggested deporting Kosovars, asserting they would be in no danger in their own country.[157]

155 EurActiv.rs. "Poverty Spurs Mass Migration from Kosovo," February 16, 2015.

156 Ibid.

157 EurActiv.com. "German Police Sent to Serbia-Hungary Border to Stem Kosovo Exodus," February 13, 2015.

Albania

According to the Cooperation and Development Institute, Albania is neither a migrant destination nor a preferred transit country. The nation doesn't offer the benefits of Germany, France, or Austria. Nor does its geography facilitate asylum seekers on their way to elsewhere. It's more than thirty kilometers (ca. eighteen miles) from the frontier to the nearest useful bit of public transport. And, unfortunately, the system is not integrated, having higher costs than elsewhere. Moreover, Albania's railroad net has no connection to the European system. Additionally, if migrants were to enter the country en route to Austria, they would have to choose: either take to the sea or cross four national borders before reaching Central Europe.

Nature also plays a role in discouraging the illegal-alien tide. Mountains and forests make it difficult for the elderly, women, and children to pass through. In winter, cold and rain exacerbate the problems migrants face.

Government policy works against the illegals. Tirana [the Albanian capital] has emphatically stated, "If you came to Albania either you ask for asylum, or you will be returned," and "Everything will be decided in close cooperation with our EU partners."[158]

Citing *The Migrants' File*, the Cooperation and Development Institute asserts that, while people smuggling can be lucrative, drug smuggling pays better (€70,000, more than US$75,000, for 70 kilograms of marijuana, about 154 pounds, versus €3,000 to €5,000 for a person of equivalent weight, about US$3,200 to US$5,300). People aren't as bulky as heroin. They can't be disposed of as quickly and easily as a few kilos of marijuana. Still, there is business to be done. Between 2001 and 2015, migrants (or some entity/entities) paid €16 billion (ca. US$17.1 billion) to bring them to Europe.

Yet if there is smuggling of one item, there is more likely to be smuggling of other kinds. Drugs, people, and guns are all lucrative, portable,

158 Cooperation and Development Institute in Partnership with the Hanns Seidel Stiftung, ALBANIA IN THE WESTERN BALKANS ROUTE, August 2015–June 2016.

and interchangeable. They take up little space, are easily concealable, and their origins are generally not clear. More important than such smuggling being good business, governments see advantages as well. Drugs helped finance the Iran-Contra Affair, and drugs funded the Yugoslav wars, creating so many refugees that the rest of Europe feared being swamped. It was likely Balkan gunrunners who carried weapons and explosives to France for the November 13, 2015, attacks. The shadowy halls of government agencies don't always conceal as much as you might think.

To date, Albania has avoided the tsunami of illegals. Additionally, it is relatively unscathed by asylum seekers. In 2014, 134 people sought asylum. In 2015, it was 106. During the first five months of 2016, the total came to 303. Yet the important phrase is "to date." In March 2016, someone or some group created a Facebook page titled "Transit Albania and Italia" (https://www.facebook.com/albantrans/timeline). It urged asylum seekers to traverse Albania in reaching the European Union. It displayed a poster depicting the route through Albania to Italy across the Strait of Otranto. The site contains postings, directions, and instructions in multiple languages, including German and Arabic.[159]

Bosnia-Herzegovina

"Official statistics estimate that 1,471,594 citizens of Bosnia and Herzegovina (including second and third generation of emigrants) reside outside of the country. This accounts for approximately 39% of the total country population. These figures rank BiH [Bosnia-Herzegovina] second in Europe in terms of the magnitude of migration."[160]

But was this the result of America and its creature NATO destroying Yugoslavia?

Yes.

159 Ibid. and citing *The Migrants' File,* http://www.themigrantsfiles.com as well as *Interview* with Alma Mele, Asylum Directorate, Albanian Ministry of Internal Affair and *Interview* with Michael Gumprich and Christian Weiss, German Embassy in Albania.

160 UNDP (United Nations Development Program) in Bosnia and Herzegovina.

"As a result of political turmoil and ethnic tensions, Bosnia and Herzegovina declared its independence from Yugoslavia in March 1992, which was soon followed by a war that lasted from 1992 to the end of 1995. The war was marked by mass population displacement of about half of the entire population of the country."[161]

Again, to date, like Albania, Bosnia-Herzegovina has not suffered from the migrant tide. "'BiH has not yet been affected by the refugee crisis like neighbouring countries, but that does not mean that it could not happen quite soon,' said Hellbach [Christian Hellbach, German envoy to the country]. The German ambassador suggested that the increasingly strict controls introduced by some of the countries which are currently part of the route, such as Macedonia, Serbia, Croatia, Slovenia and Austria, might compel asylum seekers to try to find alternative routes, and BiH is a natural choice for them."[162]

Of course, Bosnia-Herzegovina has another type of crisis: a terrorist crisis. We can surmise that Saudi Arabia, the paymaster of religious fanatics, has developed an unhealthy interest in the country. Between 2014 and 2015, the number of Saudis traveling there doubled, from 2,052 to 4,386. This was a jump of nearly 114 percent.[163] Did they go there to visit the site of Archduke Francis Ferdinand's assassination? Or were they seeking a religious experience? Did they make a pilgrimage to Medjugorje in the hopes of seeing an apparition of Jesus Christ's mother? Or, being Saudis, did they go for the slivovitz?

No, they went for the terrorist training camps.

ISIL had been buying land in the Bosnian village of Osve on which to train terrorists, according to security officials. "According to Patrick Hill and Ed Wight at the *Sunday Mirror*, at least 12 jihadis trained in

161 Kačapor-Džihić, Zehra and Oruč, Nermin. *Social Impact of Emigration and Rural-Urban Migration in Central and Eastern Europe* Final Country Report Bosnia and Herzegovina, European Commission DG Employment, Social Affairs and Inclusion, April 2012.

162 Pavlic, Vedran. "Migrants to Start Entering Croatia through Bosnia and Herzegovina?" *total croatia news*, February 17, 2015.

163 Ministry of Security, Bosnia-Herzegovina. Sector for Immigration BOSNIA AND HERZEGOVINA MIGRATION PROFILE for the year 2015.

Osve and travelled to Syria in recent months. Five have reportedly been killed." The *Daily Mail* claimed that Bosnian police had "detained" some sixteen jihadists in raids across the country. The charges were financing terrorism and recruiting extremists for the fighting in Syria and Iraq.[164]

Another town, Gornja Maoca, is also tagged as a jihadist training facility. It's "home to Bosnian followers of Wahhabism, a strict form of Sunni Islam." (Wahhabism is the Saudi version of Islam.) While the evidence is somewhat thin, journalists have photographed the ISIL flag flying from local buildings and its symbol painted on a sign.[165]

Spain

At the end of 2016, sub-Saharan Africans swarmed Spain's Moroccan enclave of Ceuta. Four hundred successfully clambered over the barbed-wire border fence. Building on that achievement, more than 1,100 of them fought riot police as they unsuccessfully sought entry into the territory on the first day of the new year. Should they make it, they could claim asylum in Spain, a member of the European Union. Once in, they could then proceed to Germany, France, Sweden, or any other benefit-rich European country.

This was not a peaceful incursion. "The migrants used rocks and metal bars as they battled with police officers from Spain and Morocco, who joined forces to defend the border...Around 55 police officers were injured in the chaos—50 from Morocco and five from Spain."

Spanish and Moroccan authorities agreed that the illegals failed. However, they differed in their accounts of how many were turned back and how many were arrested. Spain asserted that all but two (being medically treated) had been pushed back. The Moroccan authorities

164 Stanton, Jenny. "ISIS Stronghold Discovered in Picturesque European Village Where Everyone Is 'Ready to Respond to the Summons to Jihad,'" *Daily Mail*, July 19, 2015.

165 Stanton, Jenny. "Inside the Bosnian Mountain Village Where Locals Fly the Black Flag of ISIS above Their Homes as Jihadists' Influence Spreads," *Daily Mail*, February 4, 2015.

claimed they arrested all eight hundred involved in the attack on the six-meter (nearly twenty-foot) barrier.[166]

Italy

In October 2013, the Italian government had ordered its navy to search for and rescue boat people in waters near the peninsula and islands. This operation, *Mare Nostrum*, brought 190,000 of them to Italy. Few claimed political asylum, few stayed in the country, and many disappeared. Almost none registered with authorities. They were initially lodged in welcome centers, each individual admitted costing the taxpayer €35 per day, €13,000 per year (about US$38/day, US$14,099/year).

Who's that swimming through the door? *More* single men? (And who's paying for their bathing suits?)

> Last year [2014], most were from sub-Saharan Africa. Top of the league table were the Nigerians, followed by the Malians and the Gambians, the Senegalese and even the Pakistanis—who together made up 70 per cent of the total. No doubt these countries are no picnic to live in, and parts of some of them are war zones, but that should not, and in theory does not, guarantee refugee status. It is also a fact that most boat people are young single men and the price of a ticket on a people-smuggling boat is €2,000 [about US$2,150] (nearly two years' pay for the average worker in Mali).[167]

More are awaited. The captain of one vessel rescuing migrants noted that there were about 450,000 to 500,000 more waiting in Libya to come over. According to British Defense Secretary Michael Fallon, "We could see hundreds of thousands trying to cross this summer [2015]." So many are coming that the Italian police dump busloads of migrants in town

166 Gutteridge, Nick. "BATTLE FOR EUROPE: More Than 1,100 Migrants Fight Riot Police as They Storm Spanish Border," *Express*, January 2, 2017.

167 Farrell, Nicholas. "Welcome to Italy: This Is What a Real Immigration Crisis Looks Like," *The Spectator*, June 20, 2015.

squares or at railroad stations. Many are diseased: 10 percent with scabies (a burrowing mite) and 25 percent with hepatitis C (a contagious liver disease).

Before the migrants streamed toward Greece in 2015, Italy had been the reservoir into which they flowed. Partially checking this flood had been maritime disasters tied to the lengthy ocean voyage. Additionally, war-torn Libya, the favorite jumping-off spot, had become still more dangerous after NATO's destruction of all order in that country. Rival governments, local militias, and terrorists all made internal travel extremely dangerous. Hundreds drowned in disasters during long voyages through dangerous waters. (The *entrepôt* then was Lampedusa, an Italian island near Tunisia.)[168] However, the "decline" was only relative. The United Kingdom's *Daily Mail* reported in April 2016 that thousands of migrants had begun swarming into Sicily. Arrivals had jumped 90 percent during the first quarter of that year, with six thousand people landing in just three days. Despite increased naval patrols, twenty thousand souls had landed in Italy in the first four months, with 90 percent coming ashore in Sicily. The previous year's tally had been ten thousand. Most of the migrants were eventually disbursed fairly evenly throughout the country. However, the largest concentrations were in Lombardy and Sicily.[169]

> Fabrice Leggeri, the executive director of the border protection agency, Frontex, is concerned about the shift in migrant routes, which he says is placing a massive burden on Italy. He said that the number of refugees traveling from Libya to Italy is 13 to 14 times greater than the number crossing to Greece from Turkey. He added that the central Mediterranean route is being used more than ever, and the number of illegal border crossings

168 "How Is the Migrant Crisis Dividing EU Countries?"

169 Simons, Wallis Jake. "EXCLUSIVE—'Welcome to the NEW Lesbos': Now Sicily Is Flooded with 2,000 Migrants EVERY DAY Since the Balkans Route Shut," *Daily Mail*, April 14, 2016.

> between Libya and Italy exceeds the number of all other illegal border crossings in the EU.[170]

Like the rest of Europe, Italy is choking on the criminal element washed up on its shore amid refugees and migrants of many types. People suspect that many of the boat people, besides the usual flotsam and jetsam strewn on the beaches, include Islamic terrorists of one flavor or another. "One of those arrested in connection with the Islamic terrorist attack on the Bardo National Museum of Tunis in March [2015] had crossed the Mediterranean from Libya to Italy in a migrant boat in February."[171]

> Violent clashes in Rome and the northern city of Treviso this month forced the police to evacuate migrants from local reception centers, after residents protested the "invasion" of foreigners from the Middle East and Africa. Leaders of the Northern League, an anti-immigration party, last month pressured local mayors to refuse orders from Rome to settle migrants in their communities.[172]

Denmark

More than thirty-six thousand migrants, mostly Muslim, have poured into Denmark, a country of 5.6 million, over the last two years. Claiming to be asylum seekers, they have enraged the locals. Natives complain that the newcomers don't seem interested in learning Danish or adapting to the country's customs and culture. They are observed to be unemployed and living in a parallel society. While 74 percent of Danes have jobs, only 48 percent of the migrants do.

---

170 Numanovic, Emir. "Austria Takes Steps to Control Migration on Balkan Route," *Deutsche Welle,* July 1, 2016.

171 "Welcome to Italy: This Is What a Real Immigration Crisis Looks Like."

172 Bohlen, Celestine. "Italy's Influx of Immigrants Is a Domestic Problem, Too," *New York Times,* July 28, 2015.

To be sure, the European Union, its member states, and their politicians created this problem—and not only in Denmark. They, the United States, and Israel drove the *Völkerwanderung* from their homes and forced them into an alien climate and culture. None of them have any facility with most European languages, and few of the Europeans know any Arabic or Pashto or Urdu. The migrants, pushed from their own countries, lack the education and skills needed to function in a modern Europe. The United States' and other countries' intelligence services have done the aliens an immense disservice. In some ways, they've made the migrants a scapegoat for their dangerous policies. Driving millions into Europe enables the perpetrators of this atrocity to hide murderers, war criminals, and human rights violators in their midst, in plain sight. This also works as a means of dividing and polarizing the growing gap between the Left and the Right, including the Alt Right. Consider that the fissure was born in part as the result of the migrant crisis in Europe and the United States. This helped give rise to the Trump phenomenon. (Hillary Clinton and now-President Trump argued bitterly in various TV debates about the effects of open borders. US migrant policy proved to be one of the decisive factors in determining the outcome of the 2016 election.)

In reaction, while "Macedonia, Hungary and Slovenia have all built border fences, Denmark imposed new identity controls on its border with Germany in January [2016]." Moreover, "a measure passed in January, though rarely enforced, empowers the authorities to confiscate valuables from new arrivals to offset the cost of settling them. Last year, Denmark placed ads in Arabic-language newspapers stressing its tough new policies, essentially suggesting: Don't come here. 'Muslims do not assimilate as easily as Europeans or some Asians,' said Denmark's culture minister, Bertel Haarder, partly because, as he put it, 'their patriarchal culture frowns on women working outside the home and often constrains freedom of speech.'"[173]

173 Zucchino, David. "'I've Become a Racist': Migrant Wave Unleashes Danish Tensions Over Identity," *New York Times*, September 5, 2016.

Crime has come along with the migrants to Denmark.

> A 36-year-old Syrian migrant sexually assaulted a 20-year-old woman in Bornhöved. The woman was showing the man an apartment that had been advertised for rent when he sexually assaulted her.[174]
>
> The Danish Immigration Authorities…shut the Børnecenter Tullebølle [asylum] center down due to numerous incidents… Last month, for instance, a massive brawl took place there. In August, five teenagers who fled the center were charged for sexual assaults—namely, groping and a rape. In July, another fight broke out, with up to 100 underage boys from the center taking part in it.[175]

There are other problems associated with the migrants, not least of which is their cost to the community. One particular Syrian is expected to annually cost the Danish taxpayer 214,128 Danish kroner (nearly €28,777, about US$31,368). The forty-seven-year-old got refugee status for himself, a wife, and eight children. Now he has obtained permission to bring over his remaining twelve children along with two more wives. The man, Daham Al Hasan, claims to be too sick to work and so can't support his family. Additionally, Al Hasan asserts his health is so poor that he can't learn Danish. Even the integration spokesman for the Conservatives, Naser Khader, said, "It is highly problematic that a Syrian refugee can be allowed to call himself sick to avoid working and learning Danish, so he can support…20 children."

> The politician added it should not be possible for someone who does not intend to work to be given such vast sums and called for Denmark to implement an upper limit for the number of children a person can claim contributions for.

---

174 www.syrianrefugeethreats.com.

175 *RT.* "Sex Acts with Boys Were Filmed at Danish Asylum Center, Report Reveals," November 1, 2016.

> Khader said: "We need to save and it can't be right that a man, who has not contributed, is granted hundreds of thousands in child support."[176]

"DANES enjoy a worldwide reputation as a tolerant, humane and liberal people."[177] But following the flood of migrants, schools in Denmark now find that alien children have become the majority in classrooms. "The Langkaer upper secondary school outside the city of Aarhus...[saw] the number of students who are migrants or the children of migrants rise from 25 per cent in 2007 to 80 per cent of this year's [2016] first-year students." Attempts to balance the number of aliens with native Danes brought forth accusations of discrimination. In response, the school's headmaster asserted that "the aim was to encourage integration." He noted that you need more than one ethnicity in the classroom for assimilation.[178]

Are these more of Kelly Greenhill's coercion costs?

Sweden

Sweden is a country the Gatestone Institute termed a "humanitarian superpower." The country now has more Chaldean Catholics than their native Iraq does. That Nordic land, with a population of 9.5 million (2013 census), has dealt with 650,000 asylum seekers in the last fifteen years, and 163,000 arrived in 2015.

But there seem to be limits—violent limits.

> For a British boy to be killed by a grenade attack anywhere is appalling, but for it to happen in a suburb of Gothenburg should shatter a few illusions about Sweden. Last week's murder of eight-year-old Yuusuf Warsame fits a pattern that Swedes have come

---

176 Stromme, Lizzie. "'Too Sick to Work Migrant' Now Wants to Bring 12 MORE Children and 2 MORE Wives to Europe," *Express*, May 27, 2016.

177 (No author). "Testing Danish Tolerance," *The Economist*, August 26, 1999.

178 Day, Harvey. "Danish School Starts Separating Students by Ethnicity: As Migrant Pupil Numbers Reach 80% Teachers Act to Make Sure Ethnic Danes Aren't Outnumbered in Classes," *Daily Mail*, September 11, 2016.

> slowly to recognise over the years. He was from Birmingham, visiting relatives, and was caught up in what Swedish police believe is a gang war within the Somali community. Last year, a four-year-old girl was killed by a car bomb outside Gothenburg, another apparent victim of gang violence.[179]

But those are not the only incidents. In Västerås, Sweden, a failed asylum seeker, under deportation orders, decapitated a woman and her twenty-eight-year-old son. He murdered them with kitchen knives in an Ikea store. The perpetrator, an Eritrean named Abraham Ukbagabir, claimed he had lost control after learning the government was sending him home.[180] A refugee claiming to be fifteen (but who was really aged nineteen) raped a twelve-year-old boy in a migrant home. Another refugee, an adult claiming to be fifteen, stabbed his caregiver to death; the woman was the twenty-two-year-old daughter of immigrants.[181]

Like other European countries, Sweden is inundated with unaccompanied minors, mostly boys, who outnumber girls five to one. "In 2014, when the number of children arriving annually hit 7,000, there were serious questions about how Sweden would cope. Last year, just over 35,000 unaccompanied children registered with the authorities... Afghans and Somalis are currently the two biggest groups. Then come Syrians, Ethiopians, Iraqis, Moroccans and Eritreans. Some are fleeing war; many are fleeing poverty and misery." And no one really knows who's an adult and who's a child since Sweden does not test for age.[182]

Each of these children costs the Swedish taxpayer £160 (roughly 1,831 Swedish krona, €190, or US$202) per day.

One observer suggested that there are always those ready, willing, and able to help child refugees struggling to integrate into society.

---

179 Lifvendahl, Tove. (Political editor-in-chief, *Svenska Dagbladet.*) "How Sweden Became an Example of How Not to Handle Immigration," *The Spectator*, September 3, 2016.

180 Miller, Michael E. "In Sweden's Ikea Attack, Two Migrants, Two Slayings and Rampant Fear of Refugees," *Washington Post*, September 29, 2015.

181 "How Sweden Became an Example of How Not to Handle Immigration."

182 Ibid.

Besides drug dealers, pimps, and gang leaders, there are jihadists offering their unique services. Tove Lifvendahl, political editor-in-chief of *Svenska Dagbladet,* said, "There have been reports of Islamic State recruitment drives, not just in public places, but inside Swedish government programmes. Last year my newspaper, *Svenska Dagbladet,* exposed how some official schemes had been infiltrated by jihadists."[183]

What would be front-page news about violence elsewhere gets buried in Sweden. Why? There's so much of it. Child prostitutes' services are being sold in parking lots. Unknown individuals likely forced a Palestinian fifteen-year-old into whoring while living in a care home. Children in such places are easy prey, and many, regrettably, disappear. In the past five years, more than a thousand have done so.[184]

> "There is basically nothing we can do," says the head of Skane border police. "In some cases, we don't even have descriptions of the children. So there is no means of identifying them...no information about relatives. We have nothing to work with." Lisa Green, who monitors human trafficking in Malmo, has reported 40 cases of suspected child trafficking to the police over the past few years but says her complaints were not even recorded. "Nobody is dealing with human trafficking," says Mattias Sigfridsson, head of the police department that deals with missing persons. "We have no ability to do that right now—there are no staff."[185]

Small wonder then that Sweden imposed identity checks on travelers from Denmark. This clampdown and its checkpoints have slowed traffic on the Øresund bridge, a major road and rail link between the two countries. All rail commuters must now change trains at Copenhagen airport.[186]

---

183 Ibid.

184 Ibid.

185 Ibid.

186 "How Is the Migrant Crisis Dividing EU Countries?"

6

Policy in Perspective

Viewpoints and Perceptions

In *Visas for Al Qaeda*, we went into detail, country by country, about how the United States recruited, trained, supplied, and directed Muslim terrorists. The goal had been and still is to dehouse, deculturalize, destabilize, and destroy South and Southwest Asia as well as North Africa. Now there seems to be an additional goal: destroy Europe. We've noted earlier how the continent, if united, would be a major economic competitor of the United States. A politically integrated Europe might not necessarily follow the US lead in all things.

We've talked a bit about the tensions migrants have created from Greece to Sweden. In all the lands in between, there has been increased crime, dissension, and hatred. The cause is not just the divisiveness of Arabs, Muslims, and other groups pouring into cultures they don't understand. Nor is it just the natives reacting to the flood of aliens. It's also the struggle between the established views on society, customs, and way of life and various organized groups seeking to change them. Remember the cultural war (*Kulturkampf*) in Germany between the *Gutbürger* and the *Wutbürger*? That was the fight between the good citizen who welcomes aliens and the angry man who wants his country back. Any political party, such as the

Alternative für Deutschland, challenging its government's welcoming migrants leaves itself open to attack. It's depicted as right-wing, neo-Nazi, illiberal. Its members are castigated as unhealthy members of society. There is no doubt that some of these people might be part of the AfD. But most of the faction's membership consists of ordinary, everyday Germans driven into the only party promising to stop the never-ending migrant influx.

Earlier in this work, we mentioned US actions in Latin America. We counted the revolutions, coups d'état, and civil wars the City upon a Hill fomented. These drove thousands, if not millions, of illegal aliens into the United States, where they live twelve to a room, working for minimal pay and no benefits.

But that's just south of the border. The countries did not change shape. They only lost population. But America is more than adept at geography. It has redrawn the map of the world.

Following World War I, the United States—led by its president, Woodrow Wilson, an Anglophile academic—participated in restructuring Europe. As a signatory to the Carthaginian Treaty of Versailles, America participated in the dismemberment of Germany and Austria, including their overseas possessions. In cooperation with other signatories, the United States also created entirely new countries, such as Czechoslovakia and Yugoslavia. Serbia vanished as an independent state while Hungary, Rumania, and Bulgaria changed size.

Twenty-five years later, at the end of World War II, the United States, in concert with the other victorious powers, again altered the world's map. Poland lost territory to the USSR and recouped its missing land from Germany, itself split into three pieces. Shortly afterward, America, ever true to democracy, self-determination, and anticommunism, divided Korea and Vietnam.

With that kind of history, it's clear to see that American goals have expanded. In the past, the aim was the creation of countries, the division of countries, and the rearrangement of countries. Now it's the destruction of entire continents.

And Kelly Greenhill Showed the Way

Discussing Yugoslavia's destruction, Greenhill noted, "What the West feared most [was] large-scale refugee flows and regional destabilization."[187] Citing former US Assistant Secretary of State for European Affairs Richard Holbrooke, Greenhill said that was "our greatest fear by far." The American government understood that bombing Yugoslavia would "simply accelerate the rate of *engineered* [emphasis added] migration in Kosovo."[188]

Greenhill and the people who read and followed her book recognized which European buttons to push. Most surprisingly, in the twenty-first century, the Europeans should have known about their past. Somehow they either forgot their buttons or ignored their effects. Here's an excerpt from Greenhill's chapter on NATO and the Kosovo conflict:

> Refugees had come to be most unwelcome sights in Western Europe since the numbers of asylum applicants had begun a steep and prolonged ascent in the mid-1980s. Fear and distrust of foreigners more generally had grown since then as well...The number of Europeans who believed there were "too many...foreigners..." rose dramatically...with clear majorities in Italy and Germany.

In a study in 1992, even before Yugoslavia came apart and migrants flowed in earnest, 78 percent of Germans were saying that immigration was their greatest problem. As part of a similar study, also conducted in 1992, Greece was seen as more hostile to immigrants than any of the fifteen other countries surveyed. Greeks tended to agree with the statement that all illegals should be sent home—no exceptions.[189]

---

187 Greenhill, 140, citing her interviews with German government officials in Sarajevo, Bosnia-Herzegovina, July 1999.

188 Ibid., citing Bronwen Maddox, Michael Evans, Anthony Lloyd, Tom Walker, and Daniel McGrory, "The 80 Days War," *Times*, July 15, 1999.

189 Ibid., 141, citing undated *Eurobarometer* surveys in the 1980s and 1990s.

In a footnote, Greenhill cites former British prime minister Tony Blair. In a remarkably truthful statement for him, he said, "When oppression produces massive flows of refugees which unsettle neighbouring countries then they can properly be described as 'threats to international peace and security.'"[190]

Given past experience, the Teutonic government certainly should have seen today's migration problems coming.

> Germany, after having taken in 350,000 Bosnians during the last Yugoslav war—more than all other EU member states combined—likewise feared it would bear the brunt of a full-scale crisis in Kosovo. As one diplomat described the situation, "Germany feels that the rest of Europe is not pulling its weight. It wants its partners to see this as a European problem, not as a German problem."[191]

And it wasn't just Germany that had been swamped by migrants when NATO destroyed Yugoslavia. Greenhill goes into detail in her above-noted chapter about Italy and Greece, documenting their fears and lining out the number of migrants that had flooded or could flood in. "In short, the general belief of the leaders in all three of these frontline states was that escalating the crisis in Kosovo promised each of them concentrated costs—including the possibility of an end to their political tenures—and few, if any, benefits."[192]

Yet they all supported, or at least did not oppose, the war. Now, twenty years later, they all were caught up in a new wave of migration. This one came from well outside Europe. This one was much larger. This one had the power to destroy an entire culture. Yet, again, no government took

190 Ibid., 142, citing "Doctrine of the International Community," transcript of a speech given before the Chicago Council of Economists, April 14, 1999.

191 Ibid., 143, citing Kondpoulou, Maragarita, "The Greek Media and the Kosovo Crisis," *Conflict & Communication Online 1* (2002), 7.

192 Ibid., 145.

effective action. On the contrary, all European governments invited them in and waved them through borders in lockstep with some apparently covert, carefully synchronized master plan.

And how does Greenhill frame the Yugoslav viewpoint on this? She tries *reductio ad absurdum.* (In plain English, that's disproving a proposition by following its implications to an absurd conclusion.) But six years after her book, in the midst of a new wave, her argument falls flat. Quoting a columnist in a state-run newspaper, she wrote:

> Kosovo represents a strategic zone of terrorism and drug trade… It is well known that this terroristic internal structure was supported by Albanian communist leader Enver Hoxha…[and] if we add to all this the fact that the terrorists are mostly Moslems, it seams [*sic*] that things are getting to quite another dimension.[193]

Greenhill then says,

> This was a masterful piece of fear-mongering, custom-tailored to push the buttons of anxious Western European politicians: the threat from Kosovo is not only refugees, but communist, drug-trading, Islamic, terrorist refugees.[194]

But isn't that what we have now, minus the communists?

But we also have NATO's successful public relations campaign and Greenhill's media machine with us. Remember our earlier allusions to German government officials playing down the migrants' attacks? Read what "Phony Tony" Blair said about Yugoslavia: "We had to take grip [*sic*] on the whole way the thing was run and organised because it was big—it

193 Greenhill, 147–148, citing Elias, Juan Pablo Cordoba, "The Reform: US Political Games on Kosovo and Metohia," *Politika*, March 4, 1999.

194 Ibid., 148.

wasn't just a military campaign it was also a propaganda campaign and we had to take our public opinions with us."[195]

This seems to have become the established pattern for shaping citizens' views on migrants now. The principal culprits in this have been the mainstream news media in both the United States and Europe. They've been leading an aggressive, flawlessly synchronized propaganda campaign selling the migrant crisis.

Greenhill added, "For several months, NATO members neutralized domestic opposition to the bombing campaign and sidestepped questions about whether it had inflamed the crisis, through the work of spokespeople who likened Kosovo to Cambodia under Pol Pot and likened FRY [Federal Republic of Yugoslavia] activities to 'the Great Terror.'"[196] (Greenhill neglected to mention which terror: During the French Revolution or in the USSR in the 1930s?)

The people who welcomed the Afghans, Syrians, Libyans, and whoever else came over the border were also carefully indoctrinated. Instead of likening the leaders of their former governments to Slobodan Milošević or Pol Pot, misinformation and disinformation were used to shape new public attitudes. The idea that the Syrian White Helmets were bravely fighting the evil Bashar al-Assad is just one example of this. It's just a continuation of the earlier

> deft NATO propaganda campaign in which Milosovic [*sic*] was compared to Hitler and the fleeing Kosovars were compared to those fleeing a Nazi onslaught. By likening the mass migration to the Holocaust [but not the *Nakba*[197]] and casting Serb behavior as genocide, the Kosovar Albanians were (at least temporarily) transformed from threats into victims. Consequently, the

---

195 Ibid., 168, citing *Moral Combat.*

196 Ibid., citing Jensen, Holger, "New Dangers Now Arise in Kosovo Crisis," *Denver Rocky Mountain News,* April 1, 1999.

197 Arabic for "catastrophe," referring to the Zionists' ethnic cleansing of Palestine in 1948.

> concentration of support for the displaced in the pro-refugee/migrant camp skyrocketed while the level of opposition to them declined, thereby radically reducing NATO vulnerability to coercion over the cost of the crisis.[198]

But no one ever charged NATO with propaganda. And no one has linked US policies to the need to receive the migrants into Europe with candy and flowers. In the previous wave of "refugees," nations feared being overrun. However, that did not happen. But today, the situation is entirely different. Europe is being swamped. And there is no finger-pointing tarantella of blame.

Was Greenhill gifted with prophecy, or is her book an instruction manual for today?

> NATO intervention in Kosovo—driven as it was, at least in part, by the actions of the KLA [Kosovo Liberation Army] and the support it garnered via intelligent use of the global media apparatus—may encourage other groups to manipulate international opinion via their own propaganda campaigns. By provoking attacks on themselves by their own governments, these groups may seek assistance with their bids for self-determination or for the overthrow of undemocratic governments, as the KLA now readily admits it did...It can also serve as a handy fig leaf for actors who wish to support self-determination movements for their own self-serving political reasons.[199]

Is this US policy in Libya? Is this US policy in Syria?

Think about it. Earlier, the author mentioned how activists and NGOs tried to use mass migration from North Korea to bring down its government. They had a two-pronged approach. One was "staging... dramatic escapes and bids for asylum, ideally captured on film and

198 Ibid., 177–178.
199 Ibid., 179.

subsequently distributed to major news outlets to maximize the international impact of these events." The other prong was to raise "public consciousness of the issue and mobilizing pressure on targets."[200]

Think back to the human waves splashing across European beaches. Remember pictures of people traveling with only the clothes on their backs? Remember pictures of families burdened with raggedy children? Remember pictures of people clawing their way through rusty, barbed-wire fences? Doesn't that take you back to the 1940s? Do you remember the wretched Poles, Russians, French, and others streaming away from the *Wehrmacht*'s vanguard?

Propaganda and Faith in America

Carefully constructed propaganda is always effective. And it is working today. And it is changing minds, clouding minds, and infecting minds. Here's a comment from a German reader of *Die CIA und der Terror*:[201]

> People here have too much faith in America...I told my sister about your book. She is a medical doctor and not stupid, but as in many cases she does not have enough time to figure out on her own the political picture. She saw what I told her from your book as a "conspiracy theory." Al-Assad is an inhuman dictator, the US helps democracy in the Near East, etc. It is almost hopeless.

Europe used to question US foreign policy and its underpinnings. In the 1950s, 1960s, and 1970s, there were mass marches in European countries and Japan against American nuclear weapons. They had good reason for their fears. There was the aggressive US Cold War policy. And there were American planes flying around the world, toting megaton-yield thermonuclear arms. In 1966, the US Air Force accidentally

200 Ibid., 235.

201 The Kopp Verlag translation for the German-speaking market of *Visas for Al Qaeda: CIA Handouts That Rocked the World.*

dropped four hydrogen bombs on Spain. While the weapons did not explode, the casings broke, releasing plutonium, a substance with a half-life of twenty-four thousand years, and irradiating the Palomares region. While there were no apparent demonstrations against the "accident," people have long memories. Spaniards there are still unhappy:

> Local barman Andres Portillo says the damage is to the town's image. "Every time the story hits the media, it hurts tourism," he says. "A lot of people don't want to come here because they think the quality of life must be low, that cancer rates are higher..."
>
> Some here say that without the negative publicity, Palomares could be every bit as popular as its more famous neighbour, Marbella.
>
> So the community finds itself trapped. When residents complain, the accident makes headlines again and there's a drop in the number of visitors, and a drop in the prices farmers get at market for their produce.[202]

In Germany, in the late 1970s, the Carter government wanted to deploy neutron-bomb-tipped cruise and Pershing II missiles. At the time, the author was there as a diplomat, and he well remembers the uproar in the German media. Germans didn't want their country to become a nuclear battleground, ultimately becoming a radioactive slag heap. Carter's successor, Ronald Reagan, stuck to that plan. United Press International (UPI) reported:

> An estimated 250,000 people poured into Bonn Saturday [October 10, 1981] to denounce the deployment of U.S. nuclear missiles in Western Europe in the biggest demonstration in West German history.

202 Hadden, Gerry. "Palomares Bombs: Spain Waits for US to Finish Nuclear Clean-Up," *BBC News*, October 22, 2012.

> "Americans go west," "Get out of NATO," "No Nukes," read banners that underlined Chancellor Helmut Schmidt's complaint that the demonstration was directed at his government's foreign and security policies.[203]

Thousands demonstrated against the American war in Indochina. In London, in Paris, in Berlin, and in Belgrade, the people were out in the streets. In fact, there were probably fewer countries and capitals where protests did not take place.

But today? Too many people, as noted above, quietly accept America's foreign policy. They even accept the consequences, such as the migrant wave, without question.

The Establishment's Dilemma and Merkel's Muddles

And when people do question what happens, the establishment rounds on them. The people who count, the media that count, denounce them as radical right-wing racists. In Austria on December 4, 2016, those that count successfully lambasted Norbert Hofer as a radical rightist. As candidate for the largely ceremonial position of president, both he and the Austrian Freedom Party (*Freiheits Partei Österreich*, FPÖ) were loudly and vaguely criticized. One paper objected to the blue of campaign posters because it was similar to a color used by the Austrian Nazis in the 1930s.[204] Another asserted the party was extremist because it distributed a book with the phrase "we need more army tents than party tents."[205]

But, as we noted earlier about Germany, not all of the ordinary people accept the elites' view of the world. Hofer's support came from

203 Fleming, Joseph B. "Denounce US in Biggest West German Demonstration," *UPI*, October 10, 1981.

204 Walser, Harald. "Eure Schande heißt Norbert Hofer!" (Your Shane is Called Norbert Hofer), *der Standard*, November 6, 2013.

205 No author. "FPÖ-Hofer gab Buch heraus: So 'rechtsextrem' ist der Inhalt" (FPÖ-Hofer Handed Out a Book: The Contents Are Extreme Right-Wing), *Heute*, September 30, 2016.

all over Austria, except in the far west and north center. Comments in *Zero Hedge* echo what Silvia Germek, an astute observer of the European scene, told us in 2015: Europe will be jerked further to the right. The Left's migrant policies harbor compound Trojan horse agendas that are destroying Europe.

> Nevertheless the strong showing by the Freedom party is still likely to be seen as a boost for Marine Le Pen, leader of France's National Front [a further right party] ahead of her country's presidential election next year. Herbert Kickl, who ran Mr. Hofer's campaign, described the vote as a "historic" for the Freedom party.
>
> Don't count the Freedom Party out yet though: according to oppinion [*sic*] polls, Freedom party could become Austria's largest political party after parliamentary elections due by September 2018 but expected to be called early. That could see the party's leader Heinz-Christian Strache becoming the country's next chancellor.
>
> "This may be only a temporary relief for European leaders if it strengthens the Freedom Party's chances in parliamentary elections," said Heather Grabbe, European politics expert at the [George Soros] Open Society European Policy Institute in Brussels.[206]

Continuing migrant crime and "gover-ups" will likely drive Germany further to the right. Because of this, Chancellor Merkel, who declared she will stand again for the office, may have more troubles. On October 16, 2016, an Afghan migrant, Hussein Kavari, raped and murdered Maria Ladenburger, daughter of a high-ranking EU official. The seventeen-year-old Afghan attacker caught the young medical student as she was bicycling home from a party in the university city of Freiburg.

---

206 Durden, Tyler. "Freedom Party's Hofer Defeated by Greens' Van der Bellen in Austria's Presidential Election," *Zero Hedge*, December 4, 2016.

The beautiful nineteen-year-old reputedly worked in her spare time in refugee homes there. (But, apparently, she did not know her attacker.)

The crime was brutal (murder by drowning). And Merkel will likely face questions as to why the police kept a lid on the matter for nearly two months. The details and the involvement of the migrant criminal came out no earlier than December 2.[207] More questions are out there now. The asylee, according to new press reports, was a known criminal. He had received a "ten-year sentence in Corfu for attempting to kill a 20-year-old woman he hurled off a cliff face after following her as she walked home." Released for good behavior after twenty-eight months, he skipped parole and fled the country. Kavari applied for and received asylum in Freiburg, the city where he violated Maria Ladenburger and sent her to a watery grave.[208]

In mid-November 2016, a German contact (who voted for Merkel) told the author she found this crime terrible. This, coupled with another, unsolved murder not far from Freiburg, disturbed her greatly—so much so, she said, she could hardly stand to listen to the news anymore.

In the hope of avoiding an election disaster, Merkel may be reexamining her views. While still welcoming migrants, she is now objecting to some of their clothing. The *Washington Post* is suggesting that Frau Merkel's new opposition to full-veil coverings is tied to her damaged approval ratings. The article fails to specify what the religious coverings are (e.g., face veils [*niqabs*] or head-to-foot robes [*burkas*]). However, it ties the chancellor's new attitude to "the arrests of two asylum seekers in five days in connection with three sexual assaults," including Maria Ladenburger's. Continuing, the *Post* wrote, "Right-wing politicians are openly blaming Merkel's policy for what they decry as a migrant-fueled

---

207 Virtue, Rob; Hall, Allan; Pallenberg, Monika. "Daughter of Top EU Official Raped and Murdered in Germany—Afghan Migrant Admits Killing," *Express*, December 5, 2016. Thanks to Wayne Madsen for sending us the story.

208 Hall, Allan. "Why Was He Allowed In?: EU Free Movement Under Fire as Migrant 'Murderer' ALREADY Jailed," *Express*, December 15, 2016. (Thanks to waynemadsen-report.com.)

crime wave."[209] In another article, the *Post* quoted a Friedrich Ebert Foundation survey highlighting the chancellor's problems with the electorate. The Foundation, associated with the German Socialist Party and funded by the government, claimed 40 percent of the country thought Islam was undermining German society.[210] Moreover, the Foundation claimed that 50 percent of Germans were prejudiced against asylum seekers. Still worse for Merkel, 43 percent of the country thought the government was "concealing the truth from people."[211]

---

209 Faiola, Anthony. "Merkel Urges Ban on Islamic 'Veil,'" *Washington Post*, December 8, 2016.

210 Lane, Charles. "In Germany, a Lesson in Good Intentions," *Washington Post* December 8, 2016.

211 Friedrich Ebert Stiftung (Foundation). "Out of the Shadows: The NEW-RIGHT in Germany," December 1, 2016.

7

Migrants, Costs, Targeting

Another Look at Germany

THERE IS MORE behind the targeting of the Federal Republic with migrants.

George Friedman of *Stratfor* (a provider of "strategic intelligence") has asserted that the German Question "is the key issue of our time." In a speech delivered to the Chicago Council on Global Affairs on February 4, 2015, he elaborated on this.

> It is not in the American interest to see German, European let's say, European industrialism and technology united with Russian natural resources. This is not what US grand strategy really wants to see happen.

Friedman claimed that US geopolitics in Europe is based on driving a wedge between Europe and Russia.

An extremely knowledgeable political scientist corroborated this. Our contact, a high-level European government official writing especially for this book, said (in translation),

> And Bashar el Assad would have long been history had Moscow not intervened in this particular war. This prevented the lateral

> attempt of delivering oil and gas through Syria and further west in order to weaken Russian influence, which is essential because of the oil and gas provided by Moscow. Leaks of the information site "WikiLeaks" showed that the US continues to see Germany as unreliable and wants to separate it in any way possible from Russia. What worries the US is Russian oil and gas and German technology. One must also view the refugee crisis in this context.

Our interlocutor added,

> Ankara is the key to further destabilization of Europe and Germany, and this development now depends not only on Washington and the European Union, but increasingly Moscow, to whom Berlin is a very important political and trading partner.[212]

One author, Gearóid Ó Colmáin, asserted that US military planners have long opposed the integration of Germany and Russia. They saw this as something in Germany's geopolitical interests and not in those of America.[213]

Are the Americans, as Ó Colmáin suggests, looking to provoke an armed conflict between Germany and Russia? A wave of migrants has and will continue to destabilize Germany. The flood of illegals is pushing the country further to the right and driving down respect for authority. Would this be enough to install a man on horseback and strike out at real or imaginary threats to the east? Certainly, as the reader of *Die CIA und der Terror* said, "People here have too much faith in America." And it is the United States that insists that Russia is dangerous, that Russia

---

212 Official statement by Pavle Kalinic for this publication, December 23, 2016. Translation. He is equivalent to Croatia's DHS chief, and he is also their top terrorism specialist.

213 Ó Colmáin, Gearóid. "The Balkanization of Europe: Neo-Prometheism and Neo-Ottomanism," *Dissident Voice*, January 27, 2016.

interfered in US elections, that Russia is expansionist. It is the United States that conducts military operations on Russia's borders, and it is the United States that keeps expanding NATO eastward.

Anakonda 2016 involved more than thirty thousand soldiers (half from the United States) and thousands of combat vehicles in maneuvers across Poland. In spring 2015, Operation Dragoon Ride sent 120 US armored vehicles through Poland, Lithuania, Estonia, Latvia, and the Czech Republic, ending in Germany. The following spring, the American army repeated its road march, this time sending two armored columns through the Czech Republic, Poland, Latvia, and Lithuania, concluding in Estonia. Tens of thousands of soldiers and hundreds of armored vehicles maneuvering along the Russian frontier are threatening and blatantly provocative. This can result in war by miscalculation.

Following America's lead, German Chancellor Merkel claimed that Russia may try to interfere in 2017's elections. In Clintonesque fashion, without supplying facts, the chancellor alleged that Russia is engaged in cyberattacks against her country. Moreover, she said, it is supplying false news.[214]

The drumbeat of false news about Russia and its intentions toward Germany goes on. Now, Gustav Gressel, a supposed Russian expert at the European Council on Foreign Relations (which calls itself a pan-European think tank), has devised a new fairy tale. He "said small numbers of refugees with links to the Kremlin and Syrian security services could be mobilised to sway public opinion against the Chancellor [Merkel]." Alluding to the December 31, 2015, migrant attacks across Germany, Gressel declared "similar attacks could provoke Germans to turn on Merkel at next September's [2017] election." True to a government supportive of the United States and hostile to Russia, Hans-Georg Maaßen declared that "a Russian disinformation campaign was likely." Maaßen,

214 Burke, David. "Merkel Warns Russia Could Interfere in German Election through Cyber Attacks and Propaganda Campaigns," *Daily Mail,* November 8, 2016.

the BfV head, told Reuters, "This could happen again next year and we are alarmed."[215]

This is all speculation.

Angela Merkel and her government created the migrant mess. Angela Merkel and her government now seem desperate to end it—without taking substantive action. Instead of sending the illegals back home, Merkel now wants to ban "Islamic coverings," whatever they might be. Instead of owning up to migrant crimes, Merkel's government conceals them. Instead of admitting her mistake, Merkel blames the Russians for something that hasn't happened and won't happen. This appears to be a government out of control, out of touch with the people, and out of touch with reality. It looks like a government headed for failure.

With wild accusations from surrogates along with her own rants about "enemies," the chancellor sounds like Hillary Clinton. Hillary blamed her failure to become president on Russian intervention. The former secretary of state also claimed FBI Director Comey's e-mail probe caused her loss. It was Clinton, in her failed electoral campaign, who said, "Angela Merkel was her favorite world leader."[216] Given that Hillary's hysteria failed miserably, can we expect the same of Merkel's? Or will she conjure up such bogeymen that Germany lurches far to the right so as to fight them? Or will she fail, leaving the further-right parties to repudiate her policies and install a government of rightists?

What will Merkel do next? If the electorate boots her out of office, would the further-right parties, such as the AfD, get enough votes to reverse her policies? Would they be able to form a coalition government from a mix of the Left Party (*die Linke*), the Greens, and a rightist, business-oriented group, the Free Democrats?

---

215 Burke, David. "Pro-EU Think-Tank Says Russia and Syria Could Be Orchestrating Migrant Sex Attacks to Swing the Upcoming German Elections," *Daily Mail*, December 14, 2016. Original statement appeared as Mössbauer, Karina and Röpcke, Julian. "Propaganda-Feldzug sogar mit Sexmobs" (Propaganda Campaign Even with Sexmobs), *Bild*, December 9, 2016.

216 McCaskill, Nolan D. "In Swipe at Trump, Clinton Names Merkel as Her Favorite World Leader," *Politico*, September 30, 2016.

Or would there be more of the same?

Gearóid Ó Colmáin suggests that the present situation will continue, driven by US policy. Based on independent German TV station K-TV information, he notes that the migrant wave likely came from retired American General Thomas P. M. Barnett. Barnett, a former advisor to one-time US defense secretary Rumsfeld, now works with Wikistrat. The firm, an American company with ties to Israel, monitors intelligence, among other things. It also works with AFRICOM, the US military's Africa Command, headquartered in Stuttgart, Germany.

Barnett has developed the "five flows of globalization" concept: the free flow of money, security, food, energy, and people. Ó Colmáin alleges that this notion breaks down nation-state structures, allowing American corporate pillaging. Another key feature, the free flow of people, inundated Europe with migrants from all over the Third World. Additionally, Ó Colmáin links the migrant flood to Europe's declining birth rate. Citing German sociologist Gunnar Heinsohn, the Irish author compares and contrasts Merkel's "y'all come" attitude with other countries' immigration policies. Noting that the *Völkerwanderung* has resulted in a crushing burden of unskilled, uneducated troublemakers in Europe, Ó Colmáin states that Australia and Canada give preference to educated, talented settlers.

As the Irishman writes, "What we are witnessing here is a covert war being waged by the Anglo-Saxon Zionist elite against the German Federal Republic. The low-intensity war is using people as weapons to create conditions of social chaos in order to prevent Berlin's inevitable rapprochement with Moscow." Continuing, he observes that Barnett's view is connected with Oliver Roy's *Globalized Islam.* Quoting that work, Ó Colmáin writes, "There are now in the West only two movements of radical protest that claim to be 'internationalist': the antiglobalization movement and radical Islam. For a rebel, to convert is to find a cause."

Furthermore, Ó Colmáin opines that the population movements into the continent "will help increase and further entrench globalization, imperialism, and class warfare." Quoting from Barnett, he adds that the population flow isn't just a political safety valve but also an economic one. Europe needs workers to replace those dying or retiring, and the Middle East needs to drain off some of its youth.

In the end, Ó Colmáin suggests that the object is to "divide and conquer the workers of the world on the basis of religious and ethnic sectarianism, as well as bourgeois values such as human rights, thereby making the world 'safe for capitalism' and global imperialist domination."[217]

To put it another way, "the migrant crisis is actually part of a large-scale aggression against the EU aimed at collapsing the Schengen-Dublin-Frontex system as the key step toward foreign-power penetration and domination over Europe."[218] As we have seen, the European Union's continent-wide free movement of people has been called into question. Moreover, the Dublin program of requiring asylum applicants to change their status in the first country reached has ended. Additionally, Frontex's promotion, coordination, and development of European border management have collapsed. Nationalism is on the rise.

A high-ranking European official, Pavle Kalinic, touched on this as well. Writing as a special contribution to this publication, he noted,

> The migrant crisis, which has significantly affected the European Union, has shown that it does not function as a regulated system but is instead more of a paper tiger. The main direction of the movement and destination of choice by migrants is Germany! Of course, Germany is a collateral victim of the dissolution of the agreement of Sykes-Picot of 1916 which was a British-French agreement which was subsequently joined by the Russians and Italians to agree on the division of spheres of interest after the collapse of the Ottoman Empire. The Arab Spring, which was less of a spring, served as prelude to further destabilization of the Middle East in which a series of internationally recognized governments was destroyed. In Libya, Gaddafi was killed so he

217 Ó Colmáin, Gearóid. "Barnett's Five Flows of Globaisation," *Dissident Voice*, January 21, 2016.

218 Germek, Silvia. Unpublished 2015 MS.

could not demand repayment of debts owed for the sale of oil, also to prevent him from replacing the Franc of former French colonies with the Libyan Dinar as gold-backed currency.

Of course, the dead Gaddafi can not specify with how many million dollars he co-financed the political campaign of [Nicholas] Sarkozy [the former French president]. Mubarak was overthrown in Egypt, illustrating that Washington does not care for even its most faithful allies. But democratic elections brought Morsi to power which was backed by the Muslim Brotherhood, which forced Washington to pull the brakes. Overnight, Morsi was arrested and replaced by Sisi who had been appointed to the post of Chief of Staff Egyptian army by Morsi.[219]

Germek's unpublished manuscript goes on to say that the US government is deeply involved in making this happen. CIA case officers work with "human-rights groups, the pro-migrant movement and their criminal transporters, providing wads of cash and debriefing their paid operatives after cargo deliveries. On the other side of the counter, consular officials and immigration officers can reap bribes and sex from visa applicants, as shown in scandals in Kathmandu and Shanghai."[220]

Costs

Raising the pressure in the European pot is the vast pool of illegal labor that has poured across the various frontiers. In the short term, employment shortages disappear. In the longer term, there will be greater

219 Official statement for this publication, December 23, 2016. Kalinic, as noted, is equivalent to Croatia's DHS chief, and he is also their top terrorism specialist.

220 Germek, Silvia. Unpublished 2015 MS, citing Farrell, Amy; McDevitt, Jack; Perry, Noam; et al. "Review of Existing Estimates of Victims of Human Trafficking in the United States and Recommendations for Improving Research and Measurement of Human Trafficking: Final Report to ATEST," *Alliance to End Slavery and Trafficking*, 2010. NB Corrupt visa officers are noted *passim* in *Visas for Al Qaeda*.

social friction and crime. Anti-immigrant tension will rise and figure more prominently in European politics.[221]

Another force ratcheting up these tensions will come from education and training. Advanced economies and the modern administrative state require skilled labor and superior schooling. Far too many of the migrants have neither. Nor do they have sufficient language ability. Few of them are fluent in German, French, Italian, or other European tongues. Certainly, there is no ethnically European community speaking fluent Dari, Pashto, Arabic, or other exotic languages. The flood of illegals will stream downhill, to positions for garbage collectors, street sweepers, and grass cutters. Will the benefits of filling such jobs compensate for the welfare burden of carrying the migrants while they find them?

Here's one British paper's view:

> A survey by Germany's Ifo think-tank showed that most companies believed the greatest employment potential for refugees was as unskilled workers, with only 22pc of the 3,000 firms polled believing they could do skilled work and just 3pc that saw "leadership potential."
>
> The biggest barrier was communication, with 92pc citing a lack of language skills as a barrier to employment, while 71pc cited a lack of qualifications.[222]

Additionally, how many of the aliens bring religious baggage with them? Should they follow the Salafist/Wahhabi hard line, what then? That variety of Islam has proscriptions against women joining with men in the workforce. Will they refuse to deal with pork, seen as an unclean animal? If so, what happens in restaurants, cafeterias, and other food-service institutions? Some have already demanded swimming and gym workouts

221 Ibid.

222 Chan, Szu Ping. "Mapped: How a Demographic Time Bomb Will Transform the Global Economy," *The Telegraph*, January 2, 2016.

segregated by sex. Low-level jobs in certain manufacturing or entertainment industries are forbidden to devout Muslims. Examples include working in a brewery or distillery or working in a bar or nightclub.[223] Unless some migrant attitudes toward gainful employment change, there will be greater demands placed on the social welfare system.

Then There's Money, the Root of All Evil

One economist, Bernd Raffelhüschen, has warned that Germany will have financial problems soon. Instead of reaping the benefits of cheap labor and more taxes paid into social welfare programs, Teutonia will pay out €878 billion in migrant costs (about US$912 billion). Worse, the practitioner of the dismal science, one definition of economics, suggested the price tag could go as high as €1.5 trillion (ca. US$1.6 trillion). This will depend, he said, "on how well the 'second generation' fits in with life in Germany." According to Raffelhüschen, "Germany can't afford uncontrolled immigration permanently." Another source, *Marktwirtschaft* (translated as "market economics"), commented that Germany is gaining nothing from the migrant wave. Michael Eilfort, its chairman, stated, "Uncontrolled migration doesn't bring the country fiscal return, but will cost the country money long-term."[224]

Warnings Not Heeded

In 2009, the *Telegraph* warned that Europe did not see that a fuse on a population powder keg had been lit.

> Britain and the rest of the European Union are ignoring a demographic time bomb: a recent rush into the EU by migrants,

---

223 Ibid.

224 Oliphant, Vickie and Pallenberg, Monika. "GERMANY WOES CONTINUES: Migrant Crisis to Cost Merkel's Government over a TRILLION Pounds," *Express*, July 21, 2016.

> including millions of Muslims, will change the continent beyond recognition over the next two decades, and almost no policy-makers are talking about it.
>
> The numbers are startling. Only 3.2 per cent of Spain's population was foreign-born in 1998. In 2007 it was 13.4 per cent. Europe's Muslim population has more than doubled in the past 30 years and will have doubled again by 2015. In Brussels, the top seven baby boys' names recently were Mohamed, Adam, Rayan, Ayoub, Mehdi, Amine and Hamza.[225]

Continuing, the paper noted additional unseen and ignored issues connected with integrating a large number of immigrants. This was years before the migrants began flooding in. "America's Pew Forum on Religion & Public Life, part of the non-partisan Pew Research Center, said in a report: 'These [EU] countries possess deep historical, cultural, religious and linguistic traditions. Injecting hundreds of thousands, and in some cases millions, of people who look, speak and act differently into these settings often makes for a difficult social fit.'"

Clarifying its discussion of the population time bomb, the paper reported,

> EU numbers on general immigration tell a story on their own. In the latter years of the 20th century, the 27 countries of the EU attracted half a million more people a year than left. "Since 2002, however," the latest EU report says, "net migration into the EU has roughly tripled to between 1.6 million and two million people per year."
>
> The increased pace has made a nonsense of previous forecasts. In 2004 the EU thought its population would decline by

225 Michaels, Adrian. "Muslim Europe: The Demographic Time Bomb Transforming Our Continent," *The Telegraph*, August 8, 2009.

16 million by 2050. Now it thinks it will increase by 10 million by 2060. Britain is expected to become the most populous EU country by 2060, with 77 million inhabitants. Right now it has 20 million fewer people than Germany. Italy's population was expected to fall precipitously; now it is predicted to stay flat.[226]

226 Ibid.

8

Behind the Scenes, Behind the History

What's Driving This *Now*?

BESIDES AMERICAN POLICY, its war machine, and its intelligence services, are there any other groups behind this migration of the peoples? Does the European Union pressure other states to consent to its refugee policies? Do people see the dangerous effects of open-ended resettlement? Are democracies prone to destabilization? Is the United States responsible for the present crisis? Do the immigrants get help? Are there problems with German internal security?

The answer to all of these questions is yes.

As for groups behind this problem, there are several. And they are all shadowy organizations that don't reveal their contacts or sources of income. Given their obscure nature, it's possible to surmise that they have connections to the spooks.[227]

Past and current groups include the following:

- W2eu.info—Welcome to Europe
- Lesvos09.antira.info (Its registration has been deleted.)
- No Borders (now a Facebook page: No Borders)

227 Germek, Silvia. Unpublished 2015 MS.

- Borderline.eu (a German site)
- Sea-watch.org
- International Migration Initiative

The European Union is now attempting to force nonmember states to accept its decisions on migrants. In 2014, Switzerland voted to limit immigration into the country through a quota system. "But Brussels fat cats refused to agree a negotiated deal [*sic*] to limit EU migration across the Swiss border, despite Switzerland not being part of the EU." This implies that the European Union will limit Swiss access to its markets unless the Helvetian Republic reverses its previous vote.[228]

However, the Swiss federal government, despite internal efforts to thwart the 2014 plebiscite, has seemingly rejected a revote. To do so "would annul the mandate that the people and the cantons [States] gave to the government to limit immigration."[229] RASA (*Raus Aus Der Sackgasse*, or Break the Deadlock) is a group campaigning to bring more migrants into the country. Its goal is another poll to reverse the earlier one rejecting open borders. RASA, formed in summer 2014 (after the February immigration vote), claims that it is a group of scientists, politicians, cultural leaders, sportsmen, businessmen, and labor unions. It professes a membership of one thousand. Somewhat shadowy, it has raised CHF500,000 (roughly €465,000 or US$390,000) in two years to support its operations. (The Swiss billionaire and Hillary Clinton supporter Hansjörg Wyss contributed CHF180,000 of this amount, about €168,000 or US$175,000.)[230] Although aliens are prohibited from financing US election campaigns, Wyss gave US$100 million to support voter registration in the United States during the run-up to the 2016 elections. He seems to have shared information about this with the Democratic

---

228 Perring, Rebecca. "EU Dealt ANOTHER Blow over Migrant Quotas as Now Switzerland to Hold Crucial Referendum," *Express*, October 27, 2016.

229 No author. "Swiss Government Rejects Call for Second Immigration Vote," *The Local ch*, October 27, 2016.

230 http://www.initiative-rasa.ch/. CHF=Swiss Francs.

Party.[231] Hilary Clinton and her political group have long embraced the "Open Borders" concept. Evidently, Wyss does too.

Analysis

So is it really, "Good-bye, Europe, hello, chaos"?

You decide. One of the author's high school teachers, George J. Schemel, SJ, once said that a book is a machine to think with. The writer hopes he's given you enough information and statistics and events throughout the preceding pages to consider. Lest we fail to make our point, we'll tell you again: Angela Merkel's migrants have destroyed the old Europe. What follows will be chaos.

First, let's look at Europe as it was. The countries and major cities had histories going back millennia. Many of them had been part of the Roman Empire. They had their own languages with their own dialects. They repulsed invasions from outside the continent, the first by the Moors in Spain in AD 1492. (That took centuries, after Tariq ibn-Ziyad led an African army across the Straits of Gibraltar in AD 711.) The second set of invasions came from the Ottoman Turks throughout the sixteenth century. The third time came again from the Ottomans, repulsed from the gates of Vienna in 1683. Although Austria and Hungary were freed, the Turks held a good bit of the Balkans until the late nineteenth century.

While Europe had almost destroyed itself through disastrous wars in the names of religion, capitalism, and conquest, it still remained Europe. The French spoke French; the Germans, German; and the Italians, Italian. There were distinct national differences. Yet there was a distinct European way of life, a *joie de vive*, a love of learning and culture.

The University of Bologna was founded in AD 1088, *la Sorbonne*, the University of Paris, between 1160 and 1250. Karl IV, King of Bohemia and Holy Roman Emperor, established the first German-language

---

231 Markay, Lachlan. "Memo Reveals Clinton Foundation Donor's $100 Million Registration, Turnout Push," *The Washington Free Beacon*, June 22, 2016.

university at Prague in 1348. Rupert I, Elector of the Palatinate, started the University of Heidelberg in 1386.

Russian ballet troupes, the Bolshoi and the renamed Mariinsky Ballet, are the epitome of classical dance. European composers, such as Beethoven and Mozart, are known throughout the world—and admired all across the continent.

The French and Italian love of food and wine produced a lifestyle that is treasured by all who visit those countries. One US diplomat once remarked that German bread is worth the trip to Central Europe.

But no foreign army threatens this. No nation-state is attempting to bring this all crashing down. The horde of migrants comes from American and European government policies. And it is the people of Europe that are opposing these policies. It is the people of Europe who see the dangers. It is the people of Europe who want to preserve their ancient culture. And it is the people of Europe who cannot effect any change.

Outside Europe, some see more clearly. This is especially true of academics.

> The sheer mass of those new comers is already causing problems in the receiver countries similar to those encountered by the Irish in their mass migration to the United States. The kind of assimilation eventually achieved by the descendents of Irish immigrants in America, however, is unlikely for many Africans, Near Easterners and Pakistanis, perhaps even for most of them, for the conditions conducive to assimilation which existed in nineteenth century America do not exist in post-modern Europe, for there are no moving settlement frontiers incorporating new land that requires new settlers and no industrial surge that absorbs new, unskilled workers. Moreover manufacturing in Europe with its unskilled and semiskilled labor force has given way to the service industries with an emphasis on education and developed cognitive skills. The migrants now flooding

into Europe are ill equipped to easily fit into such an economy and their sheer numbers, unless curtailed, will mean that many will be permanently marginalized and with this marginalization resentment will build as it has in France with its migrants from its former North African possessions, and in Britain and the Netherlands with migrants from their former colonies.

The cost of all this will exert stress on the welfare states of Europe which in turn will raise the resentment of the native population, many of which are already vociferously opposed to the uncontrolled influx, thereby increasing social division and strife. A not insignificant dimension of those factors is religion, for a majority of those newcomers are Muslim, and there is a powerful strain of Islam that feeds off such discontent in order to advance its own cause among the Moslem [*sic*] communities living in enclaves in European urban areas, impeding their assimilation and further dividing what once were more stable societies...On top of that is the change in attitude of the elite that now administers the country. Until now the attitude of the elites was characterized by a sense of...self consciousness and national distinctiveness which supported the collection and the appreciation of folk tradition and its expression in song, theater and literature. Today, however, the elites that rule Ireland, like their counterparts across Europe, are characterized by a very different spirit, one which ignores national uniqueness, even national interests, and which appears to be suppressing, in terms of official support...[native] culture in favor of a transnational vision and a transnational policy within a wider association, the European Union.[232]

Here's another pertinent observation from a scholarly journal:

232 Custred, Professor Glynn. California State University East Bay. Fourth Conference of the International Congress of Irish Studies University of California Berkeley, April 22–24, 2016.

Consider what this means. Germans have been warned that it is their duty to accommodate themselves to newly arrived refugees and not to place politically incorrect demands upon them—that is, not to demand that the refugees adapt to German ways. Some have advised German women in particular that if they don't wish to be harassed by male refugees, they should cover their heads and be accompanied outside of the home by a male.[233]

Merkel, like Obama, bases her immigration policy on a globalist view of the world. Secretary of State John Kerry propounded this view in a recent commencement address, warning Americans that we must prepare ourselves for a "borderless world." But a world without borders is a world without citizens, and a world without citizens is a world without the rights and privileges that attach exclusively to *citizenship*. Rights and liberties exist only in separate and independent nations; they are the exclusive preserve of the nation-state. Constitutional government only succeeds in the nation-state, where the just powers of government are derived from the consent of the governed. By contrast, to see the globalist principle in practice, look at the European Union. The EU is not a constitutional government; it is an administrative state ruled by unelected bureaucrats. It attempts to do away with both borders and citizens, and it replaces rights and liberty with welfare and regulation as the objects of its administrative rule. Constitutional government—to say nothing of liberal democracy—will not be a part of the politically correct, borderless world into which so many of our political leaders wish to usher us.[234]

The common-sense citizen is forgiven for thinking this train of thought insane [admitting and tolerating those pledged to

233 Erler, Edward J. "Who We Are as a People—The Syrian Refugee Question," *Imprimis* October 2016; Volume 45, Number 10; Hillsdale College (Hillsdale, MI).
234 Ibid.

> destroy your way of life]. But what other explanation could there be for the insistence of so many of our political leaders on risking the nation's security—in light of what we see in Europe, one might even say their willingness to commit national suicide—by admitting refugees without regard to their hostility to our way of life and their wish to destroy us as a nation?
>
> Note that these leaders show no such enthusiasm for admitting Christian refugees from Middle Eastern violence, or even Yazidis, who have suffered horribly from the ravages of Islamic terror. These refugees, of course, represent no danger to America. Only by admitting those who do represent a danger can we display to the world "who we are as a people"—a people willing to sacrifice ourselves to vouchsafe our commitment to tolerance.[235]

This ties directly to Greenhill's view that democracies are uniquely open to coercive migration and its costs:

- Audience (reputation) costs are supposed to make democracies more credible in crisis situations (but don't); the higher the anticipated costs, the more likely it is that the democracy backs down to protect its reputation.[236]
- Liberal democracies are particularly susceptible to hypocrisy costs (discrepancy between professed commitment to liberal values and actions that contravene them). This is because policy making is relatively transparent, aiding the challengers in target evaluation. There are codified human rights and migrant policies.[237]
- Democracies are vulnerable to coercive engineered migration costs through their adherence to international human rights conventions. This prevents states from strictly controlling their

235 Ibid.

236 Greenhill, 10.

237 Ibid., 4.

> borders. They are trapped by their own norms. Additionally, opposition groups within and without the society can use these agreements as political fodder.[238]

Essentially, democracies have a built-in Achilles's heel. Liberalism makes them open to sacrificing themselves to maintain their core values, which then collapse under the migrant onslaught.

What is going through Europe? We've been told privately by contacts in Germany that they want their country back. In the Netherlands, populist parliament member Geert Wilders voiced it in open court when he was tried for his comments about Moroccans. "'I am not a racist and my voters are neither. They are people who want their country back and who are sick and tired of not being listened to,' said Wilders."[239]

One effect of the backlash against the invaders from elsewhere, the out-of-touch migrants, could well be increased nationalism. This might not take the form of "my country above your country." However, it might well be "my country and my countrymen above total strangers."

We've Said It Before, and We'll Say It Again

The United States of America and certain countries are largely responsible for Europe's migrant crisis. More to the point, other people are saying it as well.

> No one seems eager to talk about it, but the roots of this crisis lie in a long succession of bad Western policies in the Middle East and other regions now hemorrhaging their people. This, in a single sentence, takes care of causality and responsibility.
>
> The European powers shaped oil states a century ago that have since done little for their populations. More immediately,

238 Ibid., 60–63.

239 *AFP*. "Wilders Unapologetic as Dutch Hate Speech Trial Ends," November 23, 2016.

> operative, the 2003 [US] invasion of Iraq and now the [US] campaign to oust the Assad regime in Syria have shattered the region such that it now suffers what may be an unprecedented degree of lawlessness and violence.
>
> However, one may analyze the Iraqi and Syrian disasters, the U.S. plainly shares responsibility for the migrants now flooding into Europe. Two statistics will tell you how deeply this thought sinks in: Of the four million Syrians who have fled the civil war against Assad, the U.S. has accepted 1,500…
>
> Few of us seem to grasp the extent to which many decades of bad American policy helped shape a continent ridden with poverty and violence…
>
> As right-wing populist parties such as Alternative für Deutschland and France's Front Nationale regularly remind everybody, Europeans haven't yet come to terms on questions of race, ethnicity, and altogether what it means to be a European.[240]

Are American government officials really so stupid, as far too many believe, that none of this was calculated? Are American government officials so incompetent, as far too many believe, that they cannot deal with the results of their own actions?

"Would-be refugees hoping to flee war in the Middle East are using Facebook as their compass for finding the people smugglers they hope will get them to a better life in Europe."[241] US social media organizations provide the wherewithal for the migrants overrunning Europe. The companies, particularly Facebook, provide a wealth of information to the illegals. Want to learn the cost of bribing a Bulgarian border guard? Want to figure out the fees to pay a trafficker? Want to contact

240 Smith, Patrick. "Why Europe's Migrant Crisis Also Belongs to America," *The Fiscal Times*, September 7, 2015.

241 Than, Krisztina; Chambers, Madeline; Macdonald, Alastair; Malla, Naline; Yackley, Ayla Jean; Dunai, Marton; Vasovic, Aleksandar. "For Many Refugees, Journey to Europe Begins on Facebook," *Reuters*, September 1, 2015.

friends and family en route? Want to map out your journey? Looking for telephone numbers of connections? What's the price of being smuggled from Turkey to Germany? Find the right page on Facebook—in English, Arabic, Turkish, or another tongue.

> Facebook guides refugees before they even leave Syria, said Muhammed Salih Ali, head of the Izmir-based Association for Solidarity With Syrian Refugees.
>
> Many are told on Facebook pages to make their way to the Izmir district of Basmane, the informal headquarters in Turkey for traffickers and those hoping to make the passage.[242]

And where did Facebook come from? It's a CIA partner. It is reportedly a recipient of seed money from the CIA venture capital and technology incubator firm IN-Q-TEL.[243] Do you believe that the CIA doesn't engage in data mining on Facebook? Do you believe that it does not have any idea of what the company is doing or puts up on its migrant pages? Do you believe that it doesn't assist Facebook with help for the illegals?

Remember, esteemed reader, a book is a machine to think with.

And here is some more food for thought.

Are the governments and their intelligence services truly evil? Or are they just bad at planning? Or is there a dark fifth column running the spooks?

Consider this: Anis Amri, who allegedly drove the Polish truck into the Berlin Christmas market crowd, had more than one identity. How do we know? One of his documents was left in the cab of the truck. (You kill a dozen people and leave your calling card behind? This is like the September 11, 2001, hijacker documents: the planes were totally destroyed, but the visa of Satam al-Suqami and the passports of Ziad

242 Ibid.

243 Madsen, Wayne. *The Almost Classified Guide to CIA Front Companies, Proprietaries, & Contractors* (Research Triangle Park, NC: Lulu Press, 2016), 130.

Jarrah and Saeed al-Ghamdi were found intact.)[244] But *RT* quotes the German tabloid *Bild* as saying the police had found several passports in different names (the paper did not tell where they were found or what nationality they were). The *RT* article also reported the *Süddeutsche Zeitung* as saying that Amri had been a refugee who had applied for asylum.[245] (Another *RT* piece asserted that Amri had arrived in 2015, but in July 2016, his application had been denied.)[246]

And consider this: despite a nationwide manhunt, Amri left Berlin, left Germany, likely traveled through France, and ended up in Italy. How was he found? A routine check in Milan found Amri walking down the street. The stop resulted in a gun battle, with the Italian police shooting him dead.[247] The BfV is supposed to be an internal security and counter-espionage service. Its job is to prevent such things from happening. That is also the role of the *Bundeskriminalamt* (BKA), the Federal Criminal Police. It is Germany's central criminal investigation agency. It coordinates federal and state cooperation in police investigations. (The BKA has an office in Berlin. It, like the BfV, is part of the Interior Ministry.)

And consider this: an *RT* item had noted that Amri had been jailed in Italy before coming to Germany. After his asylum application had been denied, he couldn't be deported because he had no papers! German authorities had followed the murderer for months before ending their surveillance in September 2016.

> Amri was also being tracked by US intelligence, according to the New York Times. He had reportedly searched for information on making explosive devices and had communicated with IS at

244 Baker, Russ. "The Lost and 'Found ID' Oddity in Terror Cases—Stupid or Sinister?," *Who.What.Why.* (whowhatwhy.org) February 1, 2015.

245 *RT.* "Berlin Market Attack: Police Searching for Tunisian Man after Finding ID in Truck—Reports," December 21, 2016.

246 *RT.* "Internet Abuzz after PEGIDA Founder Shared Info on Berlin Attacker before German Police," December 22, 2016.

247 Siddique, Haroon. "Berlin Attack Suspect Pledged Allegiance to Isis in Video—Live Coverage," *The Guardian*, December 23, 2016.

> least once, via the Telegram messenger app, said an American security official who spoke on condition of anonymity. He was also on a US no-fly list.[248]

And consider yet another thing: according to *Deutsche Welle*, the BfV had been closely following Amri. In November 2015, he had told an informant for the BKA in North-Rhine Westphalia that he wanted to "do something in Germany." As stated by a document obtained by the daily *Süddeutsche Zeitung*, he also claimed that he could get an AK-47 rifle for an attack. "The BfV noted that he was traveling through Germany under various aliases. Further, he was apparently aggressively seeking an opportunity to undertake an attack in Germany. Information pointing to his dangerous potential became so overwhelming that authorities designated him a threat last February [2016]." Yet in July 2016, Germany's GTAZ joint counterterrorism center, along with the Interior Ministry, including the Federal Criminal Police and the BfV, discussed what was known about Amri. Their finding? "Currently, evidence of an acute threat is not in a legally sufficient form."

Once the Breitscheidplatz attack occurred, Justice Minister Heiko Maas said, "We had no legal basis to issue a warrant. We are going to create one now."[249]

As Traute Lopata, a secretary in Stuttgart's commercial section, used to say, *Menschenskinder nochmals!* (Good heavens yet again!)

Some conspiracy sites, such as *Aangirfan*, go a bit further and say that failing to arrest Amri wasn't stupidity or incompetence; it was intentional. "Anis Amri was driven to Berlin by an undercover informant of the German Intelligence Service—the BfV." In other words, "German intelligence (BfV) agent drove Anis Amri."[250]

---

248 *RT.* "Internet Abuzz after PEGIDA Founder Shared Info on Berlin Attacker before German Police." December 22, 2016.

249 Knipp, Kersten. "All the Cracks That Berlin Suspect Amri Slipped Through," *Deutsche Welle*, January 16, 2017.

250 No author. "BERLIN MARKET ATTACK—FALSE FLAG INSIDE JOB," *Aangirfanblogspot.com*, January 1, 2017.

Since this is a machine to think with, it's up to you, the reader, to make a decision.

Portents? Slight Changes Presaging Greater Ones?

While, as we've noted, the *Wutbürger* are under attack everywhere in Germany, attitudes might be changing. There is one straw in the wind already. While this might be a trite, hackneyed expression, it certainly fits an article originally appearing in the Swiss newspaper *SonntagsBlick*.

Where's the background on Anis Amri? Frank A. Meyer, chief publicist for the Ringer Group, started asking the unthinkable. He listed the connections forbidden to be made with Amri's attack on the Breitscheidplatz Christmas market in Berlin:

- First, no one has linked the crime to the mass migration from North Africa, Arabia, or Afghanistan.
- Second, no one has coupled the attacker to Islam.
- Third, no one related the welcoming culture for migrants to the striking failure of the security services.

Meyer went on to inquire if German journalists have added a new branch to their profession, becoming "moral executioners." He noted that anyone making forbidden inquiries is punished. He said they are denounced as racist, right-wing populists, in extreme cases as fascists. Continuing, he wrote that the mainstream media metes out the punishment. It is done through public television, public radio, and daily and weekly newspapers.

The Swiss publicist laid the blame for the attack on a variety of causes:

- First, German Chancellor Merkel issued an authoritarian order to open her country's borders. She then temporarily lost control of the migrants. To date, he asserted, German government offices have lost track of more than three hundred thousand immigrants. No one knows where they are or who they are. Therefore, he said, Germany has become a land of milk and honey for them. Their goal is not to live in a constitutional state but to engage in criminal acts, from the drug trade to terrorism. (Unfortunately, the easy exploitability of Germany's social service system and immigration policies also encourages the predators. They mingle among the migrants to engage in unlawful deeds.)

- Second, Amri traveled everywhere in the Salafist scene, from which he came. He cultivated the closest relations with imams preaching hate.
- Third, the morally overburdened culture of welcome has created an atmosphere of rebellion. The security services have to fight this when they move against unqualified migrants. Howls of protest accompany every deportation.

Meyer also laid into the police, characterizing them as delaying and denying admissions about the market attacker being a risk. He said further that this was well known. Yet Amri could travel throughout the country because the enthusiasm for migrants caused delays in taking action.

Moreover, he wrote, the German media doesn't discuss this. He commented that one entire talk show on the Second German Public Television channel (ZDF) was devoted to Amri being a revenge-seeking, crazy person rather than a religiously motivated terrorist. Additionally, Meyer said the politically correct were playing word games, seeking to minimize "Islamic" so as not to offend anyone.

Additionally, the Swiss journalist condemned the politicians, publicists, and pastors for acting as teachers of the citizens. The power elites in their Berlin bubble, he said, swore that the people were secure. They could travel anywhere in safety. However, Meyer noted, the officials making these statements are surrounded by bodyguards and travel in armored limousines with police escorts.

Meyer also said that the German president (the head of state) had told the citizens not to allow themselves to be divided. Nevertheless, President Joachim Gauck has himself split the citizenry. In private, Meyer held, he opposes Merkel's migration policy. In public, he sings the praises of the welcome culture.

According to Meyer, the migrants and the Muslims should be suspected of everything. And that suspicion should not be dropped. The same should be true of the government's immigration policy. Moreover, he recommended the view of the *Frankfurter Allgemeine Zeitung*: policy has much too long been tied to the culture of welcome, a viewpoint that has shielded what was not in keeping with the harmonious and narcissistic picture created.[251]

251 Meyer, Frank A. "Berlin-Anschlag Deutscher Winter 2016" (Berlin Attack German Winter 2016), *Focus Online*, December 25, 2016.

9

Nationalism by Country, Limits on Rights

Nationalism

Merriam-Webster DEFINES NATIONALISM as "loyalty and devotion to a nation; *especially*: a sense of national consciousness exalting one nation above all others and placing primary emphasis on promotion of its culture and interests as opposed to those of other nations or supranational groups."

Minus the phrase about "exalting one nation above all others," nationalism is increasing all across Europe. This is the direct result of Angela Merkel's invitation to the world: move to Germany and solve all your problems. In the past year or so, Merkel's mistake, if you can call it that, has driven the creation and/or expansion of dissident groups across the continent. Merkel's migrants and their crimes, which her government has minimized, have provoked a stunning backlash everywhere, not just in Germany. Yet the mainstream media always ties the nationalists in whatever country to Adolf Hitler and the Nazis. They generally fail to analyze the situation and report accurately.

Once in a while, some do.

> In a detailed legal argument widely cited by the German media, Udo di Fabio, a former judge of Germany's Constitutional Court,

> warned this month [January 2016] that in opening Germany to the enormous new wave of migrants from North Africa and the Middle East, Chancellor Angela Merkel and her government have "created a historic breach of law," involving a direct conflict between present government policy and the constitutional obligation to defend the country's borders, territorial integrity and democracy.[252]

The people in other nations of Europe see this and, perhaps, do not express it quite so eloquently. The reality, which the establishment politicians don't seem to grasp, is this:

- We, the people, protest.
- Austerity has exhausted us.
- The nation-state should protect us.
- We need to build barriers, not mend them.
- People are asking, "What has the European Union done for us?"[253]

Here's a Short Country Guide to Nationalism

Greece

The Golden Dawn, which the BBC describes as a Far Right, neo-Nazi party, wants to expel migrants. It came into action as the result of the European Union's imposition of austerity on the country. Then it targeted the migrants, seeking to present the facts about them. Golden Dawn's base is mainly those hardest hit in the economic collapse. The party distributes food only to those with Greek nationality. Despite criticism directed against it, Golden Dawn has become the third-largest force in Greek politics, winning eighteen seats in parliament.

---

252 Lieven, Anatol. "Will the Migration Crisis Destroy European Democracy?," *Valdai Discussion Club*, January 26, 2016.

253 Foster, Peter. "Why Is Europe So Fed Up?," *The Telegraph*, May 31, 2016.

Hungary

"Far-right Jobbik is the third strongest party in Hungary—it won 20.7% of the vote in the 2014 general election." The group backed Prime Minister Viktor Orbán's erection of a razor-wire fence to block the migrant flow from Serbia. "Jobbik describes itself as 'a principled, conservative and radically patriotic Christian party' on its website. 'Its fundamental purpose is protecting Hungarian values and interests,' the message in English says." Yet the BBC asserts, "Critics see it as a far-right, even neo-Nazi movement."

Slovakia

Although the country has taken in few migrants, the nationalist People's Party–Our Slovakia entered parliament for the first time in 2016. It won fourteen seats. Immigration became a major issue in the election.

Switzerland

The country has a large population of foreigners and, while not a member of the European Union, participates in the Schengen open-borders agreement. However, in 2014, it capped migration into Helvetia, as mentioned earlier, running afoul of the European Union. Reflecting the will of the people, the antimigrant Swiss People's Party (SVP) won nearly 30 percent of the vote. It gained a record sixty-five slots in the two-hundred-seat National Assembly, the lower house of the Swiss Federal Assembly.

Austria

As noted earlier, the Austrian Freedom Party (*Freiheits Partei Österreich*, FPÖ) is vilified as an ultraright-wing group. However, it has set the Austrian establishment on its ear. Austria's familiar, centrist, consensus-oriented politics dominated the government since 1945, even under the ten-year foreign military occupation. Now, with H. C. Strache's FPÖ nearly winning the presidency in 2016, things may change. Its presidential candidate, Norbert Hofer, got nearly 90 percent of his support from blue-collar workers. About 40 percent of the white-collar workers backed him. With the independent, Alexander Van der Bellen, it was the reverse: 60 percent of the white-collar workers voted for him, with just over 10 percent of blue-collar workers espousing that candidate at the polls.

Although there are reports that 40 percent of Austrians voted for the FPÖ at least once, the BBC lists that party as winning 35 percent of the vote. Yet, according to the media, it racked up 46.7 percent of the ballots cast.

Italy

That country's Northern League seems, at present, to be rather small potatoes, garnering about 4 percent of the vote in the 2013 general election. However, the party is opposed to the migrant wave sweeping through the country. Consequently, it is doing well in local elections, chalking up 20 percent of the vote in left-leaning Tuscany in 2015.

France

Marine Le Pen leads the *Front National,* an anti-European Union, anti-migrant party. It has two seats in the French National Assembly. The nationalist party collected nearly seven million votes in 2015's regional elections. Initially expected to lose in the second round of voting in the April 2017 presidential election, her prospects appear to be improving at this writing. She has the solid support of a third of the electorate. Nevertheless, whatever the outcome, the *Front National* has been and will still be a force to be reckoned with.

Germany

The Federal Republic's main force for nationalism is AfD, *Alternative für Deutschand* (Alternative for Germany). Established in 2013 in opposition to a European Union–centric Germany, the party has expanded its resistance to include Mama Merkel's migrants. Coming out of nowhere, the AfD has gained seats in half of the country's sixteen states (Länder). Winning big in spring 2016 elections in Saxony-Anhalt (24 percent of the vote), Rhineland-Palatinate (nearly 13 percent), and

Baden-Württemberg (15 percent), the new party is a serious threat to the status quo.

Since the restoration of Germany's sovereignty in 1955, the right-of-center Christian Democratic Union (CDU) and its Bavarian counterpart, the Christian Socialist Union (CSU), have alternated governing with the left-of-center Socialist Party of Germany (SPD). Occasionally, they have formed coalitions with each other or together with minor parties. Much like Americans, Germans are increasingly fed up with unresponsive politics and politicians. They see the AfD as a grouping that will change the country, returning it to the way it was before Merkel and her CDU/CSU flooded the land with aliens.

PEGIDA (in translation as Patriotic Europeans against the Islamization of the West) comes out of Dresden in what was once East Germany. It holds massive marches all over the country, often with as many as twenty-five thousand demonstrators. Strongly opposed to the migrant wave and demanding strict enforcement of existing laws on asylum, the group attracts counterdemonstrations and government hostility. Chancellor Merkel denounced them as xenophobic and racist. PEGIDA plans to support the AfD in 2017's general election.

Netherlands

Geert Wilders's anti-European Union Party for Freedom (PVV) is now the second-largest party in Holland, winning twenty seats in 2017's parliamentary elections on March 15. This was a one-third increase over the faction's 2012 strength. Prime Minister Mark Rutte's VVD lost eight positions.[254] Wilders and his party are strongly opposed to migrants. In a move that only strengthened his hand and his party, the Dutch government tried him for hate speech; Wilders had apparently implied there should be fewer Moroccans in Holland. Slamming the prosecution in open court, he stated that it was "a charade, a disgrace for the

254 "VVD Wins 33 Seats But Coalition Partner Labour is Hammered," *DutchNews.nl*, March 26, 2017.

Netherlands, a mockery for our society..." Moreover, he asserted that, as a member of parliament, he must be free to talk about Dutch problems.[255]

Sweden

Sweden's Social Democrats have dominated politics for years, emphasizing tolerance of minorities. The nationalist Sweden Democrats (SD) have now challenged this. The SD demands strict immigration controls and opposes multiculturalism. In 2014, the SD became the third-largest party, winning 13 percent in the general election. However, other parties in parliament avoid dealing with them. Presumably, the establishment doesn't recognize that more than 160,000 asylum seekers arrived in Sweden in 2015—the highest per capita rate in the European Union.

Denmark

The antimigrant Danish People's Party (DPP) garnered 21 percent of the vote, a record, in 2015's general election. (Its previous high had been 12 percent in 2011.) The ruling coalition now depends on it. Opposing multiculturalism, its power has helped make Denmark's immigration rules some of the toughest in Europe. Danish police have "the authority to seize valuables worth more than 10,000 kroner (£1,045; $1,514; ca. €1,350) from refugees to cover housing and food costs."[256]

Sodele, As the Swabians Say

So Mama Merkel's migrants are pushing Europe further to the right, and they are demonstrating that the Left's policies are a failure. But what kind of rightward move are we talking about? What sort of Europe will emerge from the present chaos, assuming one will come to light from its cocoon? Will it become more like the United States, with the Federal Bureau of Investigation, the Department of Homeland Security,

255 "Populist Lawmaker Slams Trial as 'Charade,'" *Associated Press*, November 24, 2016.

256 The foregoing section comes mainly from "Guide to Nationalist Parties Challenging Europe," *BBC*, May 23, 2016.

the National Security Agency, and Fusion Centers observing you online, on the telephone, and on your computer? FinCen, the Financial Crimes Enforcement Network, already examines your financial transactions in real time.

Currently, in the European Union, your information is protected, at least on paper.

> Under EU law, personal data can only be gathered legally under strict conditions, for a legitimate purpose. Furthermore, persons or organisations which collect and manage your personal information must protect it from misuse and must respect certain rights of the data owners which are guaranteed by EU law.[257]

So far, European politicians on the right have called only for reinstating national borders and damming the migrant tide. However, there have been worrisome lines about losing privacy printed in the *Washington Post*, house organ of the American intelligence services.

Citing statements by left-leaning and/or establishment European officials, the *Post* wrote that in December 2016, "E.U. leaders proposed… border controls that would run checks on most people as they enter or exit Europe…the European Parliament approved the creation of an air-passenger database…long shunned based on privacy concerns."

According to the article, privacy advocates now fear that Europe may be moving toward the American model of security. (The US idea of protection is more security theater than actual security.)[258] Jos Vander Velpen, head of Belgium's Human Rights League, claimed "he is worried about the direction of the new security proposals."

And well he should be. The *Post* went on to say that "Britain has long pursued an American-style approach to surveillance, [and] France has

257 European Commission: Justice/Data Protection; Updated November 24, 2016.

258 For an excellent discussion of this, see Trento, Susan B. and Trento, Joseph J., *Unsafe at Any Altitude,* (Hanover, NH: Steerforth Press, 2006).

moved the furthest of any European nation toward trading away civil liberties in the name of security."[259]

Up to now, the movement has been to more closely watch citizens and control their access to weapons. On November 16, 2015, the European Union Commission "adopted a package of measures to make it more difficult to acquire firearms in the European Union, better track legally held firearms, strengthen cooperation between Member States, and ensure that deactivated firearms are rendered inoperable...The Commission today proposed to establish a European Travel Information and Authorisation System (ETIAS) to strengthen security checks on visa-free travellers. The ETIAS will gather information on all those travelling visa-free to the European Union to allow for advance irregular migration and security checks...The Commission is actively driving the implementation of the EU Passenger Name Record (PNR) Directive."[260]

On January 25, 2016, the European Union, in conjunction with the European Police Agency (Europol), established the European Counter Terrorism Center (ECTC).[261] Remarkably vague in its activities, the ECTC focuses on

- tackling foreign fighters;
- sharing intelligence and expertise on terrorism financing (through the Terrorist Finance Tracking Programme and the Financial Intelligence Unit);
- online terrorist propaganda and extremism (through the European Union Internet Referral Unit);
- illegal arms trafficking; and
- international cooperation among counterterrorism authorities.[262]

259 Birnbaum, Michael. "Terror May Be New Normal in Europe," *Washington Post*, December 25, 2016.

260 European Agenda on Security: Second Report on Progress toward an Effective and Sustainable Security Union. Brussels, November 16, 2015.

261 European Commission News, January 25, 2016.

262 EUOPOL: European Counter Terrorism Centre—ECTC. January 2016.

But look who their counterterrorism contacts are:

> European officials have been talking to U.S. law enforcement and intelligence agencies, including the Department of Homeland Security and the FBI, which have already grappled with similar issues.
>
> "We're trying to benefit from each other's experiences," said Kshemendra Paul, Program Manager of the Information-Sharing Environment at the U.S. Office of the Director of National Intelligence.[263]

See How This Plays Out in Germany

> The government of Nazi Germany was a fascist, totalitarian state. Totalitarian regimes, in contrast to a dictatorship, establish complete political, social, and cultural control over their subjects, and are usually headed by a charismatic leader. Fascism is a form of right-wing totalitarianism which emphasizes the subordination of the individual to advance the interests of the state.[264]

The Nazis implemented this through the Secret State Police (*Geheime Staatspolizei*, Gestapo).

> This was "the political police of Nazi Germany. The Gestapo ruthlessly eliminated opposition to the Nazis within Germany and its occupied territories...The functions of the Gestapo often overlapped with those of other security departments, with which the Gestapo had both to cooperate and compete. Owing to its relatively small size—approximately 32,000 personnel at the end

---

263 Seldin, Jeff. "Europe's New Counterterror Center Unlikely to Make Quick Impact," *VOA*, February 22, 2016.

264 "Nazi Fascism and the Modern Totalitarian State," *remembrance.org*.

> of 1944—the Gestapo relied extensively on the use of denunciations from among the local German populace in order to conduct its investigations...The Gestapo operated without civil restraints. It had the authority of "preventative arrest," and its actions were not subject to judicial appeal.[265]

V for Victory or V for V Men?

Then there were the V men. Presumably, this term comes from the German for such a trusted person, *Vertrauensmann*. "Hitler was recruited to be a 'V' man while in the post-war [1914–1918] army. 'V' men were to spy upon German citizens for the army and government."[266] V men popped up later as one of the classes of people the Nazi Security Service (*Sicherheitsdienst*, SD) dealt with. An organization of vast power, it involved itself deeply in the lives of those suspected to be enemies of the state. To the SD, as an intelligence-gathering agency, V men were people who could be relied on.[267]

Na ja, a German might say. So? Didn't we de-Nazify after the war? *Yanni*, an Arab might say. What does this mean? The Federal Republic's constitution, the *Grundgesetz* (Basic Law), fixed this undemocratic activity, right?

Wrong.

In the 1950s, the German government banned Communist Party affiliates from public service. It did not ban the entirety of Nazi Party membership (only Gestapo members or those deemed "main culprits"). However, there were investigations. About 125,000 people were examined for membership in an anticonstitutional organization, with perhaps 7,000 found guilty. "Even where there was no conviction, the proceedings usually led to the loss of a person's job. Journalists, editors

265 *Encyclopedia Britannica* (online).

266 *History 20* (online).

267 Trueman, C. N. "The SD," *History Learning Site*, August 16, 2016.

and publishers faced Berufsverbot (banned from following their profession), newspapers were prohibited and confiscated."

"In the 1970s, in reaction to the terrorist acts of the Red Army Faction (RAF) the principles of due process during proceedings involving state security were drastically curtailed; with the same applying to freedom of opinion. A critical word could result in criminal proceedings for 'exhibiting sympathy' for the RAF."[268]

So perhaps that was then, and this is now.

No. Absolutely not. After mysterious attacks in Paris and Brussels (and claims there might be some in Germany), the Federal Republic began examining its internal controls. After another shove from Mama Merkel's migrants and the sudden "appearance" of ISIL,

> Germany has grown its security apparatus steadily in response.
>
> The country's 2009 anti-terrorism law has been sharpened to grant federal police and intelligence services more powers. Police presence has been boosted. The interior minister has proposed expanding video surveillance significantly, to include shopping centres, buses and sports events. And the government has stepped up cooperation between Germany's intelligence agency, the Bundesnachrichtendienst (BND), and its European counterparts with a joint European intelligence database.
>
> Berlin maintains that these measures are crucial to protecting Germany and its allies from myriad challenges, particularly "terrorism."
>
> Yet, in a country where privacy is paramount and government surveillance raises the spectre of a totalitarian past, opposition legislators, lawyers and activists are sounding the alarm over changes they say take direct aim at fundamental rights, and many have vowed to fight back in court.[269]

268 Leicht, Justus. "The Grundgesetz: 60 Years of Germany's Post-War Constitution," *World Socialist Web Site,* May 29, 2009.

269 Somaskanda, Sumi. "Is Big Brother Coming to Germany?," *Al Jazeera,* December 14, 2016.

But why is the BfV, the Federal Office for the Protection of the Constitution, the internal security service, presumably with its own V men, not mentioned?

The chancellor's office submitted, and the parliament (*Bundestag*) passed sweeping authority for, the security services to spy not only on foreigners but also on German citizens. The October 21, 2016, law tries to make weasel-worded differences between natives and aliens. However, the German constitution makes no such distinction.[270] In fact, many civil rights and industry groups say that modern communications are far too complex. "When you tap a telecommunications line nowadays, you always get a mix of foreign traffic, national traffic and national-to-international traffic. But the way the law is written, they can access any line as long as there is some foreign communication on it," according to Klaus Landefeld, a board member of an Internet trade association, Eco International. "EU citizens and companies are also subject to surveillance, if the data they share is relevant to German or European security policy. Until now, the BND could only tap into individual lines and access up to 20 percent of communications, but those limitations have been lifted with the new legislation."[271]

In the past, Germans were outraged at being spied upon. They still remember the domestic political surveillance of the Nazis and the East German *Stasi*. They were more outraged when they learned "German intelligence services had been working in close cooperation with the NSA, and had even spied on European allies at the behest of the Americans."

But in Germany, just as in the United States, the established political parties go their own way, regardless of common sense and the constitution. "The coalition government hailed the law as a major contribution to both transparency and security. Uli Groetsch, a Social Democrat (SPD) member of the Committee on Domestic Affairs and the Parliamentary

270 Basic Law: Article 10 [Privacy of correspondence, posts and telecommunications] (1) The privacy of correspondence, posts and telecommunications shall be inviolable.

271 "Is Big Brother Coming to Germany?"

Control Panel, said it was the most extensive legislation of its kind in the world. 'As domestic affairs lawmakers, we put a lot of stock in making sure our intelligence services have the necessary resources,' he told Al Jazeera."[272]

There's a thread running through Merkel's million-migrant march. Who's coordinating it? How? We know why: to destabilize South and Southwest Asia, North Africa, and Europe. We've mentioned the American and other "intelligence" services with their spooks. But what about Germany?

Earlier, this writer noted how Henriette Reker had been elected lord mayor of Cologne after an attack by a man ostensibly opposed to migrants. The knife shown in pictures about the alleged throat slashing looked big enough to chop up a buffalo. Was this guy some sort of V man connected to the BfV or the Federal Criminal Police?

Volker Beck, representing Cologne as internal policy spokesman for the Greens, noted that there was secrecy surrounding the attacker's file. He said the secrecy made you want to prick up your ears. The mystery about the dossier's classification led to suspicions that the man, Frank S., might have connections to the BfV as some sort of V man. The Green Party asked the BfV, the BKA, and state police agencies what they knew of Frank S. Daniel Schwerd, a member of North Rhine-Westphalia's state legislature with no party affiliation, posed a similar question to his government.[273]

Reker acquired enough sympathy support (nearly 53 percent of the vote) to win handily. The first woman to gain the position, Reker defeated her closest competitor, Jochen Ott of the Social Democrats (SPD), who had just 32 percent. And it was Reker who could not or would

---

272 Ibid.

273 Wiermer, Christian. "Reker-Attentat Grüne fragen: Gab es Verbindungen von Frank S. zum Verfassungsschutz? " (Reker Attack Greens Ask, Were There Connections between Frank S. and the Office for Protection of the Constitution?), October 21, 2015. Also http://www.daniel-schwerd.de/geheimnisse-in-der-arbeitslosengeschichte-des-reker-attentaeters/(Secrets in the Jobless History of Reker Attacker). October 25, 2015.

not use the police and water cannons on the raping, rioting migrants around the railroad station during *Silvester* 2015.

One of the activities of the BfV is infiltration of groups. How? Here's what the agency says:

> For the collection of information, the use of intelligence means is an indispensable instrument, too. This includes the handling of trusted contacts (individuals recruited from the extremist scene, no domestic intelligence staff) in extremist circles, covert surveillance, and, if necessary, mail and telephone interception.[274]

Could the carefully coordinated attacks on women in Germany (and elsewhere) have had the assistance of V men? If so, what might have been the political motives behind it? Was the suppression of news about the *Silvester* assaults their work as well? What about welcoming the invaders with candy and flowers? Who created such elaborate PSYOPs? Indeed, the news about the rape and murder of Maria Ladenburger was kept under wraps for months. How was this kept secret?

More importantly, why? The role of both the BfV and the BKA, the Federal Criminal Police Office, is to fight threats to the German Republic. Here's the BfV (with about 2,800 employees)[275] in its own words:

> The Federal Office for the Protection of the Constitution (Bundesamt für Verfassungsschutz, BfV) and the intelligence services of the federal states, have been tasked with the collection and the analysis of information on
>
> 1. efforts
>   - directed against the free democratic basic order or
>   - against the existence and the security of the Federation or one of its States or

274 www.verfassungsschutz.de.

275 E-mail from BfV Press Spokesman's Office, January 3, 2017.

- aimed at unlawfully hampering constitutional bodies of the Federation or one of its States or their members in the performance of their duties or
- jeopardising foreign interests of the Federal Republic of Germany by the use of violence or the preparation thereof or
- directed against the idea of international understanding (article 9, para. 2 of the Basic Law (Grundgesetz, GG)), especially against the peaceful coexistence of peoples

2. intelligence activities carried out on behalf of a foreign power (counter-intelligence).
3. Moreover, in conformity with section 3 (2) of the BVerfSchG, BfV contributes to counter-sabotage and personnel/physical security.[276]

Here's the BKA in its own words.

> The Bundeskriminalamt (BKA) [is] the criminal police of the Federation...
>
> The orientation, build-up and expansion of the Bundeskriminalamt are, and always have been, closely tied to the national and international development of crime and the specific role of the BKA within the existing security architecture in Germany, Europe and the world...
>
> As of the mid-80's, besides continuing its battle against terrorism, the Bundeskriminalamt concentrated above all on dealing with the growth of international drug trafficking and the spread of organized crime...
>
> The resulting new organisation of the state security division of the Bundeskriminalamt distinctly strengthens our investigative potential in the fight against international terrorism. With

276 Homepage BfV: https://www.verfassungsschutz.de/en/index-en.html.

> the creation of the "Joint Counter-Terrorism Centre" (GTAZ) at our site in Berlin in December 2004, in which information on international terrorism is collated and analysed by various agencies, the fight against terrorism has taken a major step forward. These measures are supplemented by the newly founded division "International Coordination" in January 2005, which should bring about a further improvement of the co-operation with our international partners...
>
> The successful performance of the duties of the Bundeskriminalamt is guaranteed by more than 5,500 employees from 70 different professional groups, whose dedication and creativity ensure the BKA's excellent reputation the world over as a competent partner in the fight against crime.[277]

This is scarcely believable. Eight thousand people carpeting Germany, tied to state criminal and intelligence offices, can't ward off known criminals. Eight thousand people connected to domestic and foreign computerized databases can't find known criminals. Eight thousand people with great skills and training can't search for migrants.

This isn't a banana republic. This is Germany. This is a country with records going back to the Thirty Years' War. This is a country whose national motto could be "There must be order" (*Ordnung Muß Sein*). Yet for over a year, migrants from the whole world have created a crime wave. And the authorities appeared to be oblivious, if not complicit. Again, is there some sort of fifth column hidden in the security services?

Or is it hidden in one of the BfV's tasks? One job is collecting and analyzing information "directed against the idea of international understanding (article 9, para. 2 of the Basic Law Grundgesetz, GG), especially against the peaceful coexistence of peoples." Does the federal office do more than just collect and analyze? Does "idea of international understanding" translate into *helping* the *Völkerwanderung*?

277 Homepage, the BKA: https://www.bka.de/EN/Home/home_node.html.

Certainly, the loyal opposition in Germany is not shy about parceling out the blame. It is Merkel, Merkel, Merkel.

After the Christmas 2016 market attack in Berlin, the AfD rounded on the chancellor. Having organized a large demonstration outside her office, the AfD took to the Internet, holding her responsible for the incident. "'These are Merkel's dead,' Marcus Pretzell, chairman of the Alternative for Germany party in the Western state of North Rhine-Westphalia, posted on Twitter."[278] "'She [Merkel] made a decision that was disastrous for Germany,' said Mr. [Alexander] Gauland [former CDU member and a founder of the AfD]. 'This is just one consequence of that. She is complicit.'"[279]

The Sleepers Awake (Maybe)

Police in Cologne and Düsseldorf evidently thwarted a repeat of last year's New Year's Eve attacks. According to a Cologne press conference, one thousand questionable individuals traveled to Cologne and another eight hundred to Düsseldorf. Many were from North Africa. There were few arrests, although the 1,500 policemen examined many, taking three hundred from one train for identity checks. As in the United States, trucks were placed strategically about the train station, and entrance to Cologne's Cathedral Square was strictly controlled. In addition, newly installed high-resolution TV cameras transmitted views of the square directly to police headquarters.[280]

278 Donahue, Patrick. "Christmas Market Tragedy Hands Merkel Critics Line of Attack," *Bloomberg Politics*, December 19, 2016.

279 Davis, Austin. "Germany's Far-Right Party Seizes on Berlin Truck Attack, says Angela Merkel 'Complicit,'" *The Washington Times*, December 28, 2016.

280 "Polizei: 2000 Fahndungsrelevante nach NRW gereist" (Police: 2000 Search-Relevant People Traveled to North Rhine-Westphalia), *Sputnik.de Panorama*, January 1, 2017. "Silvester in Köln unter Polizeischutz—Festnahmen und mehrere Übergriffe" (New Year's Eve in Cologne under Police Protection—Arrests and Several Attacks), *Sputnik.de Panorama*, January 1, 2017.

This brought immediate criticism from the Greens (who had supported Henriette Reker's candidacy for lord mayor). According to *RT*, "Party...leader Simone Peter has questioned the legality of the mass ID checks of migrants that were conducted on New Year's Eve in Cologne. *'A question of proportionality and legitimacy arises when almost 1,000 people are being checked and some detained based on how they look like,'* Peter told the *Rheinische Post*." The news service continued with a quote from Volker Beck, the party's representative for migration. *"Police measures should be based on [the person's] dangers or the behavior of a person, not their identity,"* he said, noting that *"so-called 'racial profiling'—meaning police action based only on the supposed ethnic group, religion, and national origin—would not be a legitimate method."*

The Greens also waxed wroth over police use of the abbreviation *Nafri* for *North African*.[281] Appearing on *RT TV* January 3, 2017, a Green member of Hungarian extraction characterized the term as racist. He asserted he did not want to be called a Hungaro-German.

None of the Greens commented on the Nafris' use of cell phones to coordinate their flocking to Cologne and Düsseldorf. They said little about what the Nafris planned to do this year or what they did last year. "According to local federal police spokesman Wolfgang Wurm, groups of migrants had teamed up in online messenger chats to plan a mass gathering in Cologne during the celebrations."[282]

However, the heavy police presence, widespread identity checks, institution of controlled areas, and installation of high-resolution TV cameras forebodes American-style security theater, if not increased loss of liberty. Whether this activity represented a genuine effort to prevent a repeat of last year's attacks or whether it presages reductions in personal freedom is, as yet, unknown. Addressing the foregoing, German Interior Ministry Spokesman Johannes Dimroth "did not clarify whether the tactics as applied in Cologne this year would be a *'role model'* for the future."[283]

---

281 *RT*. "Cologne Police Slammed for 'Racial Profiling' after Mass Migrant Screening on NYE," January 2, 2017.

282 Ibid.

283 Ibid.

But compare and contrast this with events in Austria on December 31, 2016.

On January 4–5, 2017, *RT* reported eighteen women were groped in Innsbruck, Austria's winter capital. At New Year's festivities, about ten men grabbed women's breasts and other parts in the midst of twenty-five thousand celebrating in the winter ski resort. The men, in their late teens, were almost invisible in the press of people.[284] In seeming contradiction, Reuters reported them as older, in their twenties or thirties. However, the news service described them as "dark skinned" and foreign looking, noting that they spoke English or poor German. A police spokesman, confirming that the attackers were aliens, said, "We have never seen anything in this form…I cannot remember (an attack) of this intensity, on this scale and with this modus operandi."[285] Adding information, the BBC noted that the men were Asian or North African.[286]

Compare and contrast this with another German city.

In Dortmund, in the old *Ruhrpott* (the once-smoky Ruhr industrial area), there were disturbances involving young North African men. Despite a reinforced police presence, a number of them were removed from Leeds Square and the railroad station area.[287] The *Ruhr Nachrichten* newspaper described *Silvester* 2016 in Dortmund as no child's birthday party. There had been forty violent attacks, dangerous use of fireworks, provocations of police, and property damage. An overwhelming number of foreign youths had gathered in large and small groups in the city center. The largest group, of about one thousand, poured into Leeds Square. They shot fireworks at other celebrants and at the police. Although there were no sexual attacks, an unknown individual fired

284 *RT.* "Innsbruck Women Suffered at Least 18 Sex Attacks amid New Year Festivities," January 4–5, 2017.

285 *Reuters.* "Austria Investigates Series of New Year's Sexual Assaults in Innsbruck," January 4, 2017.

286 BBC. "New Year's Eve Sex Assaults Prompt Police Manhunt in Austria," January 5, 2017.

287 Bandermann, Peter. "Böllerverbote und Platzverweise: Die Lage in Dortmund" (Firecrackers Forbidden and Dismissals), *WAZ.de,* December 31, 2016.

a rocket at a homeless man, seriously injuring him. In addition, the paper noted that a missile had hit and set fire to netting protecting construction at the Reinhold church. Also, a group of presumed Arabs chanting "Syria" danced about, waving the opposition's green, white, and black flag.[288]

288 Bandermann, Peter. "Wie Medien die Silvesternacht für Hass-Aufbau nutzen" (How the Media Make Use of Hate-Buildng on New Year's Eve), *Ruhr Nachrichten*, January 6, 2017.

10

Pressure to Keep the Migrants Marching

And the Beat (and the Migrants) Goes On

While tending to ignore or push aside the migration wave's origins, alleged experts urge letting the *Völkerwanderung* continue. They do not demand an end to America's wars that caused it. Here are some comments, all selected from an *Al Jazeera* report:

Rami, a Syrian refugee in Athens, said:

> Politicians wanted to stop refugees coming. Islamophobia and the problems that happened "because" of the refugees—fascists used these things in a bad way. The situation got worse. There are still people on the left who fight till the end, because they believe in "no borders," and solidarity.
>
> Detaining people in Greece or Italy is a first step to stop refugees from coming. Europe has said it doesn't want any more Muslims or refugees."

Preethi Nallu, editor at Refugees Deeply (an independent digital media project dedicated to covering the refugee crisis) asserted,

> Against the cacophonous reports of "droves" of people trying to enter Europe, we must press the reset button. We must ignite

global collective consciousness toward this new era of migration. It is the defining issue of our time.

The year 2016 proved that militarising the Mediterranean and fortifying borders are not tenable solutions. With mutating smuggling networks that extend from the Logar villages of Afghanistan to the depths of the Sahara, combating the illicit migrant "trade" is not as simple as shooting smugglers on sight or erecting new barriers.

While the EU-Turkey deal has thwarted arrivals to Greece for one season, it is merely a bandage on an infection. Italy's new record this year, with more than 171,000 arrivals by sea, is proof that such deals simply shift the routes.

Médecins Sans Frontières Sea (Doctors Without Borders Sea) claimed,

> In 2016 the world catastrophically failed millions of people fleeing war, persecution and despair. Calculating politics and egocentrism won out over moral and legal obligations to offer protection and assistance to those in need. Countries across the world implemented harmful migration and asylum policies—increasing the suffering of people on the move by routinely denying them humanitarian assistance and any form of dignity.
>
> Like a contagious disease, walls, fences and restrictive border measures disseminated all over the world with deadly consequences: 7,200 people died at borders globally, with more than 5,000 in the Mediterranean Sea alone.
>
> States continued to look for cynical measures to keep people in need out of sight, signing agreements with third countries conditioning development aid on a border control agenda. The EU-Turkey deal is perhaps the most reprehensible, as it has shown the world that you can outsource the responsibility to offer protection while dangerously restricting the right to seek asylum.

Alarmphone (an activist network providing a hotline for refugees in distress at sea) vowed to bring more migrants to Europe:

> European governments reacted violently to the historic migration movements of 2015, making unauthorised migrant journeys lengthier, costlier, more dangerous and deadly...The Dublin laws are being forcefully re-installed, and mass deportations are looming large for 2017...
>
> Nevertheless, people still do make it across: This year, more than 350,000 people arrived in Europe via the sea.
>
> We will continue to support these disobedient movements in 2017. In the year to come we will struggle on to make sea crossings a little less dangerous, as we have done in the past two years, when we supported more than 1,750 boats. We are determined to speak up against those who show hostility toward the newcomers, who preach hatred and seek to divide us.
>
> We will welcome those who had to risk their lives to find protection in a new community, a trans-border community that is inclusive and open, based upon the principles of global justice and the freedom of movement for all.
>
> We believe that a world without borders is possible, in which both Frontex and the smugglers would then have disappeared.[289]

Some See behind the Migrant Curtain

"The political leaders of the European Union are entirely wrong about the Islamic terrorist attacks in Europe and the migration to the Union of people fleeing the war zones...These are not simply the accidental consequences of conflict in the wider Middle East and Africa, but a strategic objective of the United States."[290]

289 Safdar, Anealla and Strickland, Patrick. "2016: The Year the World Stopped Caring about Refugees," *Al Jazeera*, December 29, 2016.

290 Voltairenet.org. Introduction to "The European Union Is Blind to the Military Strategy of the United States" by Thierry Meyssan, May 14, 2015.

That's right. Confronting two overwhelming events, European leaders believe they are disconnected. They are not. Terrorist attacks and migrant waves are directly related. And they are instruments of US policy.

Europeans and their leaders deliberately have shut themselves off from what has been happening in the Ukraine, in Southwest Asia, and in North Africa. Obeying American demands for embargos, few businessmen travel to those regions. Obeying American demands to shutter their embassies, they become deaf and blind to what is really happening in those regions.

Here are the European Union's basic errors in misinterpreting current events:

- No Western European leader, absolutely none, has dared to publicly express the idea that the refugees from Iraq, Syria, Libya, the Horn of Africa, Nigeria, and Mali are fleeing not dictatorships but the chaos into which we have deliberately, though unconsciously, plunged their countries.
- No Western European leader, absolutely none, has dared to publicly express the idea that the "Islamist" attacks that are affecting Europe are not the extension of the wars in the greater Middle East but are directed by those who have also directed the chaos in this region.
- No Western European leader, absolutely none, has dared to publicly express the idea that the next stage will be the Islamization of the drug market, on the model of the Contras of Nicaragua, who sold drugs to the black community of California with the aid, and under the orders, of the CIA.

Thierry Meyssan, French intellectual and founder and chairman of Voltaire Network and the Axis for Peace Conference, noted that Europeans cannot grasp the basics of US policy. They seem not to realize that America seeks control of the European Union's plans. Furthermore, the United States wants to drive a wedge between Germany and Russia. "Washington's great fear, since the speech given by Vladimir Putin at the Munich Security Conference in 2007, is that Germany will realise where its true interests lie—not with Washington, but with Moscow." One example of this is "regime change" in the Ukraine. This "cut the main communication route between the European Union and Russia."

Meyssan expects more Islamist attacks in Europe tied to the Middle East and more Nazi violence connected with the Ukraine.

> We will...discover that al-Qaïda and the Ukrainian Nazis have been connected since their common inception, in 2007 at Ternopol (Ukraine). In reality, the grand-parents of both have known each other since the Second World War. The Nazis had at that time recruited Soviet Muslims for the fight against Moscow (that was Gerhard von Mende's plan [von Mende was the director of the ministry for Occupied Eastern Territories])...At the end of the war, both organisations were recuperated by the CIA (Frank Wisner's programme...in order to carry out sabotage operations in the USSR)...
>
> [George H. W. Bush demanded a post-Soviet policy be formulated. This became] the "Wolfowitz Doctrine," [which] explained that the guarantee of US supremacy over the rest of the world demanded the curbing of the European Union.[291]

At the risk of a digression, Meyssan's allusion to Nazis and the Balkans deserves a bit more flesh. Prior to World War II, there was a strong push by Arabs and Muslims for pan-Arabism and, later, nationalism. Mohammed Amin al-Husseini, who eventually became Grand Mufti of Jerusalem (Al-Quds), had been a supporter of the short-lived Arab Kingdom of Syria. He and others opposed Zionism and fought in the 1930s Arab revolt against

291 Meyssan, Thierry. "The European Union Is Blind to the Military Strategy of the United States," *Voltairenet.org*, May 14, 2015.

the British. They sought an end to Jewish immigration and demanded freedom for Palestine. Al-Husseini, to gain support for independence, met with Adolf Hitler and threw his support behind the *Waffen SS*[292] in the Balkans. He helped recruit Bosnian Muslims for the Thirteenth Mountain Division (First Croatian) *Handschar* of the *Waffen SS*. Named for the sword carried by Turkish policemen during Ottoman rule in the Balkans, it also comprised Catholics and ethnic Germans from the region.

Later, American and British efforts to effect regime change in the Arab world occurred in the 1950s and 1960s. According to Robert Dreyfuss in his book *Devil's Game,* the Anglo-American intelligence services sought to overthrow Gamal Abdel Nasser, president of Egypt and the first Arab to challenge European colonialism in the region. Their tool of choice was the Muslim Brotherhood.[293]

Again, as stated by Dreyfuss, since its founding in 1928, the Brotherhood (*Ikhwan*) was deeply involved with British and American intelligence services. It provided them information and assistance. There is even a photo of one of its leaders, Said Ramadan, meeting with President Dwight Eisenhower in the White House. Unsurprisingly, Saudi Arabia generously financed the group.[294] (Some have suggested that the Brotherhood was the creation of the British Secret Intelligence Service, MI6.)

Remember Those Tweets about Merkel and Germany from the Arab World?

Most of them didn't come from Germany. Most of them didn't come from the Arab world. Almost half came from the United States, the United Kingdom, and Australia. Only 6.4 percent of them came from Germany itself. Another 8.3 percent came from India, Nepal, Canada,

292 The armed wing of the SS, under tactical control of the German army (*Wehrmacht*).

293 *Visas for Al Qaeda*, 223.

294 Dreyfuss, Robert. "What Is the Muslim Brotherhood, and Will It Take Over Egypt?" *Mother Jones*, February 11, 2011.

and Belgium. The tweets emphasized that Germany and Austria were "the most refugee-welcoming countries in Europe."

Netbots were behind some of this Twitter activity. According to anti-virus software company Norton, a bot is a type of malware that allows an attacker to take control over an affected computer. Also known as web robots, bots are usually part of a network of infected machines, known as a botnet, which is typically made up of victim machines that stretch across the globe. These Netbots began issuing tweets such as "A new welcome: Activists launch home placement service for refugees in Germany and Austria #News #Change #Help" and "#hot Football Fans in Germany Unite with 'Refugees Welcome' Message #prebreak #best." (The original tweets were retweeted, multiplied, and spread many times over, filling the Twitterverse.)[295]

Besides the mechanics of coordinating refugees, more astute analysis from Thierry Meyssan clarifies the questionable background of the migrant wave. Reinforcing others' statements about economic refugees, the journalist emphasizes that only a third come from war zones. The rest are, essentially, poor people from the Third World seeking their fortune in the First. Moreover, Meyssan shows that German industrialists are seeking cheap, easily exploited labor. He noted, "The President of the German Industrial Federation, Ulrich Grillo, hopes for 800,000 extra foreign workers in Germany. Since European agreements forbid this, and since public opinion is hostile to the idea, he is playing his part in the staged 'refugee crisis' in order to force the evolution of the law." Hoping to mask the benefits to German industry, Grillo has spouted platitudes about how globalization aids the labor force. Speaking to the *DPA (Deutsche Presse Agentur,* or German Press Agency), Grillo asserted, "This country has been open to immigration for a long time, and it must remain so. As a prosperous country, and also out of Christian love for our neighbours, our country should be able to welcome more refugees."

---

295 Fomin, Andrey. "Who is Twitter-Luring Refugees to Germany?," *Voltairenet.org,* September 22, 2015.

The French journalist also touched on the questionable provenance of Syrian passports. "Furthermore, at the start of the war against Syria, Qatar printed and distributed false Syrian passports to jihadists from al-Qaïda so that they could convince Atlantist [Western] journalists that they were 'rebels,' and not foreign mercenaries. False Syrian passports are today distributed by certain smugglers to non-Syrian migrants. The migrants who accept them rightly believe that these false papers will facilitate their welcome in the Union." With only the Czech and Romanian embassies open in Damascus, there is no way for the European Union to check the passports' validity.[296]

Who's That in the Driver's Seat?

Meyssan identifies three men running the migrant invasion from behind the scenes.

Peter Sutherland is the special representative of the general secretary of the United Nations for international migrations. He has an impressive and somewhat scary collection of exes: ex-director of BP, ex-president of Goldman Sachs International, ex-administrator for the Bilderberg Group, and ex-president of the European section of the Trilateral Commission.[297]

But Sutherland doesn't help with the problems underlying international migration. Nor does he seek to alleviate them. He flat-out wants to encourage it! His belief is that there are no ill consequences to unrestricted immigration.

In June 2012, speaking to the British Parliament's House of Lords, Sutherland said, "The EU should 'do its best to undermine' the 'homogeneity' of its member states." Adding to his remarks, he claimed "the future prosperity of many EU states depended on them becoming

296 Meyssan, Thierry. "The Phony Refugee Crisis," *Voltairenet.org*, September 7, 2015.
297 Meyssan, Thierry. "The Puppeteers of the Migration Crisis," *Voltairenet.org*, May 2, 2016.

multicultural. He also suggested the UK government's immigration policy had no basis in international law."

The United Nations' special representative also heads the Global Forum on Migration and Development, an organization of 160 member states. They supposedly share ideas, but its policy statements are remarkably formless.

Judging from events during the intervening years, Sutherland seems to have had great influence. Then he asserted "migration was a 'crucial dynamic for economic growth' in some EU nations [possibly Germany] 'however difficult it may be to explain this to the citizens of those states.'"

Yes, Germany. Sutherland helped light the fuse going to the powder keg.

He added, unsurprisingly, "An ageing or declining native population in countries like Germany or southern EU states was the 'key argument...for the development of multicultural states...'" But his ideas of multiculturalism are a bit odd. In his session at the House of Lords, Sutherland, former attorney general of Ireland, urged countries to allow unskilled labor to migrate. He wanted countries to forego the educated, trained type of worker. He stressed that the migrants should have freedom of choice in emigrating.[298]

A second man at the wheel is Gerald Knaus, director-founder of the European Security Initiative (ESI). "The 'Merkel [migrant] plan' actually comes initially from the Dutch government: the initial deal proposed by the Dutch presidency was to propose that a voluntary group of EU countries (Germany, Netherlands, Austria, Sweden, Belgium) accept regulated and regular flows of migrants from Turkey (around 250,000 to 500,000) in exchange of an acceptance from Turkey to take back illegal immigrants crossing the Mediterranean Sea to Greece."

Knaus was the man who devised the Dutch proposal. ESI asserts it is "Europe's think tank for South East Europe and enlargement—films and reports on the Balkans, Turkey, Central Europe and the South

298 Wheeler, Brian. "EU Should 'Undermine National Homogeneity' Says UN Migration Chief," BBC, June 21, 2012.

Caucasus." George Soros's Open Society Foundation is a key sponsor, along with the European Commission, as well as "other [unnamed] American, German, Swedish, Canadian, Austrian and other Western foundations specialized in 'democracy promotion.'" Soros, demonstrating his position as international bogeyman, "supports multiculturalist policies and mass migration into Europe."

The ESI director, a former Soros Open Society associate, claimed "that if Angela Merkel does not succeed in finding a solution similar to the solution he proposed, and integrated in the Dutch presidency, then 'political forces wanting to curb asylum, against migrants, against EU, against Turkey, for Putin, and against Muslims will be reinforced.'"

Is this full disclosure? No! Knaus had a concealed motive behind his idea. Any guesses what it was? Remember, in the past, Russia supposedly stole the 2016 American presidential election from Hillary Clinton. In the past, Russia purportedly hacked e-mails from the Democratic National Committee. In the past, Russia allegedly caused any number of ills.

Read the think tank's comment verbatim:

> *Why would it be in Turkey's interest to help Germany in this way? For many years, Turkey has resisted taking back third-country nationals who crossed its borders into Greece, despite a readmission agreement. Why would Turkey act differently now?*
>
> *In fact, this agreement could make a significant contribution to Turkey's security. In recent times, a resurgent Russia has been revising borders, annexing territories and supporting separatists in the northern Black Sea. It has moved its military into annexed territories in the Southern Caucasus. Now, it has launched a major military intervention on Turkey's southern border, attacking groups that the US and Turkey have long supported. Turkey today finds itself surrounded by hostile states and armed groups, in a more precarious strategic position than at any time since the end of the Cold War.*

At such a time, good relations with Europe are a key anchor for Turkish security. The rise of an anti-Muslim, pro-Putin far right in European politics should therefore be a cause for real concern. It brings the prospect of EU politics moving in the direction of aligned its foreign policy more with the Kremlin.[299]

There's another aspect to this that Knaus doesn't mention.

The focus of the think tank on the interest of Turkey is in accordance with the "American Europe" model. The United States systematically declared that European Union should be extended to Turkey, according to geostrategic objectives of the United States and its close Euro-Atlanticist allies. They want to prevent the emergence of a "European Europe" on a continental scale with a closer relationship with Russia and similar to the vision of general de Gaulle (Europe from Atlantic to Ural). [*sic*]

The underlying objective of the European Stability Initiative is obviously to match Turkish and American objectives. and [*sic*] the migrations crisis is an opportunity to accelerate their vision.

Their narrative is also based on a manipulative tactic to discredit any political alternative accused of being "Islamophobic," "far right extremist" and "pro-Putin" fascist. Contrary to these accusations, growing skepticism from citizens in EU Member States to the mass migration flows are supported in reality by political parties and movements based on patriotic, conservative and euro-realist views shared by citizens attached to the nation state model and the preservation of the European civilization. They express deep skepticism toward the current evolution of Europe leading to chaos and internal conflicts. Their ideas are in accordance with Gaullist ideas and totally different from

299 No author. *European Stability Initiative*, "The Merkel Plan—a Proposal for the Syrian Refugee Crisis," October 4, 2015.

> "neo-fascist" ideologies. This "Reductio ad Hitlerum" narrative on the internet site of the European Stability Initiative think tank is dishonest, but reveals more profound geopolitical rival models at European and global level.[300]

This breaks down into two opposing camps: (1) Merkel's coalition government in Germany, linked to those of the Netherlands and Sweden, and (2) the more nationalist and patriotic electorates there and in the rest of Europe.

Merkel's position is to keep the borders unlocked and let the migrants roll. They want wide-open frontiers for "commerce, finance and migration flows." Yet they attempt to regulate immigration for alleged security reasons and under pressure from the voters.

The opposition wants the illegal wave to end. They have seen the *Kulturkampf* between the invaders, often Muslim, and European culture. They see the Paris, Brussels, and Berlin attacks as becoming a pattern and practice. They see the 2015 New Year's street battles along with attendant rapes and robberies as major political failures, flowing directly from George Soros and his Open Borders Society.

Clearly or only intuitively, they see the likely involvement of the United States and Turkey.

The flood of combatants leaving Bashar al-Assad's Syria weakens the country. (This is in accordance with Kelly Greenhill's proposition.) This helps Turkey push for regime change there. Recep Tayyip Erdoğan can use the migrant flow to blackmail Europe, extract concessions, and promote the continent's Islamization.

From the capitalist view, the marching millions form a cheap workforce. They can become new customers for business. Forced mixing of ethnicities aids the American and Euro-Federalist viewpoint. It fragments societies and destroys traditional national identities. "Migration flows

300 Thomann, Pierre-Emmanuel. "The Geopolitical Dimension of the 'Merkel Plan' and the 'Migration Weapon': Struggle between Two Rival Models of Europe," *Eurocontinent.eu*, first posted in *Allemagne, Union européenne*, March 17, 2016.

are a weapon to subdue European citizens to the unipolar and globalist approach of the United States and its Euro-atlanticist closest allies… European nations historical identities [may] dissolve…because of mass Muslim migrations from Middle East, Turkey, Maghreb [North Africa], South West Asia, Africa…" When this happens, Western Europeans will discover it harder "to find closer cooperation with Eastern Europeans, mainly Belarussians and Russians, more attached to European traditional values." This may well produce what French president Charles de Gaulle once termed an "American Europe" versus a "European Europe."

Migration tides may well prevent Europe-wide cooperation based on "sovereignty, traditional values, Christianity, and a more mixed and balanced economic model between the state and private sector." This will push the continent toward American control of a unipolar political system. It will prevent the emergence of a multipolar world that might challenge US supremacy.

Why are we astonished? "NGO's, globalist organizations and think tanks like the European Stability Initiative are behind these proposals to promote an 'open border,' ultra-liberal, multiculturalist, and Atlanticist Europe."[301]

The third member of the troika is Diederik Samsom, Dutch parliamentary representative and president of the Workers' Party. It was his plan to work out a deal on the migrant river with the Turks. In exchange for Anatolia taking back illegal aliens reaching Greece, the European Union would accept "a couple of hundred thousand refugees per year" from Turkey in return. Samsom's "idea [was] to distribute 'between 150,000 and 250,000' refugees among EU countries who voluntarily take part in the plan." Samsom asserted he, with the support of the Dutch premier (Rutte), had engaged in intensive talks with Germany, Sweden, and Austria on the matter. Samsom's justification for those particular countries was that they had social democrats in their governments.[302]

---

301 Ibid.

302 Teffer, Peter. "Dutch Want Migrant Swap Deal with Turkey," *EUobserver,* January 28, 2016.

Here's some background on his mind-set.

> *Samsom called the European agreements to stem the flow of migrants across the sea "hard and humane."...*
>
> *What role did Samsom actually play in this story [less illegal migration (return) in exchange for more legal migration (airlift)]? According to Gerald Knaus of the think tank European Stability Initiative he was "very important." Knaus is the spiritual father of the deal. But his ideas, he says, only took off when Samsom and German Chancellor Angela Merkel made them political.*
>
> *Chancellor Angela Merkel was already working on it by then?*
>
> "Yes, much earlier. Only she put emphasis on the legal migration..."
>
> *On March 3rd you added something else: Europe had to start soon with resettlement from Turkey. You received strong criticism.*
>
> "Angela Merkel was just before state elections then, so she simply could not say this. It would have been much better if she would have done it, because, who am I? But someone had to say out loud that the EU wants make legal immigration possible."[303]

Samsom's plan is *sans réalité*. According to the *Migrant Report*'s "Spotlight," the Dutchman's concept appears to be useless, if not dangerous. The European Union does not consider Turkey to be a "safe country." Asylum seekers there have no status or right of residence or right to work. Because of this, Samsom's arrangement might be contrary to international law. Additionally, the *Report* noted that the plan's existence could well encourage a greater flow of migrants. The alien tide surged in January 2016 to more than 50,000 crossing the Aegean in the dead of winter. In the previous January, only 1,694 attempted the trip.[304]

---

303 European Stability Initiative. "How the Merkel Plan Became the Samsom Plan—Interview with Diederik Samsom," March 30, 2016. Originally appeared in the Dutch newspaper *NRD,* March 29, 2016.

304 Micallef, Mark. "Could Dutch Plan to Ferry Refugees Back to Turkey Be Europe's Silver Bullet?" *Migrant Report* "Spotlight," January 28, 2016.

Amnesty International's comment was more pointed:

> Plans to label Turkey a "safe third country" in order to ferry back tens of thousands of people from Greece without due process or access to asylum application procedures would blatantly violate both European and international law.
>
> "No one should be fooled by the humanitarian sheen of this fundamentally flawed proposal. It is political expediency, plain and simple, aimed at stopping the flows of desperate people across the Aegean Sea," said John Dalhuisen, Europe and Central Asia Director at Amnesty International.
>
> "Any resettlement proposal that is conditional on effectively sealing off borders and illegally pushing back tens of thousands of people while denying them access to asylum procedures is morally bankrupt. The pan-European response to the global refugee crisis has long been in disarray, so solutions are needed, and fast. But there is no excuse for breaking the law and flouting international obligations in the process."
>
> "Turkey cannot possibly be considered a safe country for refugees. It is not even a safe country for many of its own citizens. In recent months refugees have been illegally returned to Iraq and Syria, while refugees from other countries face years in limbo before their applications will ever be heard," said John Dalhuisen.[305]

This Did Not Work in Korea, but It Seems to Be Working in Europe

According to Kelly Greenhill (remember her?), the NGO-driven attempt to depopulate North Korea failed. The planned regime change did not happen.

305 Amnesty International. "Dutch Plan for EU 'Refugee Swap' with Turkey Is Morally Bankrupt," January 28, 2016.

Why?

China resisted the activists' demands to open its borders. The Middle Kingdom did not class the fleeing North Koreans as refugees. And the South Koreans underwent an attitude change.

After the mid-1990s, defectors from the North moved from being philosopher-kings to becoming members of "socially disadvantaged groups." And, as in Europe today, the crime rate jumped substantially. Just in 2002, the migrants committed an average of 28.4 offenses per one thousand illegals, nearly twice the South Korean rate. Greenhill comments in her book, "As the number and socioeconomic complexity of the would-be refugees rose—and the lessons of the German experience became ever more apparent—South Korean attitudes toward fleeing North Koreans actually hardened rather than softened." The South then reversed its view. Initially, 72 percent of the region favored the migrants. After a good dose of down-market Northerners, 62 percent of South Koreans opposed them. The South also developed a more favorable opinion of the North, simultaneously hardening its outlook toward the United States.[306]

Echoing former Secretary of State Madeleine Albright's comment on the deaths of five hundred thousand Iraqi children, the *agents provocateurs* behind the illegal Korean wave thought the "deaths of...fleeing North Koreans was an acceptable price to pay...[to] overthrow the North Korean regime."[307]

> In addition, there is ample evidence to suggest that the *agents provacateurs* and the opportunists in this case tried to influence their targets by threatening to generate political crises within the target states of China and South Korea and by shaming them internationally. Evidence also suggests they attempted to do so, at least in part, through the use of the media and the imposition of

306 Greenhill, 254–255.

307 Ibid., 258.

> hypocrisy costs. This was the explicit—and well-documented—strategy of the activist *agents provacateurs*.[308]

Again, we need to go back to *Weapons of Mass Migration* to see the end of the illegal vampires. Who drove the stakes through their hearts? Who pounded the final nails into their coffins?

> Attempts to influence South Korean behavior...failed. In fact, the attempts to mobilize support for mass North Korean defections actually appeared to contribute to a further slide in support among the general South Korean public...In late 2004 and early 2005...the South Korean government tightened its policies vis-à-vis would-be defectors and cracked down on brokers who purportedly arranged mass defections. Both moves were supported by a majority of South Koreans and neither generated noteworthy dissent or pro-camp mobilization...In sum...the activists' coercive gambit in favor of "keeping North Koreans at home" increased over the course of the crisis and the concentration of interests in favor of admitting them markedly declined.[309]

Now that, as Greenhill once titled a chapter, "refugees *are* the war," what does she conclude? Swamping the target's ability to absorb, assimilate, and accept migrants is one form of victory. Another is agitating, so as to manipulate the target's willingness to do so. Coercive, engineered migration is most often aimed at and successful in influencing liberal, democratic patsies. The success is based on "merging the international and domestic concerns of a state into one and transforms its domestic normative and political virtues into international bargaining vices."

What makes this possible?

Some part of the target state's society doesn't want to bear the costs of supporting these commitments. They make it clear to the political elites,

308 Ibid., 257–258.

309 Ibid., 258–259.

who then tell them to suck it up. Liberal, democratic pigeons must deal with domestic checks and balances. To commit to policies that create domestic costs does not make you credible internationally. Hypocrisy penalties hurt when the targets back "migration-related human rights norms, but (attempt to) engage in behavior that abrogates those norms."[310]

Greenhill's recommendations to neutralize weapons of mass migration are astonishing. (1) She suggests early negotiations and concessions. (2) She advocates making contingency plans for domestic communities to take migrants, preventing the flood from being seen as a crisis. (3) She recommends targets cultivate the support of other states that could share the tidal wave. (4) She proposes forcing a radical regime change to alter the situation in "potential sending states" (possibly in reference to Syria).

Her policies don't neutralize the flood of illegals. Rather, they legitimize and increase the tsunami. Angela Merkel's Germany has obviously followed her directions. Look at this, a detail from Greenhill's second point:

> Potential target governments may choose to launch preventive education campaigns to affect the attitudes of the citizens who are the proxy targets of these punishment-based coercive strategies. Such campaigns might be aimed at improving perceptions of particular migrant or refugee groups, or of migrants and refugees in general.
>
> Other campaigns might focus on educating publics about the true costs and benefits of inflows...Immigration...represents a net gain for most industrialized countries. Educational outreach may be particularly appropriate in states facing falling birthrates and aging populations, such as Germany...
>
> Direct beneficiaries of migrant and refugee labor may even be persuaded to take up the cause...Personal exposure to members of other ethnic and racial groups significantly increases tolerance of, and greater affinity for, these groups writ large.[311]

310 Ibid., 263–264.

311 Ibid., 273–279.

11

Some Threads to be Pulled

Summation

THROUGHOUT THIS WORK, the author has developed a number of seemingly different threads. From time to time, he's referred to them in various, somewhat unrelated sections. Now's the time to examine them in more detail and propose some solutions to a number of pressing concerns.

The First Thread: America's Wars against Arabs and Muslims

American warfare in South and Southwest Asia as well as North Africa set loose the marching millions. In *Visas for Al Qaeda: CIA Handouts That Rocked the World,* this author provided the origin of this thread. He developed it country by country, in some detail. So much so that one journalist, Jeremy Bigwood, called the book "dangerous" because it named names. (This writer had identified as many people as he knew who were involved with regime change and US government-sponsored terrorism. These were the officials who created the mujahideen in Afghanistan. They later rebranded them as al-Qaeda in Yugoslavia and Iraq. Later, to sow more confusion, they labeled them ISIL or ISIS or IS.) The weapon of choice was often illegally issued America visas. With such a document, anyone could enter the United States for almost any purpose or easily obtain an equivalent from another country. (The State Department's computerized applicant analysis was seen as the toughest in the world.)

This was the origin of GWOT, the Global War On Terror. Terrorists recruited for the American war against the Soviets in Afghanistan got some of their visas in Saudi Arabia. Obtaining them mostly at the CIA's Jeddah consulate (in the Visa Section over the author's protests), the recruits came to the United States for training. Some were later connected to 9/11. In fact, Shayna Steinger, an alleged State Department official in Jeddah, issued visas to eleven of the fifteen Saudi hijackers who got their entry permits in the kingdom. You know the result.

George W. Bush then ordered war on Afghanistan, not Saudi Arabia. Later, Barack H. Obama continued both Bushs' wars against Afghanistan and Iraq. Moreover, he expanded them, removing Moammar Gaddafi from power in Libya and attempting to overthrow Bashar al-Assad in Syria. He used US soldiers, sailors, and airmen, along with CIA Clandestine Service Officers The president of hope and change also made use of Bill Clinton-wrecked Yugoslavia to fuel the Syrian war. Croatia supplied many weapons to Syrian terrorists.

What was the reason for regime change by terrorist? One reason was that it was easy. A solid, unified state with an educated population and a sound economy doesn't come apart effortlessly. The American government picked countries with sharp religious, ethnic, linguistic, and cultural differences. Another reason was, as noted earlier, implementation of the Yinon Plan.

> Back in 1982, Oded Yinon an Israeli journalist formerly attached to the Israeli Foreign Ministry, published a document titled "A Strategy for Israel in the Nineteen Eighties." This Israeli commentator suggested that for Israel to maintain its regional superiority, it must fragment its surrounding Arab states into smaller units. The document, later labelled as "Yinon Plan," implied that

> Arabs and Muslims killing each other in endless sectarian wars was, in effect, Israel's insurance policy.[312]

Zionists pushed the US government into two wars against Iraq, in the hope of destroying the last bit of Arab resistance to Israel. Bernard Henri Levy, a so-called philosopher, bragged that he was the Jew who liberated Libya by campaigning for NATO intervention. "And again, it was the exact same Jewish Lobby that was pushing for intervention in Syria, calling for the USA and NATO to fight alongside those same Jihadi forces that today threaten the last decade's American 'achievements' in Iraq."[313]

But that's military action, bombs, and bullets. There's more; there's *Kulturkampf.* Working with George Soros and his Open Society Initiative, "the Jewish so-called Left" wages war quietly. They "attempt to break the Arabs and Muslims by means of marginal and identity politics." By using money and organizations to promote antithetical homosexual, lesbian, and heterosexual groups, they hope to shatter those regions surrounding Israel.[314]

It worked. Millions of migrants are on the move. As written earlier, more than half (54 percent) of all refugees worldwide come from just three countries: the Syrian Arab Republic (4.9 million), Afghanistan (2.7 million), and Somalia (1.1 million). Iraq and Libya, following their destruction, have contributed 4,746,100 and 471,653 people respectively. The foregoing are countries that bore the brunt of American military action and intervention.

To snip this thread, to end this threat, the American people, along with the people of Europe, must bell the cat. They must end these illegal and unconstitutional wars of aggression—within six months. They must

312 Atzmon, Gilad. "The Jewish Plan for the Middle East and Beyond," *www.gilad.co.uk/writings,* June 13, 2014. (NB Atzmon is a Jew, born in Israel. He writes on political matters, social issues, Jewish identity, and culture.)

313 Ibid.

314 Ibid.

cut terrorist recruiting, financing, and training. US voters thought they had done this by electing Donald J. Trump, instead of Hillary Clinton, as president. They took him at his word when he tweeted "Hillary voted for the Iraq war, not me!"[315] Americans knew of Clinton's support for the murder of Libya's Moammar Gaddafi and her backing the destruction of Syria (and the Ukraine).

Instead of less war, however, the United States got more. President Trump increased the number of US servicemen in Syria in March 2017:

> The United States is sending an additional 400 troops to Syria to help prepare for the looming fight for Raqqa, the capital of the Islamic State's self-proclaimed caliphate...
>
> The increase, which includes a team of Army Rangers and a Marine artillery unit that have already arrived in Syria, represents a near-doubling of the number of American troops there.
>
> The United States military has declined to say how many troops it has deployed in Syria...[316]

On January 29, 2017, President Trump attacked central Yemen with Navy SEAL Team Six. One commando died, and three others suffered wounds. The US government did not state how many civilians, including women, were casualties.[317] Moreover, at the beginning of March 2017, Trump unleashed two days of airstrikes on Yemen. The thirty sorties killed an undisclosed number of alleged terrorists, but US government sources denied any civilian injuries.[318]

The next order of business for both the Americans and the Europeans is their withdrawal from NATO. A one-time defensive alliance, it has

315 Trump Tweet: 9:32 a.m., July 31, 2016.

316 Gordon, Michael R. "U.S. Is Sending 400 More Troops to Syria," *New York Times*, March 9, 2017.

317 Schmitt, Eric. "U.S. Commando Killed in Yemen in Trump's First Counterterrorism Operation," *New York Times*, January 29, 2017.

318 Starr, Barbara and Browne, Ryan. "US Launches Second Round of Airstrikes in Yemen," *CNN*, March 3, 2017.

become an aggressive institution, waging war in South and Southwest Asia as well as North Africa. NATO was a useful fig leaf concealing the vital US role in destroying Libya. Canceling NATO will cancel the means, motives, and opportunities for more war.

However, no one questions the need to end the Forever War. No one questions the need to dissolve NATO. And, naturally enough, no one questions the benefits of stopping the endless warfare. How many bridges could be repaired? How many water mains fixed? How many sewage treatment plants could be renovated? In the United States? In Europe? In Iraq? In Libya? In Syria? How many migrants could be educated? How many migrants could be trained for useful occupations? At home? Abroad?

Here are some numbers listing military support funds. Think about where they could be better spent.

NATO has its "own military budget worth €1.29 billion (US$1.4 billion), which is used to fund some operations and the NATO strategic command center, as well as training and research. But it is miniscule compared to overall spending on defense by NATO countries, which NATO estimates will total more than €851.4 billion or US$921 billion in 2017.

The alliance also has a civilian budget of €234.4 million ($252 million), used mainly to fund the NATO headquarters in Belgium, and its administration."[319]

Got potholes? Got crumbling bridges? Got lead or worse in your water supply? Their fixes lie in the NATO budget and not in more migrants, do they not?

The Second Thread: Weapons of Mass Migration

Kelly Greenhill's book, *Weapons of Mass Migration*, as noted earlier, formulated a new concept: regime change by population bomb. This idea works

319 Kottasova, Ivana. "How NATO is Funded and Who Pays What," *CNN*, March 20, 2017.

in two directions: one by emptying out a country, the other by flooding another country. Using force or threat of force to effect "coercive engineered migration," an actor drives a population out of its home country and into another (e.g., Iraq and Syria). The land losing people has its educational system and economy disrupted. The government strains to hold on to its credibility and legitimacy. The recipient country must deal with a flood of aliens, migrants who don't speak the language, may practice a different religion, know nothing of its culture, and have a different educational level. The net effect is to induce strains in the body politic, setting not only the immigrants against the citizens but also the citizens against the immigrants. It also sets the citizens against each other—those who want to help the migrants' struggle against those who don't.

Another side to this strategy has been to embroil the receiving state, in this case, most of Europe, in conflicts in the migrants' regions. As noted, the clash of cultures has, in places, turned brutal. To stop this, individuals and governments have stepped into the wars producing the refugees. Remember, their mistaken belief is that air strikes, naval bombardments, and foot soldiers will stem the alien tide.

What's the solution? Build an impenetrable, multistory wall topped with barbed wire? Send the migrants packing? Spend a great deal of taxpayers' money educating them in language, culture, and *mores*? Find them jobs commensurate with their education?

The Good European is quite taken with the US way of dealing with migrants. He is mesmerized by decades of propaganda that convinced Americans of their duty to accommodate all illegal aliens crossing their border. This benefits business, primarily. It harms the citizens, usually. Workers, grateful for any wage, will accept positions supplying no benefits. Citizens pay for the illegals' children's schooling and medical care. (Robert A. Stella, PhD, once told the author that 25 percent of his town's budget [San Diego, California] pays for services to illegal aliens.) The Good European is more concerned with the concept of social justice than with hard reality.

Then, there are the political parties, salivating at the millions of prospective new voters, if only they can be shoehorned into local society.

Isn't there a better way? One in which most benefit and few lose?

Recall, if you will, the vast sums spent on war, on preparations for war, on the results of war. Think of the soldiers and civilians killed or horribly maimed, and their burden on European and American future generations. Think of the same people in the war-torn regions. Sure, many want to leave their devastated lands. Sure, many want to avoid the fates of their murdered or mutilated neighbors. But, isn't it time for a change? Isn't time to end the Forever War?

Suppose instead of using astonishing riches to destroy countries, we use the staggering sums to rebuild them. Give the Syrians, the Iraqis, the Libyans, and all those peoples from all those shattered countries new places to live and work and play—back home. Establish migrant camps, not in the squalor of Greece or the Balkans but in South Asia, Southwest Asia, and North Africa. Provide real, comfortable, temporary buildings like those used to house POWs or displaced persons during and after World War II. Build classrooms to educate future teachers, computer experts, and civil engineers. Teach them languages other than their native Arabic or Pashto or Dari. Create a new Marshall Plan for the area, helping the people repair the United States–ruined infrastructure.

Out of the migrant tsunami inundating the continent, there might be many legitimate asylum applicants. In those cases, it would make sense to provide them housing, education, and medical care—but not to the disadvantage of Europeans. No one gets tossed out of his home for an asylee, no one must submit to segregated swimming pools, no one must abandon his beliefs or customs or dress to accommodate aliens. Instead, outside of their own four walls, the asylees must adapt to those strange foreign ways.

The Third Thread: Outside Help

The *Völkerwanderung* seems to have had the "benefits" of either official help, official stupidity, or official ignorance. Perhaps it's all of the above. In addition to educating masses of migrants, perhaps the solution here is to educate governments, big businesses, and NGOs.

End French, Qatari, and other governments' practices of printing Syrian and other travel documents for their "special friends," whom they want moved into Europe. Sever the spooks' ties with counterfeit passport mills. Crack down on embassies handing out official documentation to anyone who coughs up a bribe. (Syrian embassy staff in Berlin is but one example, even selling genuine passports to non-Syrians.) It's also time to make a strenuous effort toward collecting other legitimate travel documents lost, stolen, or acquired by traffickers.

It's a long hike from Damascus to Dűsseldorf. In a straight line, it's slightly more than 3,000 kilometers (just short of 2,000 miles). By road, it's a bit more than 4,000 kilometers (about 2,500 miles), a forty-hour trip. Who pays for this? Who supplies the cell phones enabling the marchers to keep in touch and plan their route?

Many carry a variety of smartphone, making use of electronic networks such as WhatsApp, Viber, Telegram, or Facebook. They use them to find the best travel routes, area maps, and communicate with their peers. The devices are notorious energy hogs, requiring a charge every few days of regular use. Should they link up with the Internet, with its many services, the battery goes flat within hours.

Cell phones for migrants are not cheap. Smartphones are especially pricey. Here are a few of the top ten in Syria: iPhone 7 is SYP142,500; Huawei Mate 9 smartphone costs SYP120,000; Samsung Galaxy S7 Edge is SYP109,500. The least expensive of the top ten smartphones in Syria in 2017 is the Lenovo Zuk Z2 Pro. That's *only* SYP90,000. The least expensive cell phones are various Nokia Models, costing 4,000 to 6,000 Syrian pounds.[320]

Yet, in 2015, the average monthly income in Damascus, the capital, was US$50 per month (Syrian pounds: SYP15,000). That will buy you fifteen kilograms of bananas (thirty-three pounds).[321] In Aleppo (Halab), once the country's largest city, the average monthly income was US$80

320 http://www.mobilewithprices.com/syria-mobiles-5084.php.

321 *EAWorldview.com*. "Syria Snapshot: In Damascus, 1 Month's Salary = 15 Kilos of Bananas," April 28, 2015.

(SYP20,000).[322] These wages certainly didn't fund cell phone purchases or provide for smugglers to move them from their homes to Germany.

Simple arithmetic is tough for attorneys and Foreign Service Officers. However, the author's calculator indicates these telephones' prices range from one-third of a month's wages to nine-and-a-half months' wages in Damascus. While this writer can't check on every country supplying migrants, the Syrian prices are indicative of how costly these devices are. Conceivably there are used phones out there. Conceivably there are cheaper phones out there. But where do people with few assets, who leave everything behind, get them? And where do all the unaccompanied children find them?

Yet Austrian intelligence suggested that it was American money paying for the million-migrant march. If it costs €11,000 (about US$11,850) to move an asylum seeker from North Africa to Europe, what does it cost to transport one from Syria? It's 14 kilometers (ca. 9 miles) from Africa to Europe across the Straits of Gibraltar. If you go from Africa to Sicily, it's 155 kilometers (roughly 96 miles). And it's not only the United States involved in this. French government officials have been caught selling lifeboats to refugees in Turkey. And are governments or big businesses or NGOs supplying the telephones?

The solution is simple: stop the subsidies and shut down the information highway. This will inconvenience many, but it will also make it easier to get the migrants home again.

Groups, organizations, and individuals are encouraging these people to leave their homes and hearths. Why? Who?

Out of nowhere suddenly came innumerable tweets emphasizing that Germany and Austria were "the most refugee-welcoming countries in Europe." Most of these didn't come from Germany or from the Arab world. But, to date, no one's tied them to a particular agency or organization.

322 *Syrian Economic Forum.* "Average Monthly Income for Most Aleppians Is $80," May 15, 2015.

As the author noted earlier, George Soros's groups are involved. He's sponsored the Central European University in Budapest, supplying exotic, hard language speakers. They volunteer to provide much-needed translation services for the migrants. Additionally, the university set up Wi-Fi and mobile phone-charging stations along the aliens' line of march.

In addition to the Central European University, George Soros and his Open Society groups have provided other aid to migrants. Meredith Woo, as director of the International Higher Education Support Program at London's Open Society Foundation, "help[ed] refugees from the Middle East, Africa, and South Asia..."[323] (NB Neither the *Washington Post* nor the Open Society's website specify the kind of help given.)

Besides George Soros, there are other organizations helping keep migrants wired. The Belgrade Centre for Human Rights, an aid group in Serbia, built Wi-Fi networks for refugees, while the UN Refugee Agency has distributed thousands of SIM cards at Jordan's refugee camps.

And big business has jumped into migrant support. It's good to look at who's involved again.

Cisco is one. As said before, it's a huge manufacturer of computer networking equipment. It helped install Wi-Fi networks and device-charging stations along the migration route in Southern and Central Europe. Cisco has also donated substantial funds and equipment to organizations aiding refugees. Some of these were NGO partners NetHope and Mercy Corps.

Both of the foregoing have backgrounds tied to the US government. NetHope is a shadowy organization headquartered in CIA-friendly Fairfax County, Virginia. It has aided migrants by setting up twenty-four Wi-Fi hot spots and charging stations along the European immigrant road. It developed a website with maps and transit information to which refugees are directed when accessing the Wi-Fi at certain camps.

---

323 Svrluga, Susan. "New Era with New Leader for Sweet Briar [College]," *Washington Post*, February 7, 2017.

Mercy Corps is much like NetHope. It even worked in Syria, but in terrorist-controlled areas. Mercy Corps has a long history of being caught up in American war zones: Afghanistan, Iraq, the Balkans. Mercy Corps staff have been charged with espionage.

In 1986, Mercy Corps began operations in Afghanistan. In the midst of NATO's war against Yugoslavia, the organization "provide[d] medicines, supplies and services to Bosnians during the Balkans wars." In Iraq, in 1991, it shipped blankets, medicine, and food to Kurds. Mercy Corps spent US$3 million aiding people in Kosovo during 1993. In 1995, the outfit distributed US$20 million in supplies throughout Bosnia and Kosovo. Still deeply involved in the Balkans, during 1999, Mercy Corps provided "food and supplies to thousands more people in Kosovo and help[ed] 100,000 refugees in Macedonia." In 2003, with the new war, the group returned to Iraq, asserting it helped families displaced by conflict. It followed them and worked with them in Syria and Jordan.[324]

Think this shows CIA ties? Read on.

On June 11, 2016, *Pravda* (a privately owned Russian news service) reported that Luhansk People's Republic authorities had arrested Oksana Mikitenko, one of Mercy Corps' staff, for espionage. The article also noted that Stuart Willcuts, the Mercy Corps regional director in the Donbass area of Luhansk, also worked for the CIA. (NB Luhansk is one of the regions that seceded from the neo-Nazi–controlled Ukraine.)

This is not so unusual as it might first seem. In 2007, Kay Hiramine, the Colorado-based founder of a multimillion-dollar humanitarian organization, Humanitarian International Services Group, once received the President's Volunteer Service Award from George W. Bush. However, in reality, Hiramine was a Pentagon spy whose NGO was funded through a highly classified Defense Department program. The object was to penetrate North Korea and gather intelligence on its nuclear program.[325]

If we get the intelligence services and their cat's-paws out of the migrant flood, perhaps the flood will subside. Perhaps it will even

---

324 www.mercycorps.org.

325 Cole, Matthew. "The Pentagon's Missionary Spies," *The Intercept*, October 26, 2015.

recede. What the spooks and George Soros and the NGOs have done is stuff the *Völkerwanderung*'s heads with false hopes, false visions, and false reality. They've driven them from their countries and herded them into a hostile, alien environment.

The current process is the old carrot-and-stick approach, applied wrongly. What must be done is use it correctly, intelligently, and humanely. Use the wired aliens' routes to help them go to their homelands. Reverse the destruction of the migrants' homes. End the encouragement and assistance in leaving them. This would be an excellent way of creating a democratic, economically viable region.

The Fourth Thread: German Internal Security

Here's the problem in a few words. Germany is a country built on an almost-religious attention to order and security. It has a number of well-staffed federal and state offices devoted to internal security, some dealing with intelligence, some dealing with crime. They all cooperate.

Yet, as the result of high-level policy decisions, internal security fell apart. How? Why?

Remember, German Chancellor Angela Merkel essentially invited the whole world to move to her country. Doing little to stem the rising tide of migrants, Merkel later opened the floodgates on August 25, 2015. That was the day the Federal Office for Migration and Refugees tweeted, "We are no longer enforcing the Dublin procedures for Syrian citizens." Then, tens of thousands rushed across the border. As time went on, hundreds of thousands more came. By the end of 2015, two million people had raced into Germany, an almost 50 percent increase over the previous year's record. Twelve months later, the flood appeared to have abated somewhat: nearly three hundred thousand asylum seekers had crossed into the Federal Republic.[326]

326 Sanders IV, Lewis. "Two Million: Germany Records Largest Influx of Immigrants in 2015," *DeutscheWelle,* March 21, 2016.

With a surging level of "immigrants," with a well-organized internal security service, and with a well-developed sense of order, Germany still completely failed at keeping its citizens safe. You'd almost think that Mack Sennett's Keystone Kops were back, this time dressed in German police uniforms.[327]

First, Germany couldn't house them. One Munich city councilman demanded to know what was to be done with the fifty thousand migrants already in the city. She said they were penned up in sports stadia without enough air mattresses to sleep on. In Süßen, the city fathers housed them in a gymnasium.

Then, the country was wracked by culture clashes.

This began with migrants soiling the streets, attacking German revelers at festivals, and assaulting unescorted women in the streets. German citizens protested. The government responded by arresting and fining the protesters, claiming they were engaged in hate speech.

The real hate came later, on December 31, 2015. And it covered Germany and other countries. The author provided more detail earlier, but it's good to review the basics again.

In Cologne, about one thousand men, described as being largely of Arab or North African origin (meaning migrants), began molesting women near the train station. Females there and near the impressive cathedral reported a sense of "lawlessness." Many were sexually molested and robbed of their money and cell phones.

The city's lord mayor, Henriette Reker, implied that it was the victims' own fault for not keeping their distance from strange men.

There were migrant assaults in Berlin. Merkel's "invitees" were fully engaged in lawlessness. Their firing of strictly controlled handguns and indiscriminate use of fireworks brought fire trucks roaring through the streets, sirens screaming.

Cologne and Berlin were not anomalies.

---

327 *Encyclopaedia Britannica*: "Keystone Kops, in silent-film comedies, insanely incompetent police force, dressed in ill-fitting, unkempt uniforms, that appeared regularly in Mack Sennett's slapstick farces from 1914 to the early 1920s." January 12, 2011.

In Hamburg, the *Frankfurter Allgemeine Zeitung* (FAZ) reported January 5, 2016, that young women were verbally and sexually molested and then robbed of money and cell phones. The attackers, migrants in various-sized groups, surrounded the women who sought to flee the scene.

There were *Silvester* outbreaks in Stuttgart, on a smaller scale than Cologne, yet also with sexual gropings, robberies, and theft of cell phones. In Weil am Rhein, a town in the far southwest of Baden-Württemberg, several asylum seekers, with others, raped two German girls. In Singen, in the south of Baden-Wurttemberg, the local paper wrote that two "dark-skinned men" attacked and attempted to strip naked a thirty-year old woman sitting on a park bench behind City Hall.

In Munich, an online news service reported that ten to fifteen men swarmed two women who were taking a cigarette break outside a disco at 2:00 a.m.

There is a sense, according to some contacts, that the German federal government was pressing news outlets around the country to downplay the events of *Silvester* 2015. In Baden-Württemberg, the police certainly minimized any connection to the Cologne events. In one instance, even the State's Attorney's Office seemed to blame the victims and not the perpetrators.

For those not well traveled, the Third World's attitude toward women is an unknown quantity. When the author served as commercial attaché in New Delhi, he once hosted a Christmas party. One of the guests, a Sikh, marveled at public displays of affection he had seen on a trip to Europe. Several embassy secretaries, attractive women, later commented that the Indian, an older gentleman, had groped them at the reception. Before traveling to Jeddah to run the Non-Immigrant Visa Section, this writer attended an area studies course at the Foreign Service Institute (the State Department's educational arm). In it, a teacher noted that Arab men divide women into two types: paid whores and free whores (i.e., those who willingly go out with men).

German government officials, apparently, are not well traveled.

Nor are the security services able to deal with migrants and their attitudes. Or, perhaps, someone has told them to ignore such people. In such cases, ignorance is not bliss. Sometimes, they get educated the hard way. Sometimes, they get caught out, as the author has mentioned earlier.

In the fall of 2016, police in North Rhine-Westphalia arrested five members of a "terrorist recruiting network." One of those detained was a preacher and a major figure in Germany's jihadist movement. Unfortunately for Germany's internal security service, neither they nor the police fingered the preacher. "The arrest appears to have been facilitated by a former IS fighter…who identified…Germany's IS leader."

In April 2016, the internal security service had hired a former bank employee, supposedly converted to Islam. The fifty-one-year old mole, a homosexual porn star, sought to use his position to "help the brothers" attack his employer. The BfV asserted that it had followed its normal procedures during the interview and hiring process. If so, what, if anything, went wrong.? Was this incompetentence? Was it an effort to use the spy as an unwitting double agent? Or was it a planned intelligence coup to keep the fear alive. Or was it an effort designed to demonstrate action against the Muslim migrant flood.

Possibly, but what's clear is that the German internal intelligence service appears unwilling or incapable of doing its job. Or is it that the BfV is under political pressure from Chancellor Merkel not to do its job?

Again, here are some of the more egregious examples of Germany failing to do the minimum to protect its citizens.

On October 16, 2016, an Afghan asylee, Hussein Kavari, raped and murdered Maria Ladenburger. The seventeen-year-old Afghan caught the young medical student as she was bicycling home from a party in the university city of Freiburg. There are questions as to why the police kept a lid on the matter for nearly two months. The asylee was a known criminal who had been jailed in Greece for attempting to murder a woman he had been following.

Are the governments and their intelligence services truly evil? Or are they just bad at planning? Or is there a dark fifth column running the spooks? Earlier, the author went into this in some detail. Here are the highlights.

Anis Amri, who allegedly drove the Polish truck into the Berlin Christmas market crowd, had multiple identities and more than a few passports. Despite having an extensive criminal history, he had obtained residence but not asylum in Germany. Despite a nationwide manhunt, Amri left Berlin, left Germany, likely traveled through France, and ended up in Italy. How? The BfV is supposed to be an internal security and counter-espionage service. Its job is to prevent such things happening. That is also the role of the Federal Criminal Police (*Bundeskriminalamt*, BKA), Germany's central criminal investigation agency. Both organizations are part of the Interior Ministry.

RT had noted that Amri couldn't be deported because he had no papers! German authorities had followed the murderer for months before ending their surveillance in September 2016! And US intelligence had tracked Amri. An American security official commented that Amri had communicated with IS at least once, via the Telegram messenger app. He was also on a US no-fly list.

Stupidity? Incompetence? Intent?

And look at the *V men*. Everything old is new again. What really is their role?

Earlier, this writer mentioned the origins of the V men. After the 1914 war ended, Adolf Hitler became a V man. These were people who spied upon German citizens for the army and government. V men popped up later as people the Nazi Security Service (*Sicherheitsdienst*, SD) dealt with. The Federal Republic's constitution, the Basic Law (*Grundgesetz*), didn't fix this undemocratic activity. Instead, it continued it.

In the 1950s, the German government banned some political party members, but not others, from public service. There were investigations. Even where there was no conviction, the proceedings usually led to the loss of a person's job. Some were prohibited from practicing their professions. In the 1970s, in reaction to the terrorist acts of the Red Army Faction (RAF), the principles of due process during proceedings involving state security were drastically curtailed, with the same applying to freedom of opinion.

After mysterious attacks in Paris (2015) and Brussels (2016) and claims there might be some in Germany, the Federal Republic began examining its internal controls in light of increased insecurity. The federal police and intelligence services got more power. Merkel's government increased cooperation between Germany's external intelligence agency, the *Bundesnachrichtendienst* (BND), and its European counterparts with a joint European intelligence database.

But why is the BfV, the Federal Office for the Protection of the Constitution, the internal security service, presumably with its own V men, not mentioned?

The Chancellor's Office submitted and the parliament (*Bundestag*) passed sweeping authority for the security services to spy not only on foreigners but on German citizens.

V for Victory or V for V Men?

Echoing earlier remarks, there's a thread running through Merkel's million-migrant march. Who's coordinating it? How? The *why* we know: destabilize South and Southwest Asia, destabilize North Africa, destabilize Europe. We've mentioned the American and other "intelligence" services with their idiot spooks. But what about Germany?

Earlier, the author noted how Henriette Reker had been elected lord mayor of Cologne just after an attack by a man ostensibly opposed to migrants. Was this guy some sort of V man connected to the BfV or the Federal Criminal Police? Some people thought so. Volker Beck, a Green politician, and others wondered about that. It was Reker who could not or would not use the police and water cannons on the raping, rioting migrants around the railroad station during *Silvester* 2015.

One of the activities of the BfV is infiltration of groups.

Could the carefully coordinated attacks on women in Germany (and elsewhere) have had the assistance of their V men? Was the suppression of news about the *Silvester* assaults their work as well? What about welcoming the migrants with candy and flowers? Who developed that idea? Or why was news about the rape and murder of Maria Ladenburger kept under wraps for months? And how?

More importantly, what was the purpose? The role of both the BfV (2,800 employees) and the Federal Criminal Police (5,500 staff) is fighting threats to the German Republic (national and international crime) and terrorism investigation (including a Joint Counter-Terrorism Centre, GTAZ, in Berlin).

This is scarcely believable. Eight thousand people carpeting Germany, tied to state criminal and intelligence offices, can't ward off known criminals. Eight thousand people connected to domestic and foreign computerized databases can't find known criminals. Eight thousand people with great skills and training can't search for dangerous migrants.

This isn't a banana republic; this is Germany. Yet, for over a year, aliens from all over have created a crime wave. And the authorities appeared to be oblivious to it, if not complicit in it. Is there a troop of Trojan horses hidden in the security services?

How can Germany resolve the issue?

1. To learn about the decision making that created the migrant wave, the German people should use their government's Freedom of Information Act (*Informationsfreiheitsgesetz*, FOIA). "It gives any person a right of access to official information from agencies of the federal government or those organizations or persons conducting public duties. Information must be provided within one month. It can be provided orally, in writing or electronically." Naturally enough, the law, as in the United States, has gaping loopholes for loosely defined national security matters. (But the mere fact of asking will put the politicians on notice.) Some German states have gone forward with their own FOIAs. "The states of Brandenburg, Berlin, Hamburg, Nordrhein-Westfalen [North Rhine-Westphalia], and Schleswig-Holstein have also

adopted combination FOI and Data Protection laws each with its own commissioner."[328]

2. The German people must publicly and in large numbers question Angela Merkel and her ministers about their actions and inactions regarding the migrant tsunami. They should demand the reasons why high government officials failed in their oaths of office "to dedicate [their] efforts to the well-being of the German people, promote their welfare, protect them from harm, uphold and defend the Basic Law [Constitution] and the laws of the Federation, perform my duties conscientiously, and do justice to all."
3. The German people must demand of their news media a complete and public accounting of the bias against criticism of aliens. They should require TV, radio, and the newspapers to own up to government influence on their reporting. The citizens ought to enquire about the media setting itself up as "moral executioner," acting as a kind of thought police on attitudes about migrants. The media have been enforcing a code of silence, blocking the people's right to know about what has been happening—and why.

Besides helping the German people regain control of their country, the previous three recommendations will assist the legitimate asylum seekers and refugees. Instead of American propaganda (which Europe adopted) portraying them as wanting a better life, they will expose the Forever War's reality: brutal conflict forcing migrants from their destroyed fatherlands.

The Fifth Thread: Nationalism

As said before, *Mutter der Nation* Merkel and her migrants appear to be reviving European nationalism. From Sweden in the north to Greece in the south, Europeans are becoming steadily outraged at aliens invading

328 http://www.freedominfo.org/regions/europe/germany/.

their historic lands and cultures. They are increasingly incensed at the idea they, and not the foreigners, must adapt. They are ever more infuriated that the migrants believe in their right to be there. And they are taking it out on the Establishment parties at the ballot box.

A new European nationalism is not a bad thing. Globalism, of the sort that Angela Merkel, George Soros, and their adherents espouse, denies nations, denies their history, and denies their heritage. And "he who denies his heritage, has no heritage."[329] Merkel's globalism, by breaking down the nation-state and its people, makes it easier to accommodate the migrant inundation. If people forget their history, reject their heritage, and dismiss their identity, then why object to aliens changing European culture?

The peoples of Europe understand this. Their leaders don't. Those want to cobble together a new multicultural Europe, erasing the one that already exists. And, so far, the replacement doesn't work and likely can't be made to work—except in the minds of the globalists. The people vigorously oppose these government policies. They denounce their leaders' abandoning constitutional obligations to defend their country's borders, territorial integrity, and democracy.

Besides harming European uniqueness, a Continental consensus, and independent entities, what else does globalism harm? That's right. The migrants in the middle. Those are the peoples from Afghanistan to Zambia, whom US policy turned out of their homes and herded into alien lands.

The assorted asylum seekers, refugees, economic opportunists, and extremists no longer have homelands, no longer have cultures, and no longer have governments. What they do have is hostility, uncertainty, and unemployment. They have no language skills and little education. Yet, somehow, the idea got planted in their heads that all they needed do was go to benefit-rich Europe. In doing so, life would vastly improve.

---

329 Gibran, Khalil.

Who sold them this concept? American intelligence services? European intelligence services? Saudi, Qatari, Israeli, and Turkish intelligence services? George Soros and his Open Society organizations? Some group did and did it as a matter of policy. The migrant flood didn't go to Egypt or Israel; the migrant flood didn't go to the Gulf states; the migrant flood didn't go to Saudi Arabia. Yet the Gulf "countries" and the Kingdom of Saudi Arabia are the four richest Arab lands. Israel ranks right up there with them. The illegals did go to Turkey, a land with its own problems. Anatolia stockpiled the migrants until it could send them *en masse* to Europe.

No wonder then that Geert Wilders and his PVV Freedom Party did so well in the March 2017 elections. The PVV became the second-largest party in the Dutch parliament after forcing Prime Minister Mart Rutte's government further to the right. Marine Le Pen and her Front National appear to be gaining ground in the face of disorganized opposition and repeated street violence. The AfD in Germany is beginning to push Chancellor Merkel further to the right, forcing her to place restrictions on migrant dress and increase scrutiny of asylum applicants. All the foregoing groupings emphasize "nationalism," the distinction between "me," "my country/my countrymen," and "them." The same is happening throughout the rest of the continent. The globalist Establishment wants desperately to hang on to the status quo, wherein the migrants are painted as saviors of the social welfare system, an aging, dying population, and a moribund society.

So, you might ask, what is the solution? Continue with globalism, a borderless Continent, and the end of the nation-state? Abolish the Schengen visa-free system? Demand identity cards on the street?

Years ago, the author was political-economic officer in Stuttgart, after the Schengen agreement had been signed but before it took effect. Howls of protest came from all quarters in Europe. The most frequent dealt with the results of dropping all boundary checks. The dissenters insisted that no border controls meant increased crime, more illegal aliens, and amplified terrorism. They seem to have been vindicated. However, the old way, stopping just long enough on the French frontier to hand a passport out a car window, was never onerous. (It took longer to change marks into francs.) Nor was it hard to produce a passport at Aachen, traveling on a train from Belgium to Germany. One State Department wag commented that you could enter Germany with only a credit card.

The answer to all this has multiple parts: (1) Reintroduce border checkpoints, demanding a valid passport with visa (if required) or a current national identity card. (2) Emphasize that the European Union is not a federal government but an administrative body subject to the nation-states of Europe. (3) End NGO and Global Society meddling in national politics. (4) Bring the security services under greater control. (5) End the root cause of the migrant tsunami: American and European wars east of the Pillars of Hercules.

Implementing these points will go a long way toward ending hostility of Europeans and migrants toward each other, reduce criminal activity, and remove the opportunity for the intelligence services to stir the pot. Without constant warfare, it will be possible to send the migrants home to rebuild their lives.

The Sixth Thread: Europe's Move to the Right

Europe appears to be moving toward the right. Why? Because the Left's policies are clearly bankrupt. They planned, helped organize, and imposed the migrant wave on an entire continent. (To be sure, they had assistance from America and other forces driving the flood of aliens from their own countries.) The Left, the established parties, all promoted the "Welcome Culture." Candy and flowers were linked to "the feel-good scenes of last September [2015], when crowds gathered at [the] Munich railway station to applaud the newly arrived refugees. Selfies Syrian men took with Ms. Merkel as she visited reception camps went viral, and became symbols of Germany's welcoming culture—its Willkommenskultur."[330] Unfortunately

330 Chazan, Guy. "Germany: Welcome Wears Thin," *Financial Times*, July 29, 2016.

for the Left and for the established politicians, a good bit of Europe didn't share this welcoming culture. Moreover, many Europeans are flummoxed by the migrants' inability or unwillingness to learn social etiquette and local customs. Some, in one German town, questioned the unwillingness of Muslims boys to sit at the same school lunch table with Christian girls.[331] With this happening, is it any wonder that more and more people are voting for right-wing parties that promise to end the migrant wave?

The Left has no plan, other than more of the same. Bring more "immigrants," press for more accommodation, seek more volunteers to help the aliens fit in. Yet they still do not realize that the Europeans, especially the rightist parties, are resisting this. Moreover, the Left is attempting to wipe out the migrants' own cultures, their own languages, their own way of life. Are they to abandon their Afghan, Libyan, or Syrian identities? Should the aliens look forward to being dehoused, deculturalized, destabilized, and destroyed? Why would they welcome this?

And there is another view, one reinforcing the foregoing.

> Questioning (while not always decrying) immigration, integration, the euro, the European Union and the establishment, while promoting a stiff dose of nationalist sentiment, is now entirely "salonfaehig," as German-speakers would say.
>
> This literally means "passable for your living room," or socially acceptable.
>
> And something else has been spreading throughout Europe.
>
> Dissatisfaction, cynicism and outright rejection of traditional political parties (as well as business and banking elites), many of which have been in power in Western Europe in one way or another since the end of the World War Two.

331 Johnson, Howard and Bräuer, Tobias. "Migrant Crisis: Changing Attitudes of a German City," *BBC NEWS*, April 28, 2016.

> This, and not far-right fervour, is arguably driving voters to stage ballot-box protests or to seek alternative political homes—to the delight of Europe's populist parties.[332]

Already, as discussed, the Left, the established parties, have done the unthinkable: begun limiting their citizens' personal liberties under the guise of security. Governments supporting migrants and opposing criticism of them have

- increased cooperation with questionable American watchdog groups, such as the FBI, Homeland Security, and the CIA;
- created an air passenger database (something long resisted by privacy groups); and
- increased controls on already strictly regulated firearms.

It wasn't the right-wing parties that did this. It was the migrant-supporting establishment. Next, we might see the European Union and its backers form ties with the extremist US Southern Poverty Law Center (SPLC), the group that spies on Arabs and Muslims in the United States. In doing so, it works with the Jewish Anti-Defamation League and B'nai B'rith. The groups then share their information with various US government agencies. (The author mentioned the SPLC's activities in *Visas for Al Qaeda.*)

So, as written earlier, the danger to freedom in Europe is like the danger to freedom in the United States—it comes from the Establishment, the "mainstream" government. It does not come from outsiders. AfD, PEGIDA, FPÖ, Jobbik, Golden Dawn, among others, have only proposed pushing Mama Merkel's millions out of Europe. They haven't demanded that the security services tap their telephones. They haven't demanded that V men infiltrate their organizations. They haven't demanded that legitimate travelers be investigated at the airport.

332 Adler, Katya. "Is Europe Lurching to the Far Right?," *BBC NEWS*, April 28, 2016.

As we noted in the main body of this book and in the *Fifth Thread* section, right-wing groups are winning or increasing their influence all over Europe. The future battle over the continent's move to the right will be between the Establishment, seeking ever-increasing "security" at the expense of liberty, and the nationalist parties, seeking migrant removal at the expense of immigrants' "rights."

The solution? Let Europe move to the right. But whose "right"? Would it be the right of Merkel and Social Democratic Party (SPD) leader, now chancellor candidate, Martin Schulz? The SPD's man opposes German parties, such as the AfD, who question the migrant wave and its effects. Schulz, who likely may not win a majority of the vote, is said to be considering an alliance with the pedophile Greens and the old East German Communist Party, now morphed into *die Linke* (the Left). So leftists of one stripe or another will likely continue Merkel's failed policies.

Is the solution increased agitation by the rightist groupings opposing Merkel's migrant bomb? Would this turn into 1920s-style street violence following a collapsed German government after World War I? What would be the result? Another charismatic leader proposing a global solution to the migrants?

It would be better for all, the Europeans and the migrants, to end the Merkel madness. Move to a rightist policy aimed at grasping real issues, not fanciful ones. And only a nationalist European Union, with concern for the states of Europe with their unique history and heritage, will be able to do so.

12

The Wrap-Up

Wars generate migrants. The United States' Forever War against Arabs and Muslims generated Europe's migrants. First, they were simply people who left their countries because their countries left them. When America bombed Afghanistan, refugees poured into Pakistan and elsewhere. They had no country anymore. What little government, infrastructure, or resources there were simply disappeared. The country disappeared; it left its people. When America bombed Iraq, it turned one of the cradles of civilization into a wasteland filled with poisonous, depleted uranium dust. Two wars displaced millions and made still more millions into refugees. They poured into Syria and Jordan, countries with limited resources. A few went to Egypt, Iran, Lebanon, and Turkey. Government, health care, and education just vanished. The United States and Israel, implementing the Yinon Plan, tried to divide the country into three pieces: a Kurdish north, a Sunni center, and a Shii south. To date, the Kurds have, to all intents and purposes, split from Iraq. When America bombed Syria, it wrecked another cradle of civilization. "The secrets of the alphabet, agriculture, astronomy, geometry, literature, medicine, metallurgy, music, religion, science and trade were all born in Syria, a land saturated with history."[333] The United States backed terrorist groups with arms, money, and training. It sent CIA Clandestine Service officers into the country to aid extremists. Using Special Operations Command soldiers, America engaged in covert operations and unconventional warfare within Syria. The United States worked with Turkey, a NATO member, and Israeli Special Forces to fight the legitimate Syrian government. This destroyed the country's society, infrastructure, and ability to function. According to the United Nations High Commissioner for Refugees (UNHCR), as of September 2016, 4.8 million Syrians have fled to Turkey, Lebanon, Jordan, Egypt, and Iraq, and 6.6 million are internally displaced. This is half the 2010 Syrian population of 21.5 million souls. When America bombed Libya, it destroyed a country that had had the highest human development index in all of Africa. When the United States murdered Moammar Gaddafi, it killed the man who had "promoted economic democracy and used the nationalized oil wealth to sustain progressive social welfare programs for all Libyans. Under Gaddafi's rule, Libyans enjoyed not only free health-care and free education, but also free electricity and interest-free loans."[334] With no government, with no domestic security, with no economy, Libyans began leaving the country that had left them. Half a million people sailed from the Jamahiriya while more than four hundred thousand more were internally displaced.

Somewhere in this sordid history, someone in the US government got the idea (perhaps from Kelly Greenhill's book) to weaponize the refugees. Like the Afghan-Arab terrorists America trained (and later turned into an international fighting force), the refugees could provide

333 Salloum, Habeeb. Except from a to-be-published book on Syria. "PART I: Syria—The Fountainhead of Western Civilization," www.arabamerica.com, January 18, 2017.

334 Chengu, Garikai. "Libya: From Africa's Richest State under Gaddafi, to Failed State after NATO Intervention," *Global Research*, October 19, 2014.

extended benefits. Besides aiding the Yinon Plan, this notion also helped the United States' strategy of wrecking Germany.

Moving the marching migrants out of South Asia, Southwest Asia, and North Africa weakened the countries they left behind. The decimated middle class, the educated populace with a work ethic, had nothing more left. Like Iraq earlier, there was nothing for them at home. The working class had no work. Instead of ending its wars of aggression and devising a Marshall Plan tailored to the Arab and Muslim worlds, the United States assisted the migrants' leaving.

Brainwashing without Soap

Always concerned with plausible deniability,[335] America used some of its many cat's-paws to achieve its goals. The object was to brainwash a good many people without using soap. No ethnic group, no country, would knowingly, willingly accept its demise. To dilute society, to weaken national ties, there must be reeducation; there must be a new mindset. How better to accomplish this than to depict migrants as refugees? And these are not just any immigrants. They are people driven from their homes by the new Hitler, Bashar al-Assad; or by the new Stalin, Saddam Hussein; or by the new Mao, Moammar Gaddafi. (They had already used up Slobodan Milošević, the Serbian Satan, to justify the destruction of Yugoslavia.)

Here's more reiteration.

Peter Sutherland, the special representative of the general secretary of the United Nations for international migrations; Gerald Knaus, director-founder of the European Security Initiative (ESI); and Diederik Samsom, Dutch parliamentary representative, all proved useful.

---

335 *USLegal.com.* Plausible deniability refers to circumstances where a denial of responsibility or knowledge of wrongdoing cannot be proved as true or untrue due to a lack of evidence proving the allegation. This term is often used in reference to situations where high-ranking officials deny responsibility for or knowledge of wrongdoing by lower-ranking officials. In those situations, officials can plausibly deny an allegation even though it may be true.

Building on decades of conditioning Americans to accept millions of illegal aliens, these men found the right stuff. The propaganda they developed and spread persuaded a large chunk of Europeans to accept the migrants. Why? How? Through clever lies: These poor people would work hard and pay taxes into a near-bankrupt welfare system. Their children would flesh out an aging, dying population. Their different cultures would revitalize a stagnant, intolerant society.

In a speech to the British House of Lords, Sutherland said, "The EU should 'do its best to undermine' the 'homogeneity' of its member states." His belief is that there are no ill consequences to unrestricted immigration. Another allegation by the former Irish attorney general was that "migration was a 'crucial dynamic for economic growth' in some EU nations [possibly Germany] 'however difficult it may be to explain this to the citizens of those states.'" Sutherland added, unsurprisingly, "An ageing or declining native population in countries like Germany or southern EU states was the 'key argument...for the development of multicultural states.'"

Gerald Knaus devised and promoted the Merkel migrant plan. Working with the Dutch government, he proposed that EU countries accept regulated and regular flows of migrants from Turkey (around 250,000 to 500,000 annually). In exchange, Turkey would take illegal immigrants caught crossing the Mediterranean Sea into Greece. The ESI director, a former Soros Open Society associate, claimed "that if Angela Merkel does not succeed in finding a solution similar to the solution he proposed, and integrated in the Dutch presidency, then 'political forces wanting to curb asylum, against migrants, against EU, against Turkey, for Putin, and against Muslims will be reinforced.'"

ESI's focus was the American Europe model. According to the United States and its Atlanticist allies' geostrategic objectives, a European Europe must not emerge. It must not form a closer relationship with Russia.

With Knaus, Diederik Samsom, Dutch parliamentary representative and president of the Workers' Party, worked out the deal on the migrant river with the Turks. Samsom asserted he, with the support of the Dutch premier (Rutte), had engaged in intensive talks with Germany, Sweden, and Austria on the matter. Samsom's justification for those particular countries was that they had social democrats in their governments.

According to the *Migrant Report*'s "Spotlight," the Dutchman's concept appears to be useless, if not dangerous. Because asylum seekers in Turkey have no status or right of residence or right to work, Samsom's arrangement might be contrary to international law. Additionally, the *Report* noted, the plan's existence could well encourage a greater flow of migrants.

Help with Passports, Help with Travel Costs, Help with Electronics

The *Völkerwanderung* seems to have official help, official stupidity, or official ignorance. Perhaps it's all of them. The author wants to sharpen the reader's focus with repetition.

Passports

Prior to 2011, the French government, one of the players in the destruction of the Arab world, printed Syrian passports. Did some of these end up in the hands of migrants? Are the French still producing them? Are countries other than Qatar manufacturing them? Just how did migrants without travel documents get hold of Syrian passports or obtain other nations' travel authorizations? With increased security features, government-issued identifications can no longer be produced in someone's basement with a child's printing set. How many genuine documents have been lost, stolen, or taken by traffickers? How many authentic passes did the Syrian embassy in Berlin issue to non-Syrians who paid a little extra?

Mirabile dictu, in addition to real passports, extremely sophisticated but counterfeit travel documents are ending up in the hands of ISIL fighters. These fake Iraqi or Syrian passports are virtually indistinguishable from the real McCoy. British, French, American, or other-flavored spooks also managed to lose track of the bad boys with the bogus papers. How? Isn't it their job to follow terrorists? And by what means do these magnificent forgeries come out of a war zone? This occurred in a country short of even the most basic items.

Travel Costs

Emphasis doesn't hurt. Who's paying for the trip from Damascus to Düsseldorf? It's two thousand miles (ca. three thousand kilometers)—in a straight line. From Kabul to Karlsruhe, it's farther. In 2015, the average monthly income in Damascus, the capital, was US$50 per month (SYP15,000). That doesn't buy much. In Halab (Aleppo), once the country's largest city, the average monthly income was $80 (SYP20,000). In a devastated country like Syria, like Iraq, like Libya, like Afghanistan, who can do more than simply survive? In Afghanistan, 42 percent of the population lives on less than US$1 per day.[336] Yet somehow the migrants find funds to pay traffickers. Citing an undated *Wall Street Journal* article, the *Greek Reporter* supplied the following prices to hire smugglers *in Athens* [emphasis added]:

- Truck and ship to Italy: €1,000 to €1,200
- Foot and car to Germany or Switzerland, via Balkans: €1,500 to €2,000
- Foot and car to Norway or Sweden, via Balkans: about €2,500
- Truck to Germany, via Balkans: about €2,500
- Plane to Germany, Norway or Sweden: €3,500 to €5,000
- Plane to Canada: about €14,000[337]

(NB US$1 = €0.94 as of January 20, 2017.)

Der Spiegel, the German newsmagazine, quoted one Syrian as having paid €7,000 for travel to Italy.[338]

---

336 http://www.averagesalarysurvey.com/afghanistan. January 19, 2017.

337 Choros, Evgenia. "The Price of Escape: How Much Do Smugglers Charge Refugees and Migrants for Passage to Europe?," *Greek Reporter*, March 30, 2016.

338 Mayr, Walter. "Traffickers Profit as Asylum Seekers Head for Europe," *Der Spiegel*, November 28, 2014.

So, esteemed reader, do you have the fare for a scheduled flight to Europe in your pocket? How much more would you pay a smuggler to sneak you in, *sans* passport, *sans* visa? Wouldn't you like a nice government agency or NGO to fund your trip to the Riviera or the next *Oktoberfest*?

Electronic Help

The torrent of aliens deluging Europe likely didn't have army-quality topographical maps. They could have had global positioning systems. But they certainly had smartphones. Again, where did these come from? Apple's new iPhone 7 costs most of a year's pay for a Syrian from Damascus. (The author's iPhone 6s, last year's model, was priced at more than US$500.) Then there are the monthly service fees and Internet data. If they bought a down-market edition, if someone gave them a used phone, they could well use it. But again, where did they get what Germans call a *handy*? Most of the migrants don't come from the upper class; most of the migrants don't come from the middle class. They come from the working class. Are they all plugged in and wired? If they are, can't they be tracked? The author's phone shows where he's traveled.

Merkel's government may be belatedly realizing this. NetzPolitik. Org reports that the Interior Ministry is now planning the seizure of migrants' cell phones and downloading data, no matter how private. According to the article, no suspicion of illegal behavior or warrant is required to authorize this.[339]

Then there's the Internet.

A map showing concentrations of Internet use indicates that there is none in South Asia. In Lebanon, Libya, Syria, and Iraq, it's less than 40 percent, often far less. In Africa, it ranges from nonexistent to less than 40 percent.[340] In the Balkans, Internet penetration of the population is

339 Reuter, Markus. "Kommentar: De Maizière macht den Trump" (Commentary: De Maizière Does a Trump), *netzpolitik*.org, February 20, 2017.

340 http://gizmodo.com/heres-a-world-map-adjusted-for-each-countrys-internet-1443568309. /www.indy100.com/article/internet-access-net-neutrality-infrastructure-data-map-statistics-world-global-computing-7508551.

at least 50 percent, ranging up to 80 percent or more.[341] And without a link to the World Wide Web, the migrants can't march. They can't communicate. They can't find a trafficker. They can't find a map.

But They Have More Help: George Soros, Big Business, Strange NGOs

Following on from an earlier discussion, the George Soros–sponsored Central European University is helping. Here and elsewhere, "students who could speak Arabic, Farsi, Pashto, and other languages provided much-needed translation services on a volunteer basis. Wi-Fi and mobile phone-charging stations were set up, providing refugees with a crucial lifeline to family and friends."[342] Meredith Woo, at the Soros Open Society Foundation London, worked closely with migrants from the Middle East, Africa, and South Asia. Besides George Soros, there are other organizations helping keep migrants wired. "Noticing the importance of access to information, [the] Belgrade Centre for Human Rights, an aid group in Serbia, has set up Wi-Fi networks for refugees, while the UN Refugee Agency has distributed thousands of SIM cards at Jordan's refugee camps."

And big business has jumped into migrant support:

> Cisco's Tactical Operations...team supported by the volunteer Disaster Response Team...from the U.K. and Ireland, Google, and NetHope have installed...Wi-Fi networks and device charging stations at more than 17 sites along the migration route... Through an employee matching program, Cisco has donated a total of $745,000 to organizations aiding in the refugee crisis—including $630,000 worth of equipment to support these deployments and $200,000 in grant funding to NGO partners NetHope and Mercy Corps.

341 http://www.internetworldstats.com/stats4.htm.

342 Central European University Annual Report, 2015.

According to Frank Schott, the managing director of global programs for NetHope, the organization "has assisted refugees by setting up 24 Wi-Fi hot spots and charging stations in six countries along the European migration route as well as developing a website with maps and transit information to which refugees are directed when accessing the Wi-Fi at certain camps."

Mercy Corps has a long history of being caught up in American war zones.

In 1986, Mercy Corps began operations in Afghanistan. In the midst of NATO's war against Yugoslavia, the organization "provide[d] medicines, supplies and services to Bosnians during the Balkans wars." In Iraq, in 1991, it shipped blankets, medicine, and food to Kurds. Mercy Corps spent US$3 million aiding 175,000 people in Kosovo during 1993. In 1995, the outfit distributed US$20 million in supplies throughout Bosnia and Kosovo. Still deeply involved in the Balkans, during 1999, Mercy Corps provided "food and supplies to 250,000 people in Kosovo and help[ed] 100,000 refugees in Macedonia." In 2003, with the new war, the group returned to Iraq, asserting it helped families displaced by conflict. It followed them and worked with them in Syria and Jordan.

Think this shows CIA ties? Read on.

On June 11, 2016, *Pravda* (a privately owned Russian news service) reported that Luhansk People's Republic authorities had arrested Oksana Mikitenko, one of Mercy Corps' staff, for espionage. The article also noted that Stuart Willcuts, the Mercy Corps regional director in the Donbass area of Luhansk, also worked for the CIA. (NB Luhansk is one of the regions that seceded from the neo-Nazi-controlled Ukraine.)

Security: Failures of Policy, Education, Official Oaths, Personal Welfare

Germany has existed in one form or another since the Roman legions occupied Colonia (Cologne/Köln), Augusta Treverorum (Trier), Bonna (Bonn), and Radasbona (Regensburg). Stuttgart, the Swabian

Metropole, began as a fortified river crossing. Indeed, the first-century historian Tacitus coined the term *Germania.*

For two millennia or more, Germany has focused on security. From the time Herrmann and his *Cherusker* tribesmen destroyed three Roman legions in the *Teutoburgerwald,* the country has dealt with military upheaval. Name your cause, and it was fought in Germania: Catholics vs. Protestants, Democrats vs. authoritarians, Communists vs. capitalists, Nazis vs. everyone else.

But today, not two decades into the twenty-first century, Germany is no longer secure. It is flooded by a million aliens or more. The Roman legions brought wine and order. The migrants have brought hatred and confusion. They have dragged the country into other nations' problems.

Citizens have lost their anchor. A tradition of mutual assistance, of shared culture, and of a stable way of life is now gone. In some ways, it began with the sudden collapse of East Germany. The two lands, East and West, had grown up with greatly differing economies and lifestyles. While seeking to join the Western *Ellenbogen* (pushy, elbowing) society with the more laissez-faire, social one in the East, Germania had to deal with the *Aussiedler,* ethnic Teutons who had long been settled in the Balkans and what became the Soviet Union. As Communism and the USSR crashed, the *Aussiedler* had the right to return to Germany. And they did, bringing with them strange, foreign ways.

Now, with barely digested *Gastarbeiter* (Turks, Greeks, Italians, and Yugoslavs), Germany is overwhelmed with another torrent of people. This time, they have little in common with the natives. They differ in religion, language, history, and outlook. They come not as refugees but as economic migrants, with little education and no skills. Germany is no longer a country needing strong backs and weak minds to dig coal and make steel. Thirty years ago, the optics firm Carl Zeiss Oberkochen's proudest boast was that it had produced a space program mirror of stunning accuracy. According to a firm contact, if the surface were the size of the Bodensee (Lake of Constance), thirty-nine miles (sixty-three kilometers) long, there would be only a few millimeters' difference from one end to the other.[343]

Carl Zeiss can't hire the migrants. It and the rest of the German economy centers on high technology based on extensive education and skills.

Knowing this, knowing German history, Angela Merkel and her security services nevertheless allowed an unknown, unknowable horde into a tightly organized society. Never checking (likely unable to check) the multitude, Merkel, the Interior Ministry, the BfV, and the BKA failed their oath of office:

> *Chancellor's, President's, Federal Minister's Oath of Office*: I swear that I will dedicate my efforts to the well-being of the German people, promote their welfare, protect them from harm, uphold and defend the Basic Law [Constitution] and the laws of the Federation, perform my duties conscientiously, and do justice to all. So help me God.[344]

As the migrants flooded Germany (and the rest of Europe), the extent of the disaster became increasingly clear.

In the beginning, people and politicians wondered what to do with them. Initially, in Munich, they were housed in open-air sports stadia. But there were not enough air mattresses to keep the aliens off the ground. Some towns housed them in sports halls. Other jurisdictions, likely under pressure from the federal government, took public housing away from citizens and gave it to the migrants. People denounced Merkel's government for supporting the illegals and were fined and/or arrested.

Crime shot up. And it wasn't petty crime. It was murder. It was rape. Yet the carefully coddled wanderers were at the bottom of it all. One man

343 Conversation of author with Carl Zeiss spokesman, in Oberkochen, in the late 1970s.
344 German Parliament Official Translation: Article 56, German Basic Law. Oath of Office for Chancellor, President, and Federal Ministers.

in Austria claimed he was overcome by sexual urges and raped a small boy. An Afghan in Freiburg im Breisgau, Hussein Kavari, raped and drowned a nineteen-year-old medical student. Months later, his previous attack on a Greek woman popped up. Then there were the carefully coordinated New Year's Eve rapes, robberies, and gropings throughout Germany and Europe. Anis Amri allegedly drove a truck into a Berlin market on Christmas. Despite his history of being jailed in Italy and being rejected for asylum, Merkel and her ministers did not deport him. Still worse, he fled Berlin, fled Germany, traveled most likely through France, and ended up in Italy.

Germania's Federal Office for the Protection for the Constitution (BfV) is charged with internal security and counterespionage. It works with equivalent services in the states (*Länder*). The BKA, the federal police, is the central criminal investigation agency. It coordinates federal and state cooperation in police inquiries. The Federal Republic is not like the United States. Hotel room registrations are not just for billing and marketing. They are for controlling the registrants. The inn gives their names to the local police, who have the option, as in the rest of Europe, to investigate the guests. In Germany, like the rest of the continent, the government issues national identity cards. Unlike the United States, which uses drivers' licenses and Social Security numbers, Germany provides cards having a photo, name, date, and place of birth. If you come to the country for more than ninety days, you are required to register your place of residence with the local government and obtain a residence permit. People who change address, even within the same apartment building, must notify the authorities. If you move away, you must again inform the appropriate agency.

Yet the Bfv and the BKA, with a total staff of more than eight thousand people, somehow missed not only the small-time crooks but also the big-time criminals. Were they overwhelmed? Were they focused on other matters? Were their trusted men, their V men, engaged in other roles? Were they willing participants in a fifth column? Were they under instructions from the chancellor to hold back? Until someone talks, until someone is caught out, we may never know.

But, dear reader, consider Frank Meyer's words. He's the Swiss publicist who commented,

> First, German chancellor Merkel issued an authoritarian order to open her country's borders. She then temporarily lost control of the migrants. To date, he asserted that German government offices have lost track of more than 300,000 immigrants. No one knows where they are, or who they are. Therefore, he said, Germany has become a land of milk and honey for them. Their goal is not to live in a constitutional state but to engage in criminal acts, from the drug trade to terrorism.

Isn't that the stated role of the BfV and the BKA? Aren't they to hunt down criminals who violate the laws, who traffic in drugs, who engage in terrorism?

Were they simply unable to cope with crime?

According to Germany's Federal Criminal Police, migrants committed 142,500 crimes just in the first half of 2016. A 40 percent increase over the previous year, this amounts to 780 crimes committed by migrants daily. It wasn't just car theft and petty larceny. These offenses included rape, physical and sexual assault, stabbings, home invasions, robberies, burglaries, and drug trafficking. The Gatestone Institute claimed that police in many parts of the Federal Republic are stretched to the limit.

In all 2015, migrants engaged in 208,344 misdeeds as noted in a confidential police report provided to *Bild* (a German tabloid). These numbers, an average of 23 crimes per hour, are an 80 percent jump over the figures from 2014. According to an October 24 YouGov poll, 68 percent of Germans thought that "security in the country has deteriorated during the past several years."

What to do? Hire more policemen? Send more of the alien wave home?

Nationalism

One effect of the backlash against the out-of-touch migrants could well be increased nationalism. This might not take the form of "my country above your country." However, it might well be "my country and my countrymen above total strangers."

Love and support for your own country seem to be reviving. Derided in dictionaries and in globalist circles, nationalism is chauvinism, xenophobia, and nativism. Patriotism, like loyalty, does not and should not exist. It's possible that the migrant wave was calculated as another way to alter the attitudes and outlook of Europeans. The tsunami of pure outsiders without ties to anything helps wash away the concept of the nation-state. It dissolves the idea of France or Germany or Sweden or Greece.

Enraged at aliens invading their lands and cultures, more and more Europeans insist the foreigners adjust to them and not vice versa. Political parties who brought on and/or encouraged the flood are losing at the ballot box. They see their confident control of government failing. Old bugbears like Marine Le Pen's Front National are rising in influence. New factions, like the German AfD, are starting to appear. Old nonmainstream groupings strengthen.

The common denominator, as in the United States, is the failure of representative government, of democracy. The establishment fails to grasp what the people, its own people, want. They ignore their protests, they ignore their demands for protection, they ignore their need for barriers, and they ignore their questions about the European Union.

Nationalism is not just growing in Germany or France. Sweden, tolerant of minorities for decades, now has parties opposing multiculturalism. The once helpful, trusting, open Danes now have some of the most restrictive immigration rules on the continent. Although the Dutch government hates Geert Wilders and his anti-European Union, antimigrant Party for Freedom (PVV), it is now the second-largest party in parliament. Neutral Switzerland, established in 1291 through the union of the original three cantons, has capped migration into the confederation.

The antimigrant Swiss People's Party won nearly 30 percent of the vote. Italy's Northern League is not gaining votes nationally. However, it is doing well in local elections, garnering 20 percent of the vote in leftist Tuscany in 2015. Austria's antialien party, the Freedom Party (*Freiheits Partei Österreich*, FPÖ), just missed winning the presidency in 2016, likely due to election irregularities and propaganda. Its support, like Donald Trump's, comes from blue-collar workers.

Moving to the Right—with What Effect?

There seems to be a growing fear that nationalism will push Europe to the right. The alarm appears to stem from elections in France and Germany scheduled for spring and fall 2017. However, it's not the rise of patriotism that is limiting freedoms on the continent. It is the allegedly leftist, mainstream governments that are striking at the heart of liberty. In Socialist France,

> Hollande is suspending civil rights...The well-respected (admittedly leftist) magazine *Mother Jones* points out, "France has embraced and even surpassed some of America's most draconian responses to terror. In the name of security, the French public has been more willing than Americans ever were to let their government spy on citizens, conduct warrantless raids, and restrict rights of free speech and assembly."[345]

On November 20, 2015, the French government expanded its emergency powers to

> allow the government to impose house arrest without authorization from a judge, conduct searches without a judicial warrant and seize any computer files it finds, and block websites

345 Wile, Anthony. "Watching the Anti-Freedom Actions of Francois Hollande," *The Daily Bell*, November 28, 2015.

> deemed to glorify terrorism without prior judicial authorization. These powers interfere with the rights to liberty, security, freedom of movement, privacy, and freedoms of association and expression.[346]

In Germany, it's Angela Merkel's semisocialist, slightly right-of-center government that is circumscribing civil liberties. By executive order, it became illegal to criticize the migrants. People who did so were fined, given probation, or jailed for "hate speech." Her government and the mainstream media, termed the *Lűgenpresse* (lying press) by its targets, went after the organized opposition. The AfD, PEGIDA, and almost any group that opposed the migrant wave were castigated as a group of neo-Nazi, extremist, undemocratic hatemongers. When the AfD criticizes Germany's obsession with Israel, Merkel and others denounce them as anti-Semitic. (The German government supports ruthless attacks on Arabs while conveniently forgetting that they are also a Semitic people.)

And it's Germany that parrots the Hillary Clinton line that the Russians have influenced and will influence elections. Merkel's government alleges that Russian hacking, cyberattacks, and misinformation are interfering and will continue to interfere in Germania's politics. The idea is that the Rus will influence public perception and opinion. (This is direct misinformation and disinformation, intended to sway the voter's choice in the next election.)

In the past year, without explanation, government pronouncements have urged citizens to stockpile food, water, medicine, and other necessities. Now, unknown administration sources are claiming that terrorists will soon use chemicals in attacks on civilians.

> Weeks after the [2016] Christmas market attack in Berlin, [the] German government reportedly issued a paper stating

346 *Human Rights Watch.* "France: New Emergency Powers Threaten Rights," November 24, 2015.

> the country is at "high risk" of terrorist attacks carried out by "Islamist-motivated perpetrators."
>
> The government apparently takes the threat seriously as the paper—accessed by *Bild* magazine—directs the German armed forces, intelligence agencies and emergency services to prepare for action in the event of a chemical attack.
>
> *"A determined and well-trained terrorist group is likely to be in a position to exploit Germany's potential chemical hazards in order to stage an attack,"* says the report jointly prepared by the government and the federal police (BKA) to evaluate level of threats to civilian population.
>
> Islamist-motivated perpetrators are able to *"procure and use large amount of chemicals,"* it states, also describing *"realistic options"* in a chemical attack.
>
> There is also *"a high-risk potential"* of terrorist organizations using chemicals to target food and drinking water supplies used in large residential buildings, and attacking chemical industry's infrastructure.
>
> The German armed forces have been preparing for this *"more intensively than before,"* the report adds in conclusion.[347]

Evidently Mama Merkel, like her great admirer Hillary Clinton, thinks people have short memories. It was Merkel and her government who invited all the feared Islamists into the country. It was Merkel and her government who did not check their backgrounds as they came. It was Merkel and her government who insisted that criticism of this action was hate speech.

More to the point, it appears that Merkel and her government are planning more restrictions on civil liberties, something the rightist groups have never espoused. Look at the text above. The armed forces and the intelligence services, not the civil police, will take action in any

---

347 *RT.* "Terrorist Chemical Attack on Drinking Water Supplies Feared in Germany—Report," January 24, 2017.

emergency. They can conceivably go door to door and apartment block to apartment block looking for bogeymen. Will citizens be subject to a curfew? Will their travel be circumscribed? Will this be another Boston Marathon bombing event, with martial law, warrantless searches, and people jailed in their own homes?[348]

There are others concerned with Germany's restrictions on civil liberties. The Institute for Social Sciences at the University of Stuttgart has been studying "support for civil liberties and preferences for domestic security policies." The project asks leading questions:

- Under which circumstances and which motives citizens would accept restrictions of civil liberties through policies of domestic security?
- Do citizens have a perceived hierarchy within civil liberties—as in: some civil liberties receive more support than others?

  This project focuses on the following civil liberties (written down in the German constitution):
- Personal freedom (Art. 2 (1))
- The right to informational self-determination
- Freedom of faith and conscience (Art. 4)
- Freedom of assembly (Art. 8)
- Freedom of association (Art. 9)
- Privacy of correspondence, posts and telecommunications (Art. 10)
- Inviolability of the home (Art. 13)

  Civil rights and liberties constitute core elements of democratic systems. The extent to which they are realized give insights into the quality of democracy. However, the conditionality and situational nature of orientations toward civil liberties have rarely been examined.

348 Springmann, J. Michael. "Boston Baked BS: It Goes So Well with Turkeys When They've Come Home to Roost," *Foreign Policy Journal*, May 10, 2013.

> Investigating whether citizens accept restrictions of civil liberties through anti-terrorism policies (e.g. collection of personal data), the project will substantiate the conflict between liberty and security in this domain. It deals with the question of how citizens cope with clashes of (valued) principles in specific situations—for example in the event of terrorist threats, in the event of terror threat, for example.[349]

At a time of normalcy, this would be an interesting study. Now, when the German government is increasingly concerned with terrorism from the migrants, it's welcomed, and it could become a blueprint for extremism. Chancellor Merkel and her minions would know just how far they could go in dissolving civil liberties. With Germania's Nazi and Stasi past, Uni Stuttgart's study could become an outline for a new round of antidemocratic activity. It might well become the Teutonic *Weapons of Mass Migration.*

And the Future? *Quo Vadimus?*

The trend is, unfortunately, clear. Regime change in Syria is still the goal of American and European policy. The US Global War On Terror (GWOT), a worldwide hairball, continues in Afghanistan and Iraq. And the Old World still helps. Great Britain is one of the largest arms suppliers supporting Saudi Arabia's attacks on Yemen, a new addition to GWOT. Israel persists in destabilizing its neighbors, including those farther away, such as Iran.

This means that the migrants will keep on marching. Countries pouring out their populations into Europe will lose what's left of their middle class, the people who comprise the bedrock of any country. They are the midlevel managers, the teachers, the administrators. Working men will leave because there is no work. Doctors, lawyers, and capitalists will depart since no one is left to use or pay for their services and abilities.

349 http://www.uni-stuttgart.de/soz/avps/liberties/home/index.en.html.

The lands will lose a goodly part of their young men; they will no longer produce children in their home countries. Populations will fall.

Europe, having unsuccessfully absorbed their predecessors, will carry on its resistance to migrant-imposed change. Voters will rage at governments that refuse to help. Additionally, those who welcome and those who oppose the wanderers will continue to battle each other, straining the body politic to its limits and beyond. The clashes, cultural and otherwise, between the refugees and the Europeans will not end, creating more difficulties.

Besides social costs, there will be material costs to this *Völkerwanderung*. Higher taxes will support needed language and cultural education. More funds will go toward technical instruction, so necessary for a modern state. Will these monies be diverted from citizens, leaving them to fend for themselves? Will they rebel against the strain caused by increased government levies?

What will happen if Germany and the rest of Europe adopt Angela Merkel's Green Book? It's titled *Dialogue about the Future—Visions for 2050* (*Dialoge Zukunft—Visionen 2050*). The work's two hundred pages describe a group of youths looking backward from the year 2050 to our present day. Produced by the Sustainability Council (*Rat für Nachhaltiges*), it shows the changes that will occur. It lists forty-two concepts that will no longer exist. Some examples of these transformations are:

- Teacher-centered education will disappear. It doesn't teach children to solve problems.
- Sensing and feelings should be emphasized instead of profit.
- Migration background will replace national origin (since the population is so mixed).
- "Normal citizen" will disappear. It's unclear what is normal and abnormal.
- Sustainability will vanish. It's a concept that men, society, and politics created and the world internalized and understood.
- State borders will be eliminated.

Other changes are the disappearance of the family's traditional image. People will live together in large "communities" without necessarily being related. Children are cared for by several parents with different sexual backgrounds. The equality of loving, regardless of gender, is fixed at all levels. Marriage is abolished.

Society permits the use and consumption of drugs. Most people no longer eat meat, fish, or dairy products. People see themselves as Europeans, but the word German, English, or French is still anchored in many heads. The children of the old nations learn only that they live in Europe, where the nation-state has become irrelevant.

Finally, there are no free elections, and politics are made mostly within a political party.[350]

And Just How Far Is It from Here to There?

There are, conceivably, some advantages to new blood flowing in European veins. Migrants paying taxes could help support the social welfare system. Additional bodies filling jobs from drugstore clerk to apprentice to master craftsman would be an advantage. There would also be additional consumers for finished products from the factories. People from different cultures and backgrounds could provide a different world view. If the *Vision 2050* plan is valid, the migrants succeeded in their integration.

Deutsche Welle certainly believes this. According to an article published May 20, 2010, migrants are integrating well.

> A new report by Germany's Advisory Council for Integration and Migration says immigrants are fitting into German society better than first thought. The council found a high level of trust between Germans and immigrants.

350 https://archive.org/stream/DialogeZukunftVision2050/Dialoge%20Zukunft%20Vision%202050_djvu.txt

Many Germans and immigrants live harmoniously side-by-side.

With a handful of European member states considering bans on the Muslim full-face veil, policies aimed at encouraging integration have been pushed to the center of public debate. The stereotype of the so-called failed immigrant who can't find employment, lacks education and stands out in a crowd is fueling much of this debate.

But the first annual report by the German Advisory Council for Integration and Migration fundamentally disagrees with this stereotype. Klaus Bade, chairperson of the council, said efforts in Germany to break down barriers between ethnicities are bearing fruit.

"In this sense, integration in Germany, and also internationally, in many areas has become more successful," he said.

The council canvassed more than 5,000 people, including immigrants and Germans, for its integration barometer. Both groups were asked how they perceived the other group, with nearly two-thirds of immigrants responding that they either "more or less" or "completely" trusted Germans. Astonishingly, only 54 percent of Germans reported trusting other fellow citizens.

Two out of three immigrants also said they felt Germans were interested in their social integration. Bade said both sides also agreed on the integration problem areas that needed to be addressed.

"On both sides more than 95 percent mentioned unemployment, improving prospects for education, language courses and combating discrimination," he said...

"This report and the research that is behind this report actually shows that there is more optimism and that people are pretty much used to immigrant neighbors and immigrants are used to having people without immigrant backgrounds as their neighbors," she said. "People are actually used to living together."

> The survey also showed that most people who were questioned approved of, rather than disapproved of, the integration policies of the German government. Michalowski said this is because integration is not a central political issue in the country.
>
> "In general, the interesting thing about Germany is that if you compare it to other countries like France or the Netherlands, among the political parties there is really a big consensus about what this issue should look like and what the main problems are," she said. "And there is no main right-wing populist party in Germany right now to stir up this anti-immigrant feeling."[351]

The *Financial Times* echoes this with a tale of a Syrian would-be astronaut.

> Aziz Dyab first dreamt of becoming an astronaut in his home town of Idlib, in northern Syria, during the darkest days of the civil war. There was no electricity, "so you could always see the stars at night," the 21-year-old says. "I learnt all the constellations, and began looking at satellites." Now he is in the German city of Frankfurt an der Oder, and is a little closer to fulfilling his ambition. He is planning to start a degree course in mechatronics—a hybrid of mechanical engineering and computer science—at Karlsruhe University in south-Western Germany in October. Aziz is one of the refugee success stories—a young man who has made great strides in settling into life in Germany and is optimistic about building a future there. He has been supported at almost every stage by a network of locals determined to smooth the path for Germany's new arrivals and help them integrate.[352]

351 Mara, Darren. "Immigrant Integration in Germany a Success Story, Report Says," *Deutsche Welle,* May 20, 2010.

352 Chazan, Guy. "A Syrian Refugee in Germany: An Aspiring Astronaut Enjoys Success," *Financial Times,* June 21, 2016.

That paper had another story about a successful asylum seeker, one taking a roundabout way to Germany.

> Nazir Wakil took a somewhat circuitous route from Syria into Germany—via the Maldives. He signed up for a premium package offered by Turkey's human smugglers, a €13,000 [about US$14,054] product available only to the richest asylum-seekers...
>
> Nazir, 43, is an eye doctor from Latakia, a stronghold of President Bashar al-Assad's regime in north-eastern Syria...
>
> He sold his house and medical practice, crossed the Turkish border, only about 15km away, and from the southern Turkish town of Adana flew to Istanbul. There he got in contact with an Iraqi human smuggler who gave him a ticket for the Maldives—a popular destination for would-be refugees, because Syrians do not need a visa to go there...
>
> After a week in the Indian Ocean island nation he booked a flight to Frankfurt, using a fake Italian passport provided by the smuggler. As soon as he arrived in Germany, in December 2014, he threw away the passport. He got on a train to Hamburg, where his cousin lives, and immediately applied for asylum. Like...the other two Syrian refugees in our series, he was sent to a refugee processing centre in Eisenhüttenstadt in the east of the country and soon after moved to Frankfurt an der Oder. There he waited a total of 11 months for his asylum request to be granted. It was a difficult time as he was unable to study or work, or bring his family from Syria. "It was all banned," he says. But he began attending German lessons organised by the local volunteer community and looked into getting a job. Nazir Wakil, with his wife Heba and their sons, Shadi, Mohanad, Basel and Wael [are] in Frankfurt an der Oder. He is now navigating Germany's complex medical bureaucracy. In the next few weeks, he will send his Syrian qualifications to the Brandenburg Medical Chamber, a professional association, for review: they will decide whether he

> needs to sit more exams or gain more clinical experience before he can practice in Germany.
>
> But Nazir is assuming he will have to spend about four years working as a doctor's assistant—which he will combine with further studies—and sit a medical licence exam before he can work as an eye doctor here. He is currently doing an internship at a Frankfurt clinic, but this is mostly to improve his German. Under German rules, the clinic where he works will pay for his training.[353]

But the foregoing stories are exceptions. They are about men with talent and ability and drive to succeed. They had plenty of help once they got to Germany. The Visions 2050 Plan, making much of this integration, has holes in it.

Migration background has disappeared from use. If so, what happened to the Germans, French, Swedes, and others? Let's not forget that the migrants are peoples of widely differing languages and cultures that American and European policies have driven from their homes, their countries, and their cultures. *Coercive mass migration* has covered Europe with an avalanche of bodies, overwhelming the continent's ability to accommodate them. The human tsunami is a flood of suffering people creating misery wherever they land. George Soros's borderless world is one of hardship. Continent-wide or worldwide government is not a solution.

As this writer noted earlier, the solution is simpler and cheaper than what Europe has now. First, we stop the wars of imperial aggression, designed to force people out of South and Southwest Asia and North Africa. Then, we create a new Marshall Plan for the countries bombed back to the Stone Age. Instead of educating migrants in Europe, educate them in Syria or Iraq or Libya. Rebuild their bridges and universities, destroyed through the Bush/Obama savage conflicts. Move them out of

353 Chazan, Guy. "A Syrian Refugee in Germany: The Struggle to Return to Work," *Financial Times*, June 21, 2016.

the many refugee camps in the region. The largest are in Lebanon (Ain al-Hilweh, seventy thousand people), Jordan (Za'atri, eighty thousand), Palestine (Jabalia, eighty-three thousand), and Turkey (Suruç, eighty thousand). Let them go home to countries with a future.

And let them go home intact. Many Syrian refugees in Turkey's camps are trading their organs for survival. Kidneys and liver lobes are sold and bought on the black market. They make up for no language skills, no relatives, no work, no housing. Payments to the "donor" range from €6,000 to €11,000 (US$6,300 to US$11,600). The ARD (1st German TV Program) magazine *FAKT*'s research showed that "consumers" from the West or Saudi Arabia pay €30,000 (almost US$32,000) for transplants in a Turkish clinic.[354]

Remember, in nearly seventy years, the world, in its ignorance, has not solved the issue of Palestinian refugees. Isn't it time to start thinking now about the new torrent of people who have lost their countries? Isn't it time to do justice instead of harm?

THE END

354 *RT Deutsch*. "Es gibt keine andere Möglichkeit—Syrische Flüchtlinge in der Türkei verkaufen eigene Organe" (There Is No Other Possibility—Syrian Refugees in Turkey Sell Their Own Organs), February 21, 2017.

SELECTED BIBLIOGRAPHY

(The author has omitted periodicals and websites cited in this book.)

Greenhill, Kelly M. *Weapons of Mass Migration: Forced Displacement, Coercion, and Foreign Policy*. Ithaca, NY: Cornell University Press, 2010.

Madsen, Wayne. *The Almost Classified Guide to CIA Front Companies, Proprietaries, & Contractors*. Research Triangle Park, NC: Lulu Press, 2016.

Springmann, J. Michael. *Visas for Al Qaeda: CIA Handouts That Rocked the World*. Washington, DC: Daena Publications LLC, 2014.

Trento, Susan B. and Trento, Joseph J., *Unsafe at Any Altitude*. Hanover, NH: Steerforth Press, 2006.

INDEX

CPSIA information can be obtained
at www.ICGtesting.com
Printed in the USA
LVOW03s0904130817
544851LV00012B/550/P

9 780990 926221